The Byza

By

Charles William Chadwick Oman, M.A., F.S.A.

Fellow of All Souls College, Oxford
Author of
"Warwick the Kingmaker," "The Art of War in the Middle Ages," Etc.

Third Edition

Loki's Publishing

Contents

Interior of St. Sophia

Preface.

Fifty years ago the word "Byzantine" was used as a synonym for all that was corrupt and decadent, and the tale of the East-Roman Empire was dismissed by modern historians as depressing and monotonous. The great Gibbon had branded the successors of Justinian and Heraclius as a series of vicious weaklings, and for several generations no one dared to contradict him.

Two books have served to undeceive the English reader, the monumental work of Finlay, published in 1856, and the more modern volumes of Mr. Bury, which appeared in 1889. Since they have written, the Byzantines no longer need an apologist, and the great work of the East-Roman Empire in holding back the Saracen, and in keeping alive throughout the Dark Ages the lamp of learning, is beginning to be realized.

The writer of this book has endeavoured to tell the story of Byzantium in the spirit of Finlay and Bury, not in that of Gibbon. He wishes to acknowledge his debts both to the veteran of the war of Greek Independence, and to the young Dublin professor. Without their aid his task would have been very heavy—with it the difficulty was removed.

The author does not claim to have grappled with all the chroniclers of the Eastern realm, but thinks that some acquaintance with Ammianus, Procopius, Maurice's "Strategikon," Leo the Deacon, Leo the Wise, Constantine Porphyrogenitus, Anna Comnena and Nicetas, may justify his having undertaken the task he has essayed.

OXFORD,
February, 1892.

I. Byzantium.

Two thousand five hundred and fifty-eight years ago a little fleet of galleys toiled painfully against the current up the long strait of the Hellespont, rowed across the broad Propontis, and came to anchor in the smooth waters of the first inlet which cuts into the European shore of the Bosphorus. There a long crescent-shaped creek, which after-ages were to know as the Golden Horn, strikes inland for seven miles, forming a quiet backwater from the rapid stream which runs outside. On the headland, enclosed between this inlet and the open sea, a few hundred colonists disembarked, and hastily secured themselves from the wild tribes of the inland, by running some rough sort of a stockade across the ground from beach to beach. Thus was founded the city of Byzantium.

The settlers were Greeks of the Dorian race, natives of the thriving seaport-state of Megara, one of the most enterprising of all the cities of Hellas in the time of colonial and commercial expansion which was then at its height. Wherever a Greek prow had cut its way into unknown waters, there Megarian seamen were soon found following in its wake. One band of these venturesome traders pushed far to the West to plant colonies in Sicily, but the larger share of the attention of Megara was turned towards the sunrising, towards the mist-enshrouded entrance of the Black Sea and the fabulous lands that lay beyond. There, as legends told, was to be found the realm of the Golden Fleece, the Eldorado of the ancient world, where kings of untold wealth reigned over the tribes of Colchis: there dwelt, by the banks of the river Thermodon, the Amazons, the warlike women who had once vexed far-off Greece by their inroads: there, too, was to be found, if one could but struggle far enough up its northern shore, the land of the Hyperboreans, the blessed folk who dwell behind the North Wind and know nothing of storm and winter. To seek these fabled wonders the Greeks sailed ever North and East till they had come to the extreme limits of the sea. The riches of the Golden Fleece they did not find, nor the country of the Hyperboreans, nor the tribes of the Amazons; but they did discover many lands well worth the knowing, and grew rich on the profits which they drew from the metals of Colchis and the forests of Paphlagonia, from the rich corn lands by the banks of the Dnieper and Bug, and the fisheries of the Bosphorus and the Maeotic Lake. Presently the whole coastland of the sea, which the Greeks, on their first coming, called Axeinos—"the Inhospitable"—became fringed with trading settlements, and its name was changed to Euxeinos—"the Hospitable"—in recognition of its friendly ports. It was in a similar spirit that, two thousand years later, the seamen who led the next great impulse of exploration that rose in Europe, turned the name of the "Cape of Storms" into that of the "Cape of Good Hope."

The Megarians, almost more than any other Greeks, devoted their attention to the Euxine, and the foundation of Byzantium was but one of their many achievements. Already, seventeen years before Byzantium came into being, another band of Megarian colonists had established themselves at Chalcedon, on the opposite Asiatic shore of the Bosphorus. The settlers who were destined to found the greater city applied to the oracle of Delphi to give them advice as to the site of their new home, and Apollo, we are told, bade them "build their town over against the city of the blind." They therefore pitched upon the headland by the Golden Horn, reasoning that the Chalcedonians were truly blind to have neglected the more eligible site on the Thracian shore, in order to found a colony on the far less inviting Bithynian side of the strait.

EARLY COIN OF BYZANTIUM.

LATE COIN OF BYZANTIUM SHOWING CRESCENT AND STAR.

From the first its situation marked out Byzantium as destined for a great future. Alike from the military and from the commercial point of view no city could have been better placed. Looking out from the easternmost headland of Thrace, with all Europe behind it and all Asia before, it was equally well suited to be the frontier fortress to defend the border of the one, or the basis of operations for an invasion from the other. As fortresses went in those early days it was almost impregnable—two sides protected by the water, the third by a strong wall not commanded by any neighbouring heights. In all its early history Byzantium never fell by storm: famine or treachery accounted for the few occasions on which it fell into the hands of an enemy. In its commercial aspect the place was even more favourably situated. It completely commanded the whole Black Sea trade: every vessel that went forth from Greece or Ionia to traffic with Scythia or Colchis, the lands by the Danube mouth or the shores of the Maeotic Lake, had to pass close under its walls, so that the prosperity of a hundred Hellenic towns on the Euxine was always at the mercy of the masters of Byzantium. The Greek loved short stages and frequent stoppages, and as a half-way house alone Byzantium would have been prosperous: but it had also a flourishing local trade of its own with the tribes of the neighbouring Thracian inland, and drew much profit from its fisheries: so much so that the city badge—its coat of arms as we should call it—comprised a tunny-fish as well as the famous ox whose form alluded to the legend of the naming of the Bosphorus.[1]

As an independent state Byzantium had a long and eventful history. For thirty years it was in the hands of the kings of Persia, but with that short exception it maintained its freedom during the first three hundred years that followed its foundation. Many stirring scenes took place beneath its walls: it was close to them that the great Darius threw across the Bosphorus his bridge of boats, which served as a model for the more famous structure on which his son Xerxes crossed the Hellespont. Fifteen years later, when Byzantium in common with all its neighbours made an ineffectual attempt to throw off the Persian yoke, in the rising called the "Ionic Revolt," it was held for a time by the arch-rebel Histiaeus, who—as much to enrich himself as to pay his seamen—invented strait dues. He forced every ship passing up or down the Bosphorus to pay a heavy toll, and won no small unpopularity thereby for the cause of freedom which he professed to champion. Ere long Byzantium fell back again into the hands of Persia, but she was finally freed from the Oriental yoke seventeen years later, when the victorious Greeks, fresh from the triumph of Salamis and Mycale, sailed up to her walls and after a long leaguer starved out the obstinate garrison [B.C. 479]. The fleet wintered there, and it was at Byzantium that the first foundations of the naval empire of Athens were laid, when all the Greek states of Asia placed their ships at the disposal of the Athenian admirals Cimon and Aristeides.

During the fifth century Byzantium twice declared war on Athens, now the mistress of the seas, and on each occasion fell into the hands of the enemy—once by voluntary surrender in 439 B.C., once by treachery from within, in 408 B.C. But the Athenians, except in one or two disgraceful cases, did not deal hardly with their conquered enemies, and the Byzantines escaped anything harder than the payment of a heavy war indemnity. In a few years their commercial gains repaired all the losses of war, and the state was itself again.

We know comparatively little about the internal history of these early centuries of the life of Byzantium. Some odd fragments of information survive here and there: we know, for example, that they used iron instead of copper for small money, a peculiarity shared by no other ancient state save Sparta. Their alphabet rejoiced in an abnormally shaped B, which puzzled all other Greeks, for it resembled a Π with an extra limb.[2] The chief gods of the city were those that we might have expected—Poseidon the ruler of the sea, whose blessing gave Byzantium its chief wealth; and Demeter, the goddess who presided over the Thracian and Scythian corn lands which formed its second source of prosperity.

The Byzantines were, if ancient chroniclers tell us the truth, a luxurious as well as a busy race: they spent too much time in their numerous inns, where the excellent wines of Maronea and other neighbouring places offered great temptations. They were gluttons too as well as tipplers: on one occasion, we are assured, the whole civic militia struck work in the height of a siege, till their commander consented to allow restaurants to be erected at convenient distances round the ramparts. One comic writer informs us that the Byzantines were eating young tunny-fish—their favourite dish—so constantly, that their whole bodies had

---

[1] See coin on opposite page. The Bosphorus was supposed to have drawn its name from being the place where Io, when transformed into a cow, forded the strait from Europe into Asia [Βοῦς-πορός].

[2] See Coin.

become well-nigh gelatinous, and it was thought they might melt if exposed to too great heat! Probably these tales are the scandals of neighbours who envied Byzantine prosperity, for it is at any rate certain that the city showed all through its history great energy and love of independence, and never shrank from war as we should have expected a nation of epicures to do.

It was not till the rise of Philip of Macedon and his greater son Alexander that Byzantium fell for the fifth time into the hands of an enemy. The elder king was repulsed from the city's walls after a long siege, culminating in an attempt at an escalade by night, which was frustrated owing to the sudden appearance of a light in heaven, which revealed the advancing enemy and was taken by the Byzantines as a token of special divine aid [B.C. 339]. In commemoration of it they assumed as one of their civic badges the blazing crescent and star, which has descended to our own days and is still used as an emblem by the present owners of the city—the Ottoman Sultans. But after repulsing Philip the Byzantines had to submit some years later to Alexander. They formed under him part of the enormous Macedonian empire, and passed on his decease through the hands of his successors—Demetrius Poliorcetes, and Lysimachus. After the death of the latter in battle, however, they recovered a precarious freedom, and were again an independent community for a hundred years, till the power of Rome invaded the regions of Thrace and the Hellespont.

Byzantium was one of the cities which took the wise course of making an early alliance with the Romans, and obtained good and easy terms in consequence. During the wars of Rome with Macedon and Antiochus the Great it proved such a faithful assistant that the Senate gave it the status of a *civitas libera et foederata*, "a free and confederate city," and it was not taken under direct Roman government, but allowed complete liberty in everything save the control of its foreign relations and the payment of a tribute to Rome. It was not till the Roman Republic had long passed away, that the Emperor Vespasian stripped it of these privileges, and threw it into the province of Thrace, to exist for the future as an ordinary provincial town [A.D. 73].

Though deprived of a liberty which had for long years been almost nominal, Byzantium could not be deprived of its unrivalled position for commerce. It continued to flourish under the *Pax Romana*, the long-continued peace which all the inner countries of the empire enjoyed during the first two centuries of the imperial *régime*, and is mentioned again and again as one of the most important cities of the middle regions of the Roman world.

But an evil time for Byzantium, as for all the other parts of the civilized world, began when the golden age of the Antonines ceased, and the epoch of the military emperors followed. In 192 A.D., Commodus, the unworthy son of the great and good Marcus Aurelius, was murdered, and ere long three military usurpers were wrangling for his blood-stained diadem. Most unhappily for itself Byzantium lay on the line of division between the eastern provinces, where Pescennius Niger had been proclaimed, and the Illyrian provinces, where Severus had assumed the imperial style. The city was seized by the army of Syria, and strengthened in haste. Presently Severus appeared from the west, after he had made himself master of Rome and Italy, and fell upon the forces of his rival Pescennius. Victory followed the arms of the Illyrian legions, the east was subdued, and the Syrian emperor put to death. But when all his other adherents had yielded, the garrison of Byzantium refused to submit. For more than two years they maintained the impregnable city against the lieutenants of Severus, and it was not till A.D. 196 that they were forced to yield. The emperor appeared in person to punish the long-protracted resistance of the town; not only the garrison, but the civil magistrates of Byzantium were slain before his eyes. The massive walls "so firmly built with great square stones clamped together with bolts of iron, that the whole seemed but one block," were laboriously cast down. The property of the citizens was confiscated, and the town itself deprived of all municipal privileges and handed over to be governed like a dependent village by its neighbours of Perinthus.

Caracalla, the son of Severus, gave back to the Byzantines the right to govern themselves, but the town had received a hard blow, and would have required a long spell of peace to recover its prosperity. Peace however it was not destined to see. All through the middle years of the third century it was vexed by the incursions of the Goths, who harried mercilessly the countries on the Black Sea whose commerce sustained its trade. Under Gallienus in A.D. 263 it was again seized by an usurping emperor, and shared the fate of his adherents. The soldiers of Gallienus sacked Byzantium from cellar to garret, and made such a slaughter of its inhabitants that it is said that the old Megarian race who had so long possessed it were absolutely exterminated. But the irresistible attraction of the site was too great to allow its ruins to remain desolate. Within ten years after its sack by the army of Gallienus, we find Byzantium again a populous town, and its inhabitants are specially praised by the historian Trebellius Pollio for the courage with which they repelled a Gothic raid in the reign of Claudius II.

The strong Illyrian emperors, who staved off from the Roman Empire the ruin which appeared about to overwhelm it in the third quarter of the third century, gave Byzantium time and peace to recover its ancient prosperity. It profited especially from the constant neighbourhood of the imperial court, after Diocletian fixed his residence at Nicomedia, only sixty miles away, on the Bithynian side of the Propontis. But the military importance of Byzantium was always interfering with its commercial greatness. After the abdication of Diocletian the empire was for twenty years vexed by constant partitions of territory between the colleagues whom he left behind him. Byzantium after a while found itself the border fortress of Licinius, the emperor who ruled in the Balkan Peninsula, while Maximinus Daza was governing the Asiatic provinces. While Licinius was absent in Italy, Maximinus treacherously attacked his rival's dominions without declaration of war, and took Byzantium by surprise. But the Illyrian emperor returned in haste, defeated his grasping neighbour not far from the walls of the city, and recovered his great frontier fortress after it had been only a few months out of his hands [A.D. 314]. The town must have suffered severely by changing masters twice in the same year; it does not, however, seem to have been sacked or burnt, as was so often the case with a captured city in those dismal days. But Licinius when he had recovered the place set to work to render it impregnable. Though it was not his capital he made it the chief fortress of his realm, which, since the defeat of Maximinus, embraced the whole eastern half of the Roman world.

It was accordingly at Byzantium that Licinius made his last desperate stand, when in A.D. 323 he found himself engaged in an unsuccessful war with his brother-in-law Constantine, the Emperor of the West. For many months the war stood still

CONSTANTINE

beneath the walls of the city; but Constantine persevered in the siege, raising great mounds which overlooked the walls, and sweeping away the defenders by a constant stream of missiles, launched from dozens of military engines which he had erected on these artificial heights. At last the city surrendered, and the cause of Licinius was lost. Constantine, the last of his rivals subdued, became the sole emperor of the Roman world, and stood a victor on the ramparts which were ever afterwards to bear his name.

II. The Foundation Of Constantinople. (A.D. 328-330.)

When the fall of Byzantium had wrecked the fortunes of Licinius, the Roman world was again united beneath the sceptre of a single master. For thirty-seven years, ever since Diocletian parcelled out the provinces with his colleagues, unity had been unknown, and emperors, whose number had sometimes risen to six and sometimes sunk to two, had administered their realms on different principles and with varying success.

Constantine, whose victory over his rivals had been secured by his talents as an administrator and a diplomatist no less than by his military skill, was one of those men whose hard practical ability has stamped upon the history of the world a much deeper impress than has been left by many conquerors and legislators of infinitely greater genius. He was a man of that self-contained, self-reliant, unsympathetic type of mind which we recognize in his great predecessor Augustus, or in Frederic the Great of Prussia.

CONSTANTINE THE GREAT.

Constantine the Great

Though the strain of old Roman blood in his veins must have been but small, Constantine was in many ways a typical Roman; the hard, cold, steady, unwearying energy, which in earlier centuries had won the empire of the world, was once more incarnate in him. But if Roman in character, he was anything but Roman in his sympathies. Born by the Danube, reared in the courts and camps of Asia and Gaul, he was absolutely free from any of that superstitious reverence for the ancient glories of the city on the Tiber which had inspired so many of his predecessors. Italy was to him but a secondary province amongst his wide realms. When he distributed his dominions among his heirs, it was Gaul that he gave as the noblest share to his eldest and best-loved son: Italy was to him a younger child's portion. There had been emperors before him who had neglected Rome: the barbarian Maximinus I. had dwelt by the Rhine and the Danube; the politic Diocletian had chosen Nicomedia as his favourite residence. But no one had yet dreamed of raising up a rival to the mistress of the world, and of turning Rome into a provincial town. If preceding emperors had dwelt far afield, it was to meet the exigencies of war on the frontiers or the government of distant provinces. It was reserved for Constantine to erect over against Rome a rival metropolis for the civilized world, an imperial city which was to be neither a mere camp nor a mere court, but the administrative and commercial centre of the Roman world.

For more than a hundred years Rome had been a most inconvenient residence for the emperors. The main problem which had been before them was the repelling of incessant barbarian inroads on the Balkan Peninsula; the troubles on the Rhine and the Euphrates, though real enough, had been but minor evils. Rome, placed half way down the long projection of Italy, handicapped by its bad harbours and separated from the rest of the empire by the passes of the Alps, was too far away from the points where the emperor was most wanted—the banks of the Danube and the walls of Sirmium and Singidunum. For the ever-recurring wars with Persia it was even more inconvenient; but these were less pressing dangers; no Persian army had yet penetrated beyond Antioch—only 200 miles from the frontier—while in the Balkan Peninsula the Goths had broken so far into the heart of the empire as to sack Athens and Thessalonica.

Constantine, with all the Roman world at his feet, and all its responsibilities weighing on his mind, was far too able a man to overlook the great need of the day—a more conveniently placed administrative and military centre for his empire. He required a place that should be easily accessible by land and sea—which Rome had never been in spite of its wonderful roads—that should overlook the Danube lands, without being too far away from the East; that should be so strongly situated that it might prove an impregnable arsenal and citadel against barbarian attacks from the north; that should at the same time be far enough away from the turmoil of the actual frontier to afford a safe and splendid residence for the imperial court. The names of several towns are given by historians as having suggested themselves to Constantine. First was his own birth-place—Naissus (Nisch) on the Morava, in the heart of the Balkan Peninsula; but Naissus had little to recommend it: it was too close to the frontier and too far from the sea. Sardica—the modern Sofia in Bulgaria—was liable to the same objections, and had not the sole advantage of Naissus, that of being connected in sentiment with the emperor's early days. Nicomedia on its long gulf at the east end of the Propontis was a more eligible situation in every way, and had already served as an imperial residence. But all that could be urged in favour of Nicomedia applied with double force to Byzantium, and, in addition, Constantine had no wish to choose a city in which his own memory would be eclipsed by that of his predecessor Diocletian, and whose name was associated by the Christians, the class of his subjects whom he had most favoured of late, with the persecutions of Diocletian and Galerius. For Ilium, the last place on which Constantine had cast his mind, nothing could be alleged except its ancient legendary glories, and the fact that the mythologists of Rome had always fabled that their city drew its origin from the exiled Trojans of Æneas. Though close to the sea it had no good harbour, and it was just too far from the mouth of the Hellespont to command effectually the exit of the Euxine.

Byzantium, on the other hand, was thoroughly well known to Constantine. For months his camp had been pitched beneath its walls; he must have known accurately every inch of its environs, and none of its military advantages can have missed his eye. Nothing, then, could have been more natural than his selection of the old Megarian city for his new capital. Yet the Roman world was startled at the first news of his choice; Byzantium had been so long known merely as a great port of call for the Euxine trade, and as a first-class provincial fortress, that it was hard to conceive of it as a destined seat of empire.

When once Constantine had determined to make Byzantium his capital, in preference to any other place in the Balkan lands, his measures were taken with his usual energy and thoroughness. The limits of the new city were at once marked out by solemn processions in the old Roman style. In later ages a picturesque legend was told to account for the magnificent scale on which it was planned. The emperor, we read, marched out on foot, followed by all his court, and traced with his spear the line where the new fortifications were to be drawn. As he paced on further and further westward along the shore of the Golden Horn, till he was more than two miles away from his starting-point, the gate of old Byzantium, his attendants grew more and more surprised at the vastness of his scheme. At last they ventured to observe that he had already exceeded the most ample limits that an imperial city could require. But Constantine turned to rebuke them: "I shall go on," he said, "until He, the invisible guide who marches before me, thinks fit to stop." Guided by his mysterious presentiment of greatness, the emperor advanced till he was three miles from the eastern angle of Byzantium, and only turned his steps when he had included in his boundary line all the seven hills which are embraced in the peninsula between the Propontis and the Golden Horn.

The rising ground just outside the walls of the old city, where Constantine's tent had been pitched during the siege of A.D. 323, was selected out as the market-place of the new foundation. There he erected the *Milion*, or "golden milestone," from which all the distances of the eastern world were in future to be measured. This "central point of the world" was not a mere single stone, but a small building like a temple, its roof supported by seven pillars; within was placed the statue of the emperor, together with that of his venerated mother, the Christian Empress Helena.

The south-eastern part of the old town of Byzantium was chosen by Constantine for the site of his imperial palace. The spot was cleared of all private dwellings for a space of 150 acres, to give space not only for a magnificent residence for his whole court, but for spacious gardens and pleasure-grounds. A wall, commencing at the Lighthouse, where the Bosphorus joins the Propontis, turned inland and swept along parallel to the shore for about a mile, in order to shut off the imperial precinct from the city.

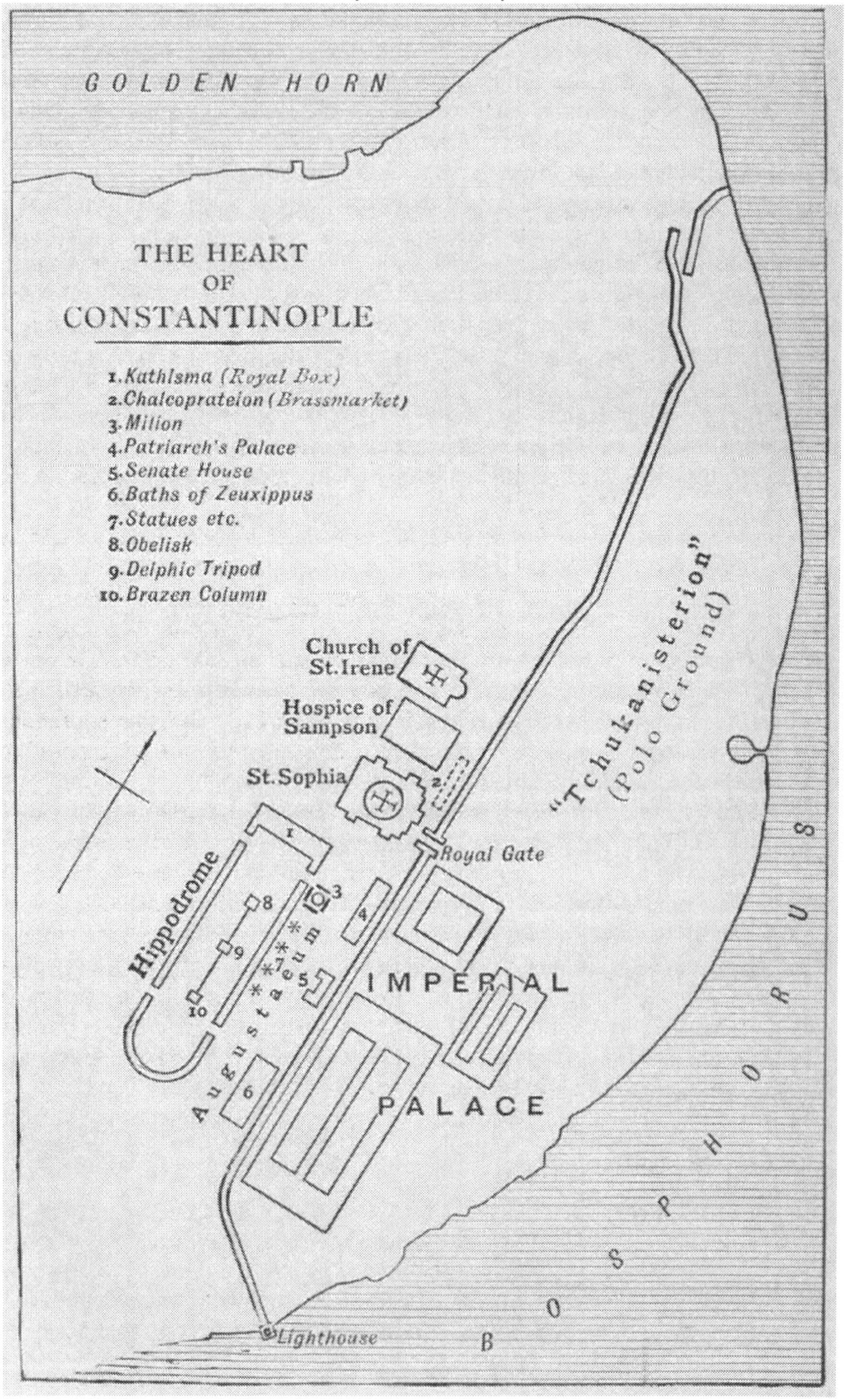
GOLDEN HORN
THE HEART OF CONSTANTINOPLE
1. Kathisma (Royal Box)
2. Chalcoprateion (Brassmarket)
3. Milion
4. Patriarch's Palace
5. Senate House
6. Baths of Zeuxippus
7. Statues etc.
8. Obelisk
9. Delphic Tripod
10. Brazen Column
Church of St. Irene
Hospice of Sampson
St. Sophia
Royal Gate
Hippodrome
Augustaeum
IMPERIAL PALACE
"Tchukanisterion" (Polo Ground)
BOSPHORUS
Lighthouse

North-west of the palace lay the central open space in which the life of Constantinople was to find its centre. This was the "Augustaeum," a splendid oblong forum, about a thousand feet long by three hundred broad. It was paved with marble and surrounded on all sides by stately public buildings. To its east, as we have already said, lay the imperial palace, but between the palace and the open space were three detached edifices connected by a colonnade. Of these, the most easterly was the Great Baths, known, from their builder, as the "Baths of Zeuxippus." They were built on the same magnificent scale which the earlier emperors had used in Old Rome, though they could not, perhaps, vie in size with the enormous Baths of Caracalla. Constantine utilized and enlarged the old public bath of Byzantium, which had been rebuilt after the taking of the city by Severus. He adorned the frontage and courts of the edifice with statues taken from every prominent town of Greece and Asia, the old Hellenic masterpieces which had escaped the rapacious hands of twelve generations of plundering proconsuls and Cæsars. There were to be seen the Athene of Lyndus, the Amphithrite of Rhodes, the Pan which had been consecrated by the Greeks after the defeat of Xerxes, and the Zeus of Dodona.

Adjoining the Baths, to the north, lay the second great building, on the east side of the Augustaeum—the Senate House. Constantine had determined to endow his new city with a senate modelled on that of Old Rome, and had indeed persuaded many old senatorial families to migrate eastward by judicious gifts of pensions and houses. We know that the assembly was worthily housed, but no details survive about Constantine's building, on account of its having been twice destroyed within the century. But, like the Baths of Zeuxippus, it was adorned with ancient statuary, among which the Nine Muses of Helicon are specially cited by the historian who describes the burning of the place in A.D. 404.

Linked to the Senate House by a colonnade, lay on the north the Palace of the Patriarch, as the Bishop of Byzantium was ere long to be called, when raised to the same status as his brethren of Antioch and Alexandria. A fine building in itself, with a spacious hall of audience and a garden, the patriarchal dwelling was yet completely overshadowed by the imperial palace which rose behind it. And so it was with the patriarch himself: he lived too near his royal master to be able to gain any independent authority. Physically and morally alike he was too much overlooked by his august neighbour, and never found the least opportunity of setting up an independent spiritual authority over against the civil government, or of founding an *imperium in imperio* like the Bishop of Rome.

THE ATMEIDAN [HIPPODROME] AND ST. SOPHIA.

All along the western side of the Augustaeum, facing the three buildings which wc have already described, lay an edifice which played a very prominent part in the public life of Constantinople. This was the great Hippodrome, a splendid circus 640 cubits long and 160 broad, in which were renewed the games that Old Rome had known so well. The whole system the chariot-races between the teams that represented the "factions"of the Circus was reproduced at Byzantium with an energy that even surpassed the devotion of the Romans to horse racing. From the first foundation of the city the rivalry of the "Blues" and the "Greens" was one of the most striking features of the life of the place. It was carried far beyond the circus, and spread into all branches of life. We often hear of the "Green" faction identifying itself with Arianism, or of the "Blue"supporting a pretender to the throne. Not merely men of sporting interests, but persons of all ranks and professions, chose their colour and backed their faction. The system was a positive danger to the public peace, and constantly led to riots, culminating in the great sedition of A.D. 523, which we shall presently have to describe at length. In the Hippodrome the "Greens" always entered by the north-eastern gate, and sat on the east side; the "Blues" approached by the north-western gate and stretched along the western side. The emperor's box, called the Kathisma, occupied the whole of the short northern side, and contained many hundreds of seats for the imperial retinue. The great central throne of the Kathisma was the place in which the monarch showed himself most frequently to his subjects, and around it many strange scenes were enacted. It was on this throne that the rebel Hypatius was crowned emperor by the mob, with his own wife's necklace for an impromptu diadem. Here also, two centuries later, the Emperor Justinian II. sat in state after his reconquest of Constantinople, with his rivals, Leontius and Apsimarus, bound beneath his footstool, while the populace chanted, in allusion to the names of the vanquished princes, the verse, "Thou shalt trample on the Lion and the Asp."

Down the centre of the Hippodrome ran the "spina," or division wall, which every circus showed; it was ornamented with three most curious monuments, whose strange juxtaposition seemed almost to typify the heterogeneous materials from which the new city was built up. The first and oldest was an obelisk brought from Egypt, and covered with the usual hieroglyphic inscriptions; the second was the most notable, though one of the least beautiful, of the antiquities of Constantinople: it was the three-headed brazen serpent which Pausanias and the victorious Greeks had dedicated at Delphi in 479 B.C., after they had destroyed the Persian army at Platæa. The golden tripod, which was supported by the heads of the serpents, had long been wanting: the sacrilegious Phocians had stolen it six centuries before; but the dedicatory inscriptions engraved on the coils of the pedestal survived then and survive now to delight the archæologist. The third monument on the "spina" was a square bronze column of more modern work, contrasting strangely with the venerable antiquity of its neighbours. By some freak of chance all three monuments have remained till our own day: the vast walls of the Hippodrome have crumbled away, but its central decorations still stand erect in the midst of an open space which the Turks call the Atmeidan, or place of horses, in dim memory of its ancient use.

Along the outer eastern wall of the Hippodrome on the western edge of the Augustaeum, stood a range of small chapels and statues, the most important landmark among them being the *Milion* or central milestone of the empire, which we have already described. The statues, few at first, were increased by later emperors, till they extended along the whole length of the forum. Constantine's own contribution to the collection was a tall porphyry column surmounted by a bronze image which had once been the tutelary Apollo of the city of Hierapolis, but was turned into a representation of the emperor by the easy method of knocking off its head and substituting the imperial features. It was exactly the reverse of a change which can be seen at Rome, where the popes have removed the head of the Emperor Aurelius, and turned him into St. Peter, on the column in the Corso.

VISIT THE ATMEIDAN

BUILDING A PALACE.
(*From a Byzantine MS.*)

North of the Hippodrome stood the great church which Constantine erected for his Christian subjects, and dedicated to the Divine Wisdom (*Hagia Sophia*). It was not the famous domed edifice which now bears that name, but an earlier and humbler building, probably of the Basilica-shape then usual. Burnt down once in the fifth and once in the sixth centuries, it has left no trace of its original character. From the west door of St. Sophia a wooden gallery, supported on arches, crossed the square, and finally ended at the "Royal Gate" of the palace. By this the emperor would betake himself to divine service without having to cross the street of the Chalcoprateia (brass market), which lay opposite to St. Sophia. The general effect of the gallery must have been somewhat like that of the curious passage perched aloft on arches which connects the Pitti and Uffizi palaces at Florence.

The edifices which we have described formed the heart of Constantinople. Between the Palace, the Hippodrome, and the Cathedral most of the important events in the history of the city took place. But to north and west the city extended for miles, and everywhere there were buildings of note, though no other cluster could vie with that round the Augustaeum. The Church of the Holy Apostles, which Constantine destined as the burying-place of his family, was the second among the ecclesiastical edifices of the town. Of the outlying civil buildings, the public granaries along the quays, the Golden Gate, by which the great road from the west entered the walls, and the palace of the praetorian praefect, who acted as governor of the city, must all have been well worthy of notice. A statue of Constantine on horseback, which stood by the last-named edifice, was one of the chief shows of Constantinople down to the end of the Middle Ages, and some curious legends gathered around it.

FIFTEENTH-CENTURY DRAWING OF THE EQUESTRIAN STATUE OF CONSTANTINE.

It was in A.D. 328 or 329—the exact date is not easily to be fixed—that Constantine had definitely chosen Byzantium for his capital, and drawn out the plan for its development. As early as May 11, 330, the buildings were so far advanced that he was able to hold the festival which celebrated its consecration. Christian bishops blessed the partially completed palace, and held the first service in St. Sophia; for Constantine, though still unbaptized himself, had determined that the new city should be Christian from the first. Of paganism there was no trace in it, save a few of the old temples of the Byzantines, spared when the older streets were levelled to clear the ground for the palace and adjoining buildings. The statues of the gods which adorned the Baths and Senate House stood there as works of art, not as objects of worship.

To fill the vast limits of his city, Constantine invited many senators of Old Rome and many rich provincial proprietors of Greece and Asia to take up their abode in it, granting them places in his new senate and sites for the dwellings they would require. The countless officers and functionaries of the imperial court, with their subordinates and slaves, must have composed a very considerable element in the new population. The artizans and handicraftsmen were enticed in thousands by the offer of special privileges. Merchants and seamen had always abounded at

Byzantium, and now flocked in numbers which made the old commercial prosperity of the city seem insignificant. Most effective—though most demoralizing—of the gifts which Constantine bestowed on the new capital to attract immigrants was the old Roman privilege of free distribution of corn to the populace. The wheat-tribute of Egypt, which had previously formed part of the public provision of Rome, was transferred to the use of Constantinople, only the African corn from Carthage being for the future assigned for the subsistence of the older city.

On the completion of the dedication festival in 330 A.D. an imperial edict gave the city the title of New Rome, and the record was placed on a marble tablet near the equestrian statue of the emperor, opposite the Strategion. But "New Rome" was a phrase destined to subsist in poetry and rhetoric alone: the world from the first very rightly gave the city the founder's name only, and persisted in calling it Constantinople.

III. The Fight With The Goths.

Constantine lived seven years after he had completed the dedication of his new city, and died in peace and prosperity on the 22nd of May, A.D.337, received on his death-bed into that Christian Church on whose verge he had lingered during the last half of his life. By his will he left his realm to be divided among his sons and nephews; but a rapid succession of murders and civil wars thinned out the imperial house, and ended in the concentration of the whole empire from the Forth to the Tigris under the sceptre of Constantius II., the second son of the great emperor. The Roman world was not yet quite ripe for a permanent division; it was still possible to manage it from a single centre, for by some strange chance the barbarian invasions which had troubled the third century had ceased for a time, and the Romans were untroubled, save by some minor bickerings on the Rhine and the Euphrates. Constantius II., an administrator of some ability, but gloomy, suspicious, and unsympathetic, was able to devote his leisure to ecclesiastical controversies, and to dishonour himself by starting the first persecution of Christian by Christian that the world had seen. The crisis in the history of the empire was not destined to fall in his day, nor in the short reign of his cousin and successor, Julian, the amiable and cultured, but entirely wrongheaded, pagan zealot, who strove to put back the clock of time and restore the worship of the ancient gods of Greece. Both Constantius and Julian, if asked whence danger to the empire might be expected, would have pointed eastward, to the Mesopotamian frontier, where their great enemy, Sapor King of Persia, strove, with no very great success, to break through the line of Roman fortresses that protected Syria and Asia Minor.

But it was not in the east that the impending storm was really brewing. It was from the north that mischief was to come.

GOTHIC IDOLS.
(*From the Column of Arcadius.*)

For a hundred and fifty years the Romans had been well acquainted with the tribes of the Goths, the most easterly of the Teutonic nations who lay along the imperial border. All through the third century they had been molesting the provinces of the Balkan Peninsula by their incessant raids, as we have already had occasion to relate. Only after a hard struggle had they been rolled back across the Danube, and compelled to limit their settlements to its northern bank, in what had once been the land of the Dacians. The last struggle with them had been in the time of Constantine, who, in a war that lasted from A.D. 328 to A.D. 332, had beaten them in the open field, compelled their king to give his sons as hostages, and dictated his own terms of peace. Since then the appetite of the Goths for war and adventure seemed permanently checked: for forty years they had kept comparatively quiet and seldom indulged in raids across the Danube. They were rapidly settling down into steady farmers in the fertile lands on the Theiss and the Pruth; they traded freely with the Roman towns of Moesia; many of their young warriors enlisted among the Roman auxiliary troops, and one considerable body of Gothic emigrants had been permitted to settle as subjects of the empire on the northern slope of the Balkans. By this time many of the Goths were becoming Christians: priests of their own blood already ministered to them, and the Bible, translated into their own language, was already in their hands. One of the earliest Gothic converts, the good Bishop Ulfilas—the first bishop of German blood that was ever consecrated—had rendered into their idiom the New Testament and most of the Old. A great portion of his work still survives, incomparably the most precious relic of the old Teutonic tongues that we now possess.

The Goths were rapidly losing their ancient ferocity. Compared to the barbarians who dwelt beyond them, they might almost be called a civilized race. The Romans were beginning to look upon them as a guard set on the frontier to ward off the wilder peoples that lay to their north and east. The nation was now divided into two tribes: the Visigoths, whose tribal name was the Thervings, lay more to the south, in what are now the countries of Moldavia, Wallachia, and Southern Hungary; the Ostrogoths, or tribe of the Gruthungs, lay more to the north and east, in Bessarabia, Transylvania, and the Dniester valley.

But a totally unexpected series of events were now to show how prescient Constantine had been, in rearing his great fortress-capital to serve as the central place of arms of the Balkan Peninsula.

About the year A.D. 372 the Huns, an enormous Tartar horde from beyond the Don and Volga, burst into the lands north of the Euxine, and began to work their way westward. The first tribe that lay in their way, the nomadic race of the Alans, they almost exterminated. Then they fell upon the Goths. The Ostrogoths made a desperate attempt to defend the line of the Dniester against the oncoming savages—"men with faces that can hardly be called faces—rather shapeless black collops of flesh with little points instead of eyes; little in stature, but lithe and active, skilful in riding, broad shouldered, good at the bow, stiff-necked and proud, hiding under a barely human form the ferocity of the wild beast." But the enemy whom the Gothic historian describes in these uninviting terms was too strong for the Teutons of the East. The Ostrogoths were crushed and compelled to become vassals of the Huns, save a remnant who fought their way southward to the Wallachian shore, near the marshes of the Delta of the Danube. Then the Huns fell on the Visigoths. The wave of invasion pressed on; the Bug and the Pruth proved no barrier to the swarms of nomad bowmen, and the Visigoths, under their Duke Fritigern, fell back in dismay with their wives and children, their waggons and flocks and herds, till they found themselves with their backs to the Danube. Surrender to the enemy was more dreadful to the Visigoths than to their eastern brethren; they were more civilized, most of them were Christians, and the prospect of slavery to savages seems to have appeared intolerable to them.

Pressed against the Danube and the Roman border, the Visigoths sent in despair to ask permission to cross from the Emperor. A contemporary writer describes how they stood. "All the multitude that had escaped from the murderous savagery of the Huns—no less than 200,000 fighting men, besides women and old men and children—-were there on the river bank, stretching out their hands with loud lamentations, and earnestly supplicating leave to cross, bewailing their calamity, and promising that they would ever faithfully adhere to the imperial alliance if only the boon was granted them."

At this moment (A.D. 376) the Roman Empire was again divided. The house of Constantine was gone, and the East was ruled by Valens, a stupid, cowardly, and avaricious prince, who had obtained the diadem and half the Roman world only because he was the brother of Valentinian, the greatest general of the day. Valentinian had taken the West for his portion, and dwelt in his camp on the Rhine and Upper Danube, while Valens, slothful and timid, shut himself up with a court of slaves and flatterers in the imperial palace at Constantinople.

The proposal of the Goths filled Valens with dismay. It was difficult to say which was more dangerous—to refuse a passage to 200,000 desperate men with arms in their hands and a savage foe at their backs, or to admit them within the line of river and fortress that protected the border, with an implied obligation to find land for them. After much doubting he chose the latter alternative: if the Goths would give hostages and surrender their arms, they should be ferried across the Danube and permitted to settle as subject-allies within the empire.

The Goths accepted the terms, gave up the sons of their chiefs as hostages, and streamed across the river as fast as the Roman Danube-flotilla could transport them. But no sooner had they reached Moesia than troubles broke out. The Roman officials at first tried to disarm the immigrants, but the Goths were unwilling to surrender their weapons, and offered large bribes to be allowed to retain them: in strict disobedience to the Emperor's orders, the bribes were accepted and the Goths retained their arms. Further disputes soon broke out. The provisions of Moesia did not suffice for so many hundred thousand mouths as had just entered its border, and Valens had ordered stores of corn from Asia to be collected for the use of the Goths, till they should have received and commenced to cultivate land of their own. But the governor, Lupicinus, to fill his own pockets, held back the food, and doled out what he chose to give at exorbitant prices. In sheer hunger the Goths were driven to barter a slave for a single loaf of bread and ten pounds of silver for a sheep. This shameless extortion continued as long as the stores and the patience of the Goths lasted. At last the poorer immigrants were actually beginning to sell their own children for slaves rather than let them starve. This drove the Goths to desperation, and a chance affray set the whole nation in a blaze. Fritigern, with many of his nobles, was dining with Count Lupicinus at the town of Marcianopolis, when some starving Goths tried to pillage the market by force. A party of Roman soldiers strove to drive them off, and were at once mishandled or slain. On hearing the tumult and learning its cause, Lupicinus recklessly bade his retinue seize and slay Fritigern and the other guests at his banquet. The Goths drew their swords and cut their way out of the palace. Then riding to the nearest camp of his followers, Fritigern told his tale, and bade them take up arms against Rome.

There followed a year of desperate fighting all along the Danube, and the northern slope of the Balkans. The Goths half-starved for many months, and smarting under the extortion and chicanery to which they had been subjected, soon showed that the old barbarian spirit was but thinly covered by the veneer of Christianity and civilization which they had acquired in the last half-century. The struggle resolved itself into a repetition of the great raids of the third century: towns were sacked and the open country harried in the old style, nor was the war rendered less fierce by the fact that many runaway slaves and other outcasts among the provincial population joined the invaders. But the Roman armies still retained their old reputation; the ravages of the Goths were checked at the Balkans, and though joined by the remnants of the Ostrogoths from the Danube mouth, as well as by other tribes flying from the Huns, the Visigoths were at first held at bay by the imperial armies. A desperate pitched battle at Ad Salices, near the modern Kustendje thinned the ranks of both sides, but led to no decisive result.

Next year, however, the unwarlike Emperor, driven into the field by the clamours of his subjects, took the field in person, with great reinforcements brought from Asia Minor. At the same time his nephew Gratian, a gallant young prince who had succeeded to the Empire of the West, set forth through Pannonia to bring aid to the lands of the Lower Danube.

The personal intervention of Valens in the struggle was followed by a fearful disaster. In 378 A.D., the main body of the Goths succeeded in forcing the line of the Balkans; they were not far from Adrianople when the Emperor started to attack them, with a splendid army of 60,000 men. Every one expected to hear of a victory, for the reputation of invincibility still clung to the legions, and after six hundred years of war the disciplined infantry of Rome, *robur peditum*, whose day had lasted since the Punic wars, were still reckoned superior, when fairly handled, to any amount of wild barbarians.

But a new chapter of the history of the art of war was just commencing; during their sojourn in the plains of South Russia and Roumania the Goths had taken, first of all German races, to fighting on horseback. Dwelling in the Ukraine they had felt the influence of that land, ever the nurse of cavalry from the day of the Scythian to that of the Tartar and Cossack. They had come to "consider it more honourable to fight on horse than on foot," and every chief was followed by his war-band of mounted men. Driven against their will into conflict with the empire, they found themselves face to face into the army that had so long held the world in fear, and had turned back their own ancestors in rout three generations before.

Valens found the main body of the Goths encamped in a great "laager," on the plain north of Adrianople. After some abortive negotiations he developed an attack on their front, when suddenly a great body of horsemen charged in on the Roman flank. It was the main strength of the Gothic cavalry, which had been foraging at a distance; receiving news of the fight it had ridden straight for the battle field. Some Roman squadrons which covered the left flank of the Emperor's army were ridden down and trampled under foot. Then the Goths swept down on the infantry of the left wing, rolled it up, and drove it in upon the centre. So tremendous was their impact that legions and cohorts were pushed together in hopeless confusion. Every attempt to stand firm failed, and in a few minutes left, centre, and reserve, were one undistinguishable mass. Imperial guards, light troops, lancers, auxiliaries, and infantry of the line were wedged together in a press that grew closer every moment. The Roman cavalry saw that the day was lost, and rode off without another effort. Then the abandoned infantry realized the horror of their position: equally unable to deploy or to fly, they had to stand to be cut down. Men could not raise their arms to strike a blow, so closely were they packed; spears snapped right and left, their bearers being unable to lift them to a vertical position; many soldiers were stifled in the press. Into this quivering mass the Goths rode, plying lance and sword against the helpless enemy. It was not till forty thousand men had fallen that the thinning of the ranks enabled the survivors to break out and follow their cavalry in a headlong flight. They left behind them, dead on the field, the Emperor, the Grand Masters of the Infantry and Cavalry, the Count of the Palace, and thirty-five commanders of different corps.

The battle of Adrianople was the most fearful defeat suffered by a Roman army since Cannæ, a slaughter to which it is aptly compared by the contemporary historian Ammianus Marcellinus. The army of the East was almost annihilated, and was never reorganized again on the old Roman lines.

This awful catastrophe brought down on Constantinople the first attack which it experienced since it had changed its name from Byzantium. After a vain assault on Adrianople, the victorious Goths pressed rapidly on towards the imperial city. Harrying the whole country side as they passed by, they presented themselves before the "Golden Gate," its south-western exit. But the attack was destined to come to nothing: "their courage failed them when they looked on the vast circuit of walls and the enormous extent of streets; all that mass of riches within appeared inaccessible to them. They cast away the siege machines which they had prepared, and rolled backward on to Thrace."[3] Beyond skirmishing under the walls with a body of Saracen cavalry which had been brought up to strengthen the garrison, they made no hostile attempt on the city. So forty years after his death, Constantine's prescience was for the first time justified. He was right in believing that an impregnable city on the Bosphorus would prove the salvation of the Balkan Peninsula even if all its open country were overrun by the invader.

The unlucky Valens was succeeded on the throne by Theodosius, a wise and virtuous prince, who set himself to repair, by caution and courage combined, the disaster that had shaken the Roman power in the Danube lands. With the remnants of the army of the East he made head against the barbarians; without venturing to attack their main body, he destroyed many marauders and scattered bands, and made the continuance of the war profitless to them. If they dispersed to plunder they were cut off; if they held together in masses they starved. Presently Fritigern died, and Theodosius made peace with his successor Athanarich, a king who had lately come over the Danube at the head of a new swarm of Goths from the Carpathian country. Theodosius frankly promised and faithfully observed the terms that Fritigern had asked of Valens ten years before. He granted the Goths land for their settlement in the Thracian province which they had wasted, and enlisted in his armies all the chiefs and their war-bands. Within ten years after the fight of Adrianople he had forty thousand Teutonic horsemen in his service; they formed the

---

[3] Ammianus Marcellinus

best and most formidable part of his host, and were granted a higher pay than the native Roman soldiery. The immediate military results of the policy of Theodosius were not unsatisfactory; it was his Gothic auxiliaries who won for him his two great victories over the legions of the West, when in A.D. 388 he conquered the rebel Magnus Maximus, and in A.D. 394 the rebel Eugenius.

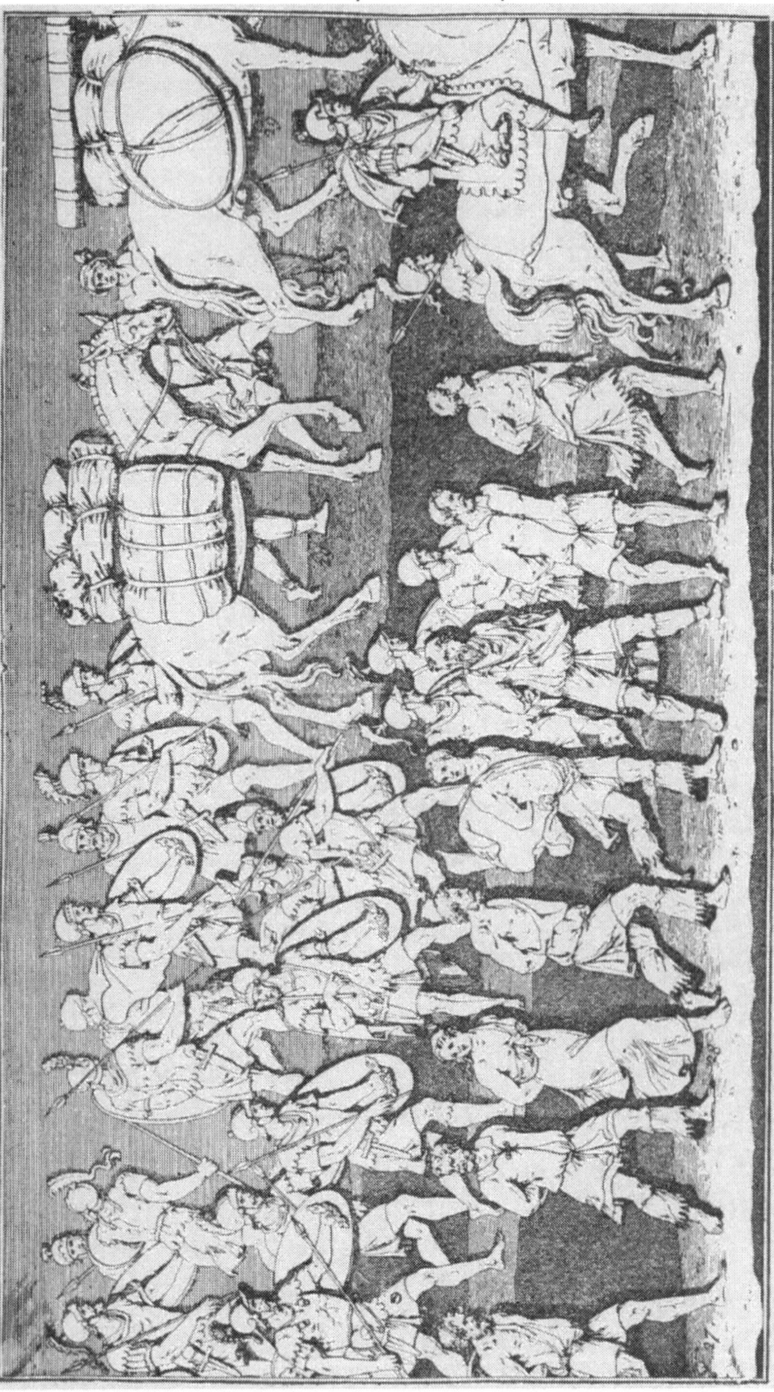

GOTHIC CAPTIVES.
(*From the Column of Arcadius.*)

But from the political side the experiment of Theodosius was fraught with the greatest danger that the Roman Empire had yet known. When barbarian auxiliaries had been enlisted before, they had been placed under Roman leaders and mixed with equal numbers of Roman troops. To leave them under their own chiefs, and deliberately favour them at the expense of the native soldiery, was a most unhappy experiment. It practically put the command of the empire in their hands; for there was no hold over them save their personal loyalty to Theodosius, and the spell which the grandeur of the Roman name and Roman culture still exercised over their minds. That spell was still strong, as is shown in the story which the Gothic historian Jornandes tells about the visit of the old King Athanarich to Constantinople. "When he entered the royal city, 'Now,'said he, 'do I at last behold what I had often heard and deemed incredible.' He passed his eyes hither and thither admiring first the site of the city, then the fleets of corn-ships, then the lofty walls, then the crowds of people of all nations, mingled as the waters from divers springs mix in a single pool, then the ranks of disciplined soldiery. And at last he cried aloud, 'Doubtless the Emperor is as a god on earth, and he who raises a hand against him is guilty of his own blood.' " But this impression was not to continue for long. In A.D. 395, the good Emperor Theodosius, "the lover of peace and of the Goths," as he was called, died, and left the throne to his two weakly sons Arcadius and Honorius.

IV. The Departure Of The Germans.

The Roman Empire, at the end of the fourth century, was in a condition which made the experiment of Theodosius particularly dangerous. The government was highly centralized and bureaucratic; hosts of officials, appointed directly from Constantinople, administered every provincial post from the greatest to the least. There was little local self-government and no local patriotism. The civil population was looked on by the bureaucratic caste as a multitude without rights or capacities, existing solely for the purpose of paying taxes. So strongly was this view held, that to prevent the revenue from suffering, the land-holding classes, from the *curialis*, or local magnate, down to the poorest peasant, were actually forbidden to move from one district to another without special permission. A landowner was even prohibited from enlisting in the army, unless he could show that he left an heir behind him capable of paying his share in the local rates. An almost entire separation existed between the civil population and the military caste; it was hard for a civilian of any position to enlist; only the lower classes—who were of no account in tax-paying—were suffered to join the army. On the other hand, every pressure was used to make the sons of soldiers continue in the service. Thus had arisen a purely professional army, which had no sympathy or connection with the unarmed provincials whom it protected.

The army had been a source of unending trouble in the third century; for a hundred years it had made and unmade Cæsars at its pleasure. That was while it was still mainly composed of men born within the empire, and officered by Romans.

But Theodosius had now swamped the native element in the army by his wholesale enlistment of Gothic war-bands. And he had, moreover, handed many of the chief military posts to Teutons. Some of them indeed had married Roman wives and taken kindly to Roman modes of life, while nearly all had professed Christianity. But at the best they were military adventurers of alien blood while at the worst they were liable to relapse into barbarism, cast all their loyalty and civilization to the winds, and take to harrying the empire again in the old fearless fashion of the third century. Clearly nothing could be more dangerous than to hand over the protection of the timid and unarmed civil population to such guardians. The contempt they must have felt for the unwarlike provincials was so great, and the temptation to plunder the wealthy cities of the empire so constant and pressing, that it is no wonder if the Teutons yielded. Cæsar-making seemed as easy to the leaders as the sack of provincial churches and treasuries did to the rank and file.

When the personal ascendency of Theodosius was removed, the empire fell at once into the troubles which were inevitable. Both at the court of Arcadius, who reigned at Constantinople, and at that of Honorius, who had received the West as his share, a war of factions commenced between the German and the Roman party. Theodosius had distributed so many high military posts to Goths and other Teutons, that this influence was almost unbounded. Stilicho *Magister militum* (commander-in-chief) of the armies of Italy was predominant at the council board of Honorius; though he was a pure barbarian by blood, Theodosius had married him to his own niece Serena, and left him practically supreme in the West, for the young emperor was aged only eleven. In the East Arcadius, the elder brother, had attained his eighteenth year, and might have ruled his own realm had he possessed the energy. But he was a witless young man, "short, thin, and sallow, so inactive that he seldom spoke, and always looked as if he was about to fall asleep." His prime minister was a Western Roman named Rufinus, but before the first year of his reign was over, a Gothic captain named Gainas slew Rufinus at a review, before the Emperor's very eyes. The weak Arcadius was then compelled to make the eunuch Eutropius his minister, and to appoint Gainas *Magister militum* for the East.

Gainas and Stilicho contented themselves with wire-pulling at Court; but another Teutonic leader thought that the time had come for bolder work. Alaric was a chief sprung from the family of the Balts, whom the Goths reckoned next to the god-descended Amals among their princely houses. He was young, daring, and untameable; several years spent at Constantinople had failed to civilize him, but had succeeded in filling him with contempt for Roman effeminacy. Soon after the death of Theodosius, he raised the Visigoths in revolt, making it his pretext that the advisers of Arcadius were refusing the *foederati*, or auxiliaries, certain arrears of pay. The Teutonic sojourners in Moesia and Thrace joined him almost to a man, and the Constantinopolitan government found itself with only a shadow of an army to oppose the rebels. Alaric wandered far and wide, from the Danube to the gates of Constantinople, and from Constantinople to Greece, ransoming or sacking every town in his way till the Goths were gorged with plunder. No one withstood him save Stilicho, who was summoned from the West to aid his master's brother. By skilful manœuvres Stilicho blockaded Alaric in a mountain position in Arcadia; but when he had him at his mercy, it was found that "dog does not eat dog." The Teutonic prime minister let the Teutonic rebel escape him, and the Visigoths rolled north again into Illyricum. Sated with plunder, Alaric then consented to grant Arcadius peace, on condition that he was made a *Magister militum* like Stilicho and Gainas, and granted as much land for his tribesmen as he chose to ask. [A.D. 396.]

For the next five years Alaric, now proclaimed King of the Goths by his victorious soldiery, reigned with undisputed sway over the eastern parts of the Balkan Peninsula, paying only a shadow of homage to the royal phantom at Constantinople. There appeared every reason to believe that a German kingdom was about to be permanently established in the lands south and west of the Danube. The fate which actually befell Gaul, Spain, and Britain, a few years later seemed destined for Moesia and Macedonia. How different the history of Europe would have been if the Germans had settled down in Servia and Bulgaria we need hardly point out.

But another series of events was impending. In A.D. 401, Alaric, instead of resuming his attacks on Constantinople, suddenly declared war on the Western Emperor Honorius. He marched round the head of the Adriatic and invaded Northern Italy. The half-Romanized Stilicho, who wished to keep the rule of the West to himself, fought hard to turn the Goths out of Italy, and beat back Alaric's first invasion. But then the young emperor, who was as weak and more worthless than his brother Arcadius, slew the great minister on a charge of treason. When

Stilicho was gone, Alaric had everything his own way; he moved with the whole Visigothic race into Italy, where he ranged about at his will, ransoming and plundering every town from Rome downwards. The Visigoths are heard of no more in the Balkan Peninsula; they now pass into the history of Italy and then into that of Spain.

While Alaric's eyes were turned on Italy, but before he had actually come into conflict with Stilicho, the Court of Constantinople had been the seat of grave troubles. Gainas the Gothic *Magister militum* of the East, and his creature, the eunuch Eutropius, had fallen out, and the man of war had no difficulty in disposing of the wretched harem-bred Grand Chamberlain. Instigated by Gainas, the German mercenaries in the army of Asia started an insurrection under a certain Tribigild. Gainas was told to march against them, and collected troops ostensibly for that purpose. But when he was at the head of a considerable army, he did not attack the rebels, but sent a message to Constantinople bidding Arcadius give up to him the obnoxious Grand Chamberlain. Eutropius, hearing of his danger, threw himself on the protection of the Church: he fled into the Cathedral of St. Sophia and clung to the altar. John Chrysostom, the intrepid Patriarch of Constantinople, forbade the soldiers to enter the church, and protected the fugitive for some days. One of the most striking incidents in the history of St. Sophia followed: while the cowering Chamberlain lay before the altar, John preached to a crowded congregation a sermon on the text, "Vanity of vanities, all is vanity," emphasizing every period of his harangue by pointing to the fallen Eutropius—prime minister of the empire yesterday, and a hunted criminal to-day. The patriarch extorted a promise that the eunuch's life should be spared, and Eutropius gave himself up. Arcadius banished him to Cyprus, but the inexorable Gainas was not contented with his rival's removal; he had Eutropius brought back to Constantinople and beheaded.

The *Magister militum* now brought his army over to Constantinople, and quartered it there to overawe the emperor. It appeared quite likely that ere long the Germans would sack the city; but the fate that befell Rome ten years later was not destined for Constantinople. A mere chance brawl put the domination of Gainas to a sudden end. He himself and many of his troops were outside the city, when a sudden quarrel at one of the gates between a band of Goths and some riotous citizens brought about a general outbreak against the Germans. The Constantinopolitan mob showed itself more courageous and not less unruly than the Roman mob of elder days. The whole population turned out with extemporized arms and attacked the German soldiery. The gates were closed to prevent Gainas and his troops from outside returning, and a desperate street-fight ranged over the entire city. Isolated bodies of the Germans were cut off one by one, and at last their barracks were surrounded and set on fire. The rioters had the upper hand; seven thousand soldiers fell, and the remnant thought themselves lucky to escape. Gainas at once declared open war on the empire, but he had not the genius of Alaric, nor the numerical strength that had followed the younger chief. He was beaten in the field and forced to fly across the Danube, where he was caught and beheaded by Uldes, King of the Huns. Curiously enough the officer who defeated Gainas was himself not only a Goth but a heathen: he was named Fravitta and had been the sworn guest-friend of Theodosius, whose son he faithfully defended even against the assault of his own countrymen, [A.D. 401.]

The departure of Alaric and the death of Gainas freed the Eastern Romans from the double danger that has impended over them. They were neitherto see an independent German kingdom on the Danube and Morava, nor to remain under the rule of a semi-civilized German *Magister militum*, making and unmaking ministers, and perhaps Cæsars, at his good pleasure. The weak Arcadius was enabled to spend the remaining seven years of his life in comparative peace and quiet. His court was only troubled by an open war between his spouse, the Empress Ælia Eudoxia, and John Chrysostom, the Patriarch of Constantinople. John was a man of saintly life and apostolic fervour, but rash and inconsiderate alike in speech and action. His charity and eloquence made him the idol of the populace of the imperial city, but his austere manners and autocratic methods of dealing with his subordinates had made him many foes among the clergy. The patriarch's enemies were secretly supported by the empress, who had taken offence at the outspoken way in which John habitually denounced the luxury and insolence of her court. She favoured the intrigues of Theophilus, Patriarch of Alexandria, against his brother prelate, backed the Asiatic clergy in their complaints about John's oppression of them, and at last induced the Emperor to allow the saintly patriarch to be deposed by a hastily-summoned council, the "Synod of the Oak" held outside the city. The populace rose at once to defend their pastor; riots broke out, Theodosius was chased back to Egypt, and the Emperor, terrified by an earthquake which seemed to manifest the wrath of heaven, restored John to his place.

Next year, however, the war between the empress and the patriarch broke out again. John took the occasion of the erection of a statue of Eudoxia in the Augustaeum to recommence his polemics. Some obsolete semi-pagan ceremonies at its dedication roused his wrath, and he delivered a scathing sermon in which—if his enemies are to be believed—he compared the empress to Herodias, and himself to John the Baptist. The Emperor, at his wife's demand, summoned another council, which condemned Chrysostom, and on Easter Day, A.D. 404, seized the patriarch in his cathedral by armed force, and banished him to Asia. That night a fire, probably kindled by the angry adherents of Chrysostom, broke out in St. Sophia, which was burnt to the ground. From thence it spread to the neighbouring buildings, and finally to the Senate-house, which was consumed with all the treasures of ancient Greek art of which Constantine had made it the repository.

Meanwhile the exiled John was banished to a dreary mountain fastness in Cappadocia, and afterwards condemned to a still more remote prison at Pityus on the Euxine. He died on his way thither, leaving a wonderful reputation for patience and cheerfulness under affliction. This fifth-century Becket was well-nigh the only patriarch of Constantinople who ever fell out with the imperial Court on a question of morals as distinguished from dogma. Chrysostom's quarrel was with the luxury, insolence, and frivolity of the Empress and her Court; no real ecclesiastical question was involved in his deposition, for the charges against him were mere pretexts to cover the hatred of his disloyal clergy and the revenge of the insulted Aelia Eudoxia. [A.D. 407.]

V. The Reorganization Of The Eastern Empire. (A.D. 408-518.)

The feeble and inert Arcadius died in A.D. 408, at the early age of thirty-one; his imperious consort had preceded him to the grave, and the empire of the East was left to Theodosius II., a child of seven years, their only son. There was hardly an instance in Roman history of a minor succeeding quietly to his father's throne. An ambitious relative or a disloyal general had habitually supplanted the helpless heir. But the ministers of Arcadius were exceptionally virtuous or exceptionally destitute of ambition. The little emperor was duly crowned, and the administration of the East undertaken in his name by the able Anthemius, who held the office of Praetorian Praefect. History relates nothing but good of this minister; he made a wise commercial treaty with the king of Persia; he repelled with ease a Hunnish invasion of Moesia; he built a flotilla on the Danube, where Roman warships had not been seen since the death of Valens, forty years before; he reorganized the corn supply of Constantinople; and did much to get back into order and cultivation the desolated north-western lands of the Balkan Peninsula, from which Alaric and his Visigothic hordes had now taken their final departure. The empire was still more indebted to him for bringing up the young Theodosius as an honest and god-fearing man. The palace under Anthemius' rule was the school of the virtues: the lives of the emperor and his three sisters, Pulcheria, Arcadia, and Marina, were the model and the marvel of their subjects. Theodosius inherited the piety and honesty of his grandfather and namesake, but was a youth of slender capacity, though he took some interest in literature, and was renowned for his beautiful penmanship. His eldest sister, Pulcheria, was the ruling spirit of the family, and possessed unlimited influence over him, though she was but two years his senior. When Anthemius died inA.D. 414, she took the title of Augusta, and assumed the regency of the East. Pulcheria was an extraordinary woman: on gathering up the reins of power she took a vow of chastity, and lived as a crowned nun for thirty-six years; her fear had been that, if she married, her husband might cherish ambitious schemes against her brother's crown; she therefore kept single herself and persuaded her sisters to make a similar vow. Austere, indefatigable, and unselfish, she proved equal to ruling the realms of the East with success, though no woman had ever made the attempt before.

When Theodosius came of age he refused to remove his sister from power, and treated her as his colleague and equal. By her advice he married inA.D. 421, the year that he came of age, the beautiful and accomplished Athenaïs, daughter of the philosopher Leontius. The emperor's chosen spouse had been brought up as a pagan, but was converted before her marriage, and baptized by the name of Eudocia. She displayed her literary tastes in writing religious poetry, which had some merit, according to the critics of the succeeding age. The austere Pulcheria—always immersed in state business or occupied in religious observances—found herself ere long ill at ease in the company of the lively, beautiful, and volatile literary lady whom she had chosen as sister-in-law. If Theodosius had been less easy-going and good-hearted he must have sent away either his sister or his wife, but he long contrived to dwell affectionately with both, though their bickerings were unending. After many years of married life, however, a final quarrel came, and the empress retired to spend the last years of her life in seclusion at Jerusalem. The cause of her exile is not really known: we have only a wild story concerning it, which finds an exact parallel in one of the tales of the "Arabian Nights."

> "The emperor," so runs the tale, "was one day met by a peasant who presented him with a Phrygian apple of enormous size, so that the whole Court marvelled at it. And he gave the man a hundred and fifty gold pieces in reward, and sent the apple to the Empress Eudocia. But she sent it as a present to Paulinus, the 'Master of the Offices,'because he was a friend of the emperor. But Paulinus, not knowing the history of the apple, took it and gave it to the emperor as he reëntered the Palace. And Theodosius having received it, recognized it and concealed it, and called his wife and questioned her, saying, 'Where is the apple that I sent you?' She answered, 'I have eaten it.' Then he bade her swear by his salvation the truth, whether she had eaten it or sent it to some one. And Eudocia swore that she had sent it to no man, but had herself eaten it. Then the emperor showed her the apple, and was exceedingly wrath, suspecting that she was enamoured of Paulinus, and had sent it to him as a love-gift; for he was a very handsome man. And on this account he put Paulinus to death, but he permitted Eudocia to go to the Holy Places to pray. And she went down from Constantinople to Jerusalem, and dwelt there all her days."

That Paulinus was executed, and that Eudocia spent her last years of retirement in Palestine, we know for certain. All the rest of the story is in reality hidden from us. The chief improbability of the tale is that Eudocia had reached the age of forty when the breach between her and her husband took place, and that Paulinus was also an official of mature years.

Theodosius' long reign passed by in comparative quiet. Its only serious troubles were a short war with the Persians, and a longer one with Attila, the great king of the Huns, whose empire now stretched over all the lands north of the Black Sea and Danube, where the Goths had once dwelt. In this struggle the Roman armies were almost invariably unfortunate. The Huns ravaged the country as far as Adrianople and Philippopolis, and had to be bought off by the annual payment of 700 lbs. of gold [£31,000]. It is true that they fell on Theodosius while his main force was engaged on the Persian frontier, but the constant ill-success of the imperial generals seems to show that the armies of the East had never been properly reorganized since the military system of Theodosius I. had been broken up by the revolt of Gainas forty years before. His grandson had neither a trustworthy body of German auxiliaries nor a sufficiently large native levy of born subjects of the empire to protect his borders.

ANGEL OF VICTORY.
(*From a Fifth-century Diptych.*)

The reconstruction of the Roman military forces was reserved for the successors of Theodosius II. He himself was killed by a fall from his horse in 450 A.D., leaving an only daughter, who was married to her cousin Valentinian III.,

Emperor of the West. Theodosius, with great wisdom, had designated as his successor, not his young-son-in-law, a cruel and profligate prince, but his sister Pulcheria, who at the same time ended her vow of celibacy and married Marcianus, a veteran soldier and a prominent member of the Senate. The marriage was but formal, for both were now well advanced in years: as a political expedient it was all that could be desired. The empire had peace and prosperity under their rule, and freed itself from the ignominious tribute to the Huns. Before Attila died in 452, he had met and been checked by the succours which Marcianus sent to the distressed Romans of the West.

When Marcianus and Pulcheria passed away, the empire came into the hands of a series of three men of ability. They were all bred as high civil officials, not as generals; all ascended the throne at a ripe age; not one of them won his crown by arms, all were peaceably designated either by their predecessors, or by the Senate and army. These princes were Leo I. (457-474), Zeno (474-491), Anastasius (491-518). Their chief merit was that they guided the Roman Empire in the East safely through the stormy times which saw its extinction in the West. While, beyond the Adriatic, province after province was being lopped off and formed into a new Germanic kingdom, the emperors who reigned at Constantinople kept a tight grip on the Balkan Peninsula and on Asia, and succeeded in maintaining their realm absolutely intact. Both East and West were equally exposed to the barbarian in the fifth century, and the difference of their fate came from the character of their rulers, not from the diversity of their political conditions. In the West, after the extinction of the house of Theodosius (455 A.D.), the emperors were ephemeral puppets, made and unmade by the generals of their armies, who were invariably Germans. The two *Magistri militum*, Ricimer and Gundovald—one Suabian, the other Burgundian by birth—deposed or slew no less than five of their nominal masters in seventeen years. In the East, on the other hand, it was the emperors who destroyed one after another the ambitious generals, who, by arms or intrigue, threatened their throne.

While this comparison bears witness to the personal ability of the three emperors who ruled at Constantinople between A.D. 457 and A.D. 518, it is only fair to remember they were greatly helped by the fact that the German element in their armies had never reached the pitch of power to which it had attained in the West; the suppression of Gainas forty years before had saved them from that danger. But unruly and aspiring generals were not wanting in the East; the greatest danger of Leo I. was the conspiracy of the great *Magister militum* Aspar, whom he detected and slew when he was on the eve of rebelling. Zeno was once chased out of his capital by rebels, and twice vexed by dangerous risings in Asia Minor, but on each occasion he triumphed over his adversaries, and celebrated his victory by the execution of the leaders of the revolt. Anastasius was vexed for several years by the raids of a certain Count Vitalian, who ranged over the Thracian provinces with armies recruited from the barbarians beyond the Danube. But, in spite of all these rebellions, the empire was never in serious danger of sinking into disorder or breaking up, as the Western realm had done, into new un-Roman kingdoms. So far was it from this fate, that Anastasius left his successor, when he died in A.D. 518, a loyal army of 150,000 men, a treasure of 320,000 lbs. of gold, and an unbroken frontier to East and West.

The main secret of the success of the emperors of the fifth century in holding their own came from the fact that they had reorganized their armies, and filled them up with native troops in great numbers. Leo I. was the first ruler who utilized the military virtues of the Isaurians, or mountain populations of Southern Asia Minor. He added several regiments of them to the army of the East, but it was his son-in-law and successor, Zeno, himself an Isaurian born, who developed the scheme. He raised an imperial guard from his countrymen, and enlisted as many corps of them as could be raised; moreover, he formed regiments of Armenians and other inhabitants of the Roman frontier of the East, and handed over to his successor, Anastasius, an army in which the barbarian auxiliaries—now composed of Teutons and Huns in about equal numbers—were decidedly dominated by the native elements.

The last danger which the Eastern Empire was to experience from the hands of the Germans fell into the reign of Zeno. The Ostrogoths had submitted to the Huns ninety years before, when their brethren the Visigoths fled into Roman territory, in the reign of Valens. But when the Hunnish Empire broke up at the death of Attila [A.D. 452], the Ostrogoths freed themselves, and replaced their late masters as the main danger on the Danube. The bulk of them streamed south-westward, and settled in Pannonia, the border-province of the Western Empire, on the frontier of the East-Roman districts of Dacia and Moesia. They soon fell out with Zeno, and two Ostrogothic chiefs, Theodoric, the son of Theodemir, and Theodoric, the son of Triarius, were the scourges of the Balkan Peninsula for more than twenty years. While the bulk of their tribesmen settled down on the banks of the Save and Mid-Danube, the two Theodorics harried the whole of Macedonia and Moesia by never-ending raids. Zeno tried to turn them against each other, offering first to the one, then to the other, the title of *Magister militum*, and a large pension. But now—as in the time of Alaric and Stilicho—it was seen that "dog will not eat dog"; the two Theodorics, after quarrelling for a while, banded themselves together against Zeno. The story of their reconciliation is curious.

Theodoric, the son of Theodemir, the ally of Rome for the moment, had surrounded his rival on a rocky hill in a defile of the Balkans. While they lay opposite each other, Theodoric, the son of Triarius [he is usually known as Theodoric the One-Eyed], rode down to his enemy's lines and called to him, "Madman, betrayer of your race, do you not see that the Roman plan is always to destroy Goths by Goths? Whichever of us fails, they, not we, will be the stronger. They never give you real help, but send you out against me to perish here in the Desert." Then all the Goths cried out, "The One-Eyed is right. These men are Goths like ourselves." So the two Theodorics made peace, and Zeno had to cope with them both at once [A.D. 479]. Two years later Theodoric the One-Eyed was slain by accident—his horse flung him, as he mounted, against a spear fixed by the door of his tent—but his namesake continued a thorn in the side of the empire till 488 A.D.

In that year Zeno bethought him of a device for ridding himself of the Ostrogoth, who, though he made no permanent settlement in Moesia or Macedonia, was gradually depopulating the realm by his incursions. The line of ephemeral emperors who reigned in Italy over the shrunken Western realm had ended in 476, when the German general Odoacer deposed Romulus Augustulus, and did not trouble himself to nominate another puppet-Cæsar to succeed him. By his order a deputation from the Roman Senate visited Zeno at Constantinople, to inform him that they did not require an emperor of their own to govern Italy, but would acknowledge him as ruler alike of East and West; at the same time they besought Zeno to nominate, as his representative in the Italian lands, their defender, the great Odoacer. Zeno replied by advising the Romans to persuade Odoacer to recognize as his lord Julius Nepos, one of the dethroned nominees of Ricimer, who had survived his loss of the imperial diadem. Odoacer refused, and proclaimed himself king in Italy, while still affecting—against Zeno's own will—to recognize the Constantinopolitan emperor as his suzerain.

In 488 A.D. it occurred to Zeno to offer Theodoric the government of Italy, if he would conquer it from Odoacer. The Ostrogoth, who had harried the inland of the Balkan Peninsula bare, and had met several reverses of late from the Roman arms, took the offer. He was made "patrician" and consul, and started off with all the Ostrogothic nation at his back to win the realm of Italy. After hard fighting with Odoacer and the mixed multitude of mercenaries that followed him, the Goths conquered Italy, and Theodoric—German king and Roman patrician—began to reign at Ravenna. He always professed to be the vassal and deputy of the emperor at Constantinople, and theoretically his conquest of Italy meant the reunion of the East and the West. But the Western realm had shrunk down to Italy and Illyricum, and the power of Zeno therein was purely nominal.

With the departure of the Ostrogoths we have seen our last of the Germans in the Balkan Peninsula; after 488 the Slavs take their place as the molesters of the Roman frontier on the Danube.

VI. Justinian.

The Emperor Anastasius died in A.D. 518 at the ripe age of eighty-eight, and his sceptre passed to Justinus, the commander of his body-guard, whom Senate and army alike hailed as most worthy to succeed the good old man. The late emperor had nephews, but he had never designated them as his heirs, and they retired into private life at his death. Justinus was well advanced in years, as all his three predecessors had been when they mounted the throne. But unlike Leo, Zeno, and Anastasius, he had won his way to the front in the army, not in the civil service. He had risen from the ranks, was a rough uncultured soldier, and is said to have been hardly able to sign his own name. His reign of nine years would have been of little note in history—for he made no wars and spent no treasure—if he had not been the means of placing on the throne of the East the greatest ruler since the death of Constantine.

Justinus had no children himself, but had adopted as his heir his nephew Justinian, son of his deceased brother Sabatius. This young man, born after his father and uncle had won their way to high places in the army, was no uncultured peasant as they had been, but had been reared, as the heir of a wealthy house, in all the learning of the day. He showed from the first a keen intelligence, and applied himself with zeal to almost every department of civil life. Law, finance, administrative economy, theology, music, architecture, fortification, all were dear to him. The only thing in which he seems to have taken little personal interest was military matters. His uncle trusted everything to him, and finally made him his colleague on the throne.

Justinian was heir designate to the empire, and had passed the age of thirty-five, giving his contemporaries the impression that he was a staid, business-like, and eminently practical personage. "No one ever remembered him young," it was said, and most certainly no one ever expected him to scandalize the empire by a sensational marriage. But in A.D. 526 the world learnt, to the horror of the respectable and the joy of all scandal-mongers, that he had declared his intention of taking to wife the dancer Theodora, the star of the Byzantine comic stage.

So many stories have gathered around Theodora's name that it is hard to say how far her early life had been discreditable. A libellous work called the "Secret History," written by an enemy of herself and her husband,[4] gives us many scandalous details of her career; but the very virulence of the book makes its tales incredible. It is indisputable, however, that Theodora was an actress, and that Roman actresses enjoyed an unenviable reputation for light morals. There was actually a law which forbade a member of the senate to marry an actress, and Justinian had to repeal it in order to legalize his own marriage. There had been scores of bad and reckless men on the throne before, but none of them had ever

[4] Certainly not by Procopius, whose name it bears.

dared to commit an action which startled the world half so much as this freak of the staid Justinian. His own mother used every effort to turn him from his purpose, and his uncle the Emperor threatened to disinherit him: but he was quietly persistent, and ere the aged Justinus died he had been induced to acknowledge the marriage of his nephew, and to confer on Theodora the title of "Patrician."

THE EMPRESS THEODORA AND HER COURT.
(From the Mosaic in San Vitale at Ravenna)

Theodora, as even her enemies allow, was the most beautiful woman of her age. Procopius, the best historian of the day, says "that it was impossible for mere man to describe her comeliness in words, or imitate it in art." All that her detractors could say was that she was below the middle height, and that her complexion was rather pale, though not unhealthy. It is unfortunate that we have no representation of her surviving, save the famous mosaic in San Vitale at Ravenna, and mosaic is of all forms of art that least suited to reproduce beauty.

Whatever her early life may have been, Theodora was in spirit and intelligence well suited to be the mate of the Emperor of the East. After her marriage no word of scandal was breathed against her life. She rose to the height of her situation: once her courage saved her husband's throne, and always she was the ablest and the most trusted of his councillors. The grave, studious, and hard-working Emperor never regretted his choice of a consort.

It cannot be said, however, that either Justinian or Theodora are sympathetic characters. The Emperor was a hard and suspicious master, and not over grateful to subjects who served him well; he was intolerant in religious, and unscrupulous in political matters. When his heart was set on a project he was utterly unmindful of the slaughter and ruin which it might bring upon his people. In the extent of his conquests and the magnificence of his public works, he was incomparably the greatest of the emperors who reigned at Constantinople. But the greatness was purely personal: he left the empire weaker in resources, if broader in provinces, than he found it. Of all the great sovereigns of history he may be most fairly compared with Louis XIV. of France; but it may be remembered to his credit in the comparison that Louis has nothing to set against Justinian's great legal work—the compilation of the *Pandects* and *Institutes*, and that Justinian's private life, unlike that of the Frenchman, was strict even to austerity. All night long, we read, he sat alone over his State papers in his cabinet, or paced the dark halls in deep thought. His sleepless vigilance so struck his subjects that the strangest legends became current even in his life-time: his enemies whispered that he was no mere man, but an evil spirit that required no rest. One grotesque tale even said that the Emperor had been seen long after midnight traversing the corridors of his palace—without his head.

If Justinian seemed hardly human to those who feared him, Theodora is represented as entirely given up to pride and ambition, never forgiving an offence, but hunting to death or exile all who had crossed her in the smallest thing. She is reproached—but who that has risen from a low estate is not?—of an inordinate love for the pomps and vanities of imperial state. High officials complained that she had as great a voice in settling political matters as her husband. Yet, on the whole, her influence would appear not to have been an evil one—historians acknowledge that she was liberal in almsgiving, religious after her own fashion, and that she often interfered to aid the oppressed. It is particularly recorded that, remembering the dangers of her own youth, she was zealous in establishing institutions for the reclaiming of women who had fallen into sin.

The aged Justinus died in 527 A.D., and Justinian became the sole occupant of the throne, which he was destined to occupy for thirty-eight years. It was less than half the century, yet his personality seems to pervade the whole period, and history hardly remembers the insignificant predecessors and successors whose reigns eke out the remainder of the years between 500 and 600.

The empire when Justinian took it over from the hands of his uncle was in a more prosperous condition than it had known since the death of Constantine. Since the Ostrogoths had moved out of the Balkan Peninsula in A.D. 487, it had not suffered from any very long or destructive invasion from without. The Slavonic tribes, now heard of for the first time, and the Bulgarians had made raids across the Danube, but they had not yet shown any signs of settling down—as the Goths had done—within the limits of the empire. Their incursions, though vexatious, were not dangerous. Still the European provinces of the empire were in worse condition than the Asiatic, and were far from having recovered the effects of the ravages of Fritigern and Alaric, Attila, and Theodoric. But the more fortunate Asiatic lands had hardly seen a foreign enemy for centuries.[5] Except in the immediate neighbourhood of the Persian frontier there was no danger, and Persian wars had been infrequent of late. Southern Asia Minor had once or twice suffered from internal risings—rebellions of the warlike Isaurians—but civil war left no such permanent mark on the land as did barbarian invasions. On the whole, the resources of the provinces beyond the Bosphorus were intact.

Justinus in his quiet reign had spent little or none of the great hoard of treasure which Anastasius had bequeathed to him. There were more than 300,000 lbs. of gold [£13,400,000] in store when Justinian came to the throne. The army, as we have had occasion to relate in the last chapter, was in good order, and composed in a larger proportion of born subjects of the empire than it had been at any time since the battle of Adrianople. There would appear to have been from 150,000 to 200,000 men under arms, but the extent of the frontiers of the empire were so great that Justinian never sent out a single army of more than 30,000 strong, and forces of only a third of that number are often found entrusted with such mighty enterprises as the invasion of Africa or the defence of the Armenian border. The flower of the Roman army was no longer its infantry, but its mailed horsemen (*Cataphracti*), armed with lance and bow, as the Parthian cavalry had once been of old. The infantry comprised more archers and javelin-men than heavy troops: the Isaurians and other provincials of the mountainous parts of Asia Minor were reckoned the best of them. Among both horse and foot large bodies of foreign auxiliaries were still found: the Huns and Arabs supplied light cavalry, the German Herules and Gepidæ from beyond the Danube heavier troops.

The weakest point in the empire when Justinian took it over was its financial system. The cardinal maxim of political economy, that "taxes should be raised in the manner least oppressive to those who pay them" was as yet undreamt of. The exaction of arbitrary customs dues, and the frequent grant of monopolies was noxious to trade. The deplorable system of tax-farming through middlemen was employed in many branches of the revenue. Landed proprietors, small and great, were still mercilessly overtaxed, in consideration of their exemption from military service. The budget was always handicapped by the necessity for providing free corn for the populace of Constantinople. Yet in spite of all these drawbacks Justinian enjoyed an enormous and steady revenue. His finance minister, John of Cappadocia, was such an ingenious extortioner that the treasury was never empty in the hardest stress of war and famine: but it was kept full at the expense of the future. The grinding taxation of Justinian's reign bore fruit in the permanent impoverishment of the provinces: his successors were never able to raise such a revenue again. Here again Justinian may well be compared to Louis XIV.

---

[5] There had been only an isolated raids of Huns in A. D. 395, which penetrated as far as Palestine. No other invasion reached as far as Antioch.

Justinian's policy divides into the departments of internal and foreign affairs. Of his doings as legislator, administrator, theologian, and builder, we shall speak in their proper place. But the history of his foreign policy forms the main interest of his reign. He had determined to take up a task which none of his predecessors since the division of the Empire under Arcadius and Honorius had dared to contemplate. It was his dream to re-unite under his sceptre the German kingdoms in the Western Mediterranean which had been formed out of the broken fragments of the realm of Honorius; and to end the solemn pretence by which he was nominally acknowledged as Emperor West of the Adriatic, while really all power was in the hands of the German rulers who posed as his vicegerents. He aimed at reconquering Italy, Africa, and Spain—if not the further provinces of the old empire. We shall see that he went far towards accomplishing his intention.

But during the first five years of his reign his attention was distracted by other matters. The first of them was an obstinate war of four years' duration, with Kobad, King of Persia. The causes of quarrel were ultimately the rival pretensions of the Roman and Persian Empires to the suzerainty of the small states on their northern frontiers near the Black Sea, the kingdoms of Lazica and Iberia, and more proximately the strengthening of the fortresses on the Mesopotamian border by Justinian. His fortification of Dara, close to the Persian frontier town of Nisibis, was the *casus belli* chosen by Kobad, who declared war in 528, a year after Justinian's accession.

The Persian war was bloody, but absolutely indecisive. All the attacks of the enemy were repelled, and one great pitched battle won over him at Dara in 530. But neither party succeeded in taking a single fortress of importance from the other; and when, on the death of Kobad, his son Chosroës made peace with the empire, the terms amounted to the restoration of the old frontier. The only importance of the war was that it enabled Justinian to test his army, and showed him that he possessed an officer of first-rate merit in Belisarius, the victor of the battle of Dara.

This famous general was a native of the Thracian inland; he entered the army very young, and rose rapidly, till at the age of twenty-three he was already Governor of Dara, and at twenty-five *Magister militum* of the East.[6] His influence at Court was very great, as he had married Antonina, the favourite and confidante of the Empress Theodora. His position, indeed, was not unlike that which Marlborough, owing to his wife's ascendency, enjoyed at the Court of Queen Anne. Like Marlborough, too, Belisarius was ruled and bullied by his clever and unscrupulous wife. Unlike the great Duchess Sarah, Antonina never set herself to thwart her mistress; but after Theodora's death she and her husband lost favour, and in declining years knew much the same misfortune as did the Marlboroughs.

The year which saw the Persian War end [A.D. 532], saw also the rise and fall of another danger, which while it lasted was much more threatening to the Emperor's life and power. We have already noticed the "Blues" and "Greens," the great factions of the Byzantine Circus.[7] All through the fifth century they had been growing stronger, and interfered more and more in politics, and even in religious

[6] "Born in Germania, a district between Thrace and Illyricum," says his secretary, Procopius. We do not know where the district—a German settlement, presumably—was situated.

[7] See Chap. ii. p. 22.

controversies. To be a "Green" in 530 meant to be a partisan of the house of the late Emperor Anastasius, and a Monophysite.[8] The "Blues" posed as partisans of the house of Justinus, and as strictly orthodox in matters ecclesiastical. From mere Circus factions they had almost grown into political parties; but they still retained at the bottom many traces of their low sporting origin. The rougher elements predominated in them; they were prone to riot and mischief, and, as the events of 532 were to show, they were a serious danger to the State.

In January of that year there was serious rioting in the streets. Justinian, though ordinarily he favoured the Blue faction, impartially ordered the leaders of the rioters on both sides to be put to death. Seven were selected for execution, and four of them were duly beheaded in the presence of a great and angry mob, in front of the monastery of St. Conon. The last three rioters were to be hung, but the hangman so bungled his task that two of the criminals, one a Blue the other a Green, fell to the ground alive. The guards seized them and they were again suspended; but once more—owing no doubt to the terror of the executioners at the menaces of the mob—the rope slipped. Then the multitude broke loose, the guards were swept away, and the half-hung criminals were thrust into sanctuary at the adjacent monastery.

This exciting incident proved the commencement of six days of desperate rioting. The Blues and Greens united, and taking as their watchword, *Nika*, "conquer," swept through the city, crying for the deposition of John of Cappadocia, the unpopular finance minister, and of Eudemius, Praefect of the city, who was immediately responsible for the executions. The ordinary police of the capital were quite unable to master them, and Justinian was weak enough to promise to dismiss the officials. But the mob was now quite out of hand, and refused to disperse: the trouble was fomented by the partisans of the house of the late emperor, who began to shout for the deposition of Justinian, and wished to make Hypatius, nephew of Anastasius, Cæsar in his stead. The city was almost empty of troops, owing to the garrison having been sent to the Persian War. The Emperor could only count on 4,000 men of the Imperial Guard, a few German auxiliaries, and a regiment of 500 "Cataphracti," mailed horsemen, under Belisarius, who had just returned from the seat of war.

Belisarius was placed in command of the whole, and sallied out to clear the streets, but the rioters, showing the same pluck that the Byzantine mob displayed against the soldiers of Gainas a hundred and twenty-five years before, offered a stout resistance. The main fighting took place around the great square of the Augustaeum, between the Imperial palace and the Hippodrome. In the heat of the fight the rebels set fire to the Brazen Porch by the Senate House. The Senate House caught fire, and then the conflagration spread east and north, till it was wafted across the square to St. Sophia. On the third day of the riot the great cathedral was burnt to the ground, and from thence the flames issued out to burn the hospital of Sampson and the church of St. Irene.[9] The fire checked the fighting, and the insurgents were now in possession of most of the city. But they could not find their

[8] To hold the view which denied the existence both of a truly human and a truly Divine nature in Our Lord Jesus Christ.

[9] See The Heart of Constantinople map.

chosen leader, for the unfortunate Hypatius, who had no desire to risk his neck, had taken refuge with the Emperor in the palace. It was not till he was actually driven out by Justinian, who feared to have him about his person, that this rebel in spite of himself, fell into the hands of his own adherents. But on the sixth day of the riots they led him to the Hippodrome, installed him in the royal seat of the Kathisma, and crowned him there with a gold chain of his wife's, for want of a proper diadem.

Charles William Chadwick Oman

THEODORA IMPERATRIX.

[*From the Painting by Val. Prinsep. The copyright is in the Artist's hands.*]

Meanwhile there was dismay and diversity of councils in the Palace. John of Cappadocia and many other ministers strove to persuade the Emperor to fly by sea, and gather additional troops at Heraclea. There was nothing left in his power save the palace, and they insisted that if he remained there longer he would be surrounded by the rebels and cut off from escape. It was then that the Empress Theodora rose to the level of the occasion, refused to fly, and urged her husband to make one final assault on the enemy. Her words are preserved by Procopius.

"This is no occasion to keep to the old rule that a woman must not speak in the council. Those who are most concerned have most right to dictate the course of action. Now every man must die once, and for a king death is better than dethronement and exile. May I never see the day when my purple robe is stripped from me, and when I am no more called Lady and Mistress! If you wish, O Emperor, to save your life, nothing is easier: there are your ships and the sea. But *I* agree with the old saying that 'Empire is the best winding-sheet.' "

Spurred on by his wife's bold words, Justinian ordered a last assault on the rebels, and Belisarius led out his full force. The factions were now in the Hippodrome, saluting their newly-crowned leader with shouts of "*Hypatie Auguste, tu vincas,*" preparatory to a final attack on the palace. Belisarius attacked at once all three gates of the Hippodrome: that directed against the door of the Kathisma failed, but the soldiery forced both the side entrances, and after a hard struggle the rebels were entirely routed. Crowded into the enormous building with only five exits, they fell in thousands by the swords of the victorious Imperialists. It is said that 35,000 men were slain in the six days of this great "Sedition of Nika."

It is curious to learn that not even this awful slaughter succeeded in crushing the factions. We hear of the Blues and Greens still rioting on various occasions during the next fifty years. But they never came again so near to changing the course of history as in the famous rising of A.D. 532.

VII. Justinian's Foreign Conquests.

After the Persians had drawn back, foiled in their attempt to conquer Mesopotamia, and after the suppression of the "Nika" sedition had cowed the unruly populace of Constantinople, Justinian found himself at last free, and was able to take in hand his great scheme for the reconquest of the lost provinces of the empire.

The enforced delay of six years between his accession and his first attempt to execute his great plan, was, as it happened, extremely favourable to the Emperor. In each of the two German kingdoms with which he had first to deal, the power had passed within those six years into the hands of a weak and incapable sovereign. In Africa, Hilderic, the king of the Vandals, had been dethroned by his cousin Gelimer, a warlike and ambitious, but very incapable, ruler. In Italy, Theodoric, the great king of the Ostrogoths, had died in A.D. 526, and his grandson and successor, Athalaric, in A.D. 533. After the death of the young Athalaric, the kingdom fell to his mother, Amalasuntha, and she, compelled by Gothic public opinion to take a husband to rule in her behalf, had unwisely wedded Theodahat, her nearest kinsman. He was cruel, scheming, and suspicious, and murdered his wife, within a year of her having brought him the kingdom of Italy as a dowry.[10] Cowardly and avaricious as well as ungrateful, Theodahat possessed exactly those vices which were most suited to make him the scorn of his warlike subjects; he could count neither on their loyalty nor their respect in the event of a war.

Both the Vandals in Africa and the Goths in Italy were at this time so weak as to invite an attack by an enterprising neighbour. They had, in fact, conquered larger realms than their limited numbers were really able to control. The original tribal hordes which had subdued Africa and Italy were composed of fifty or sixty thousand warriors, with their wives and children. Now such a body concentrated on one spot was powerful enough to bear down everything before it. But when the conquerors spread themselves abroad, they were but a sprinkling among the millions of provincials whom they had to govern. In all Italy there were probably but three cities—Ravenna, Verona, and Pavia—in which the Ostrogoths formed a large proportion of the population. A great army makes but a small nation, and the Goths and Vandals were too few to occupy such wide tracts as Italy and Africa. They formed merely a small aristocracy, governing by dint of the ascendency which their fathers had won over the minds of the unwarlike populations which they had subdued. The only chance for the survival of the Ostrogothic and Vandal monarchies lay in the possibility of their amalgamating with the Roman provincial population, as the Franks, under more favourable circumstances, did with the conquered inhabitants of Gaul. This was seen by Theodoric, the great conqueror of Italy; and he did his best to reconcile Goth and Roman, held the balance with strict

---

[10] The murder of Amalasuntha took place *after* the Roman invasion of Africa; but Theodahat was already on the throne when the Vandal war was proceeding.

justice between the two, and employed Romans as well as Goths in the government of the country. But one generation does little to assuage old hatreds such as that between the conquerors and the conquered in Italy. Theodoric was succeeded by a child, and then by a ruffian, and his work ended with him. Even he was unable to strike at the most fatal difference of all between his countrymen and the Italians. The Goths were Arians, having been converted to Christianity in the fourth century by missionaries who held the Arian heresy. Their subjects, on the other hand, were Orthodox Catholics, almost without exception. When religious hatred was added to race hatred, there was hardly any hope of welding together the two nationalities.

Another source of weakness in the kingdoms of Africa and Italy must be noted. The Vandals of the third generation and the Goths of the second, after their settlement in the south, seem to have degenerated in courage and stamina. It may be that the climate was unfavourable to races reared in the Danube lands; it may be that the temptations of unlimited luxury offered by Roman civilization sufficed to demoralize them. A Gothic sage observed at the time that "the Goth, when rich, tends to become Roman in his habits; the Roman, when poor, Gothic in his." There was truth in this saying, and the result of the change was ominous for the permanence of the kingdom of Italy. If the masters softened and the subjects hardened, they would not preserve for ever their respective positions.

The case of the kingdom of Africa was infinitely worse than that of the kingdom of Italy. The Vandals were less numerous than the Goths, in proportion to their subjects; they were not merely heretics, but fanatical and persecuting heretics, which the Goths were not. Moreover, they had never had at their head a great organizer and administrator like Theodoric, but only a succession of turbulent princes of the Viking type, fit for war and nothing else.

Justinian declared war on King Gelimer the moment that he had made peace with Persia, using as his *casus belli*, not a definite re-assertion of the claim of the empire over Africa—for such language would have provoked the rulers of Italy and Spain to join the Vandals, but the fact that Gelimer had wrongfully deposed Hilderic, the Emperor's ally. In July, 533, Belisarius, who was now at the height of his favour for his successful suppression of the "Nika" rioters, sailed from the Bosphorus with an army of 10,000 foot and 5,000 horse. He was accompanied, luckily for history, by his secretary, Procopius, a very capable writer, who has left a full account of his master's campaigns. Belisarius landed at Tripoli, at the extreme eastern limit of the Vandal power. The town was at once betrayed to him by its Roman inhabitants. From thence he advanced cautiously along the coast, meeting with no opposition; for the incapable Gelimer had been caught unprepared, and was still engaged in calling in his scattered warriors. It was not till he had approached within ten miles of Carthage that Belisarius was attacked by the Vandals. After a hard struggle he defeated them, and the city fell into his hands next clay. The provincials were delighted at the rout of their masters, and welcomed the imperial army with joy; there was neither riot nor pillage, and Carthage had not the aspect of a conquered town.

Calling up his last reserves, Gelimer made one more attempt to try the fortunes of war. He advanced on Carthage, and was met by Belisarius at Tricameron, on the road to Bulla. Again the day went against him; his army broke up, his last fortresses threw open their gates, and there was an end of the Vandal kingdom. It had existed just 104 years, since Genseric entered Africa in A.D. 429.

Gelimer took refuge for a time with the Moorish tribes who dwelt in the fastnesses of Mount Atlas. But ere long he resolved to surrender himself to Belisarius, whose humanity was as well known as his courage. He sent to Carthage to say that he was about to give himself up, and—so the story goes—asked but for three things: a harp, to which to chant a dirge he had written on the fate of himself and the Vandal race; a sponge, to wipe away his tears; and a loaf, a delicacy he had not tasted ever since he had been forced to partake of the unsavoury food of the Moors! Belisarius received Gelimer with kindness, and took him to Constantinople, along with the treasures of the palace of Carthage, which included many of the spoils of Rome captured by the Vandals eighty-six years before, when they sacked the imperial city, in 453. It is said that among these spoils were some of the golden vessels of the Temple at Jerusalem, which Titus had brought in triumph to Rome, and which Gaiseric had carried from Rome to Carthage.

CAVALRY SCOUTS.

(*From a Byzantine MS.*)

The triumphal entry of Belisarius into Constantinople with his captives and his spoils, encouraged Justinian to order instant preparations for an attack on the second German kingdom, on his western frontier. He declared war on the wretched King Theodahat in the summer of A.D. 435, using as his pretext the murder of Queen Amalasuntha, whom, as we have already said, her ungrateful spouse had first imprisoned and then strangled within a year of their marriage.

The king of the Goths, whether he was conscience-stricken or merely cowardly, showed the greatest terror at the declaration of war. He even wrote to Constantinople offering to resign his crown, if the Emperor would guarantee his life and his private property. Meanwhile he consulted soothsayers and magicians about his prospects, for he was as superstitious as he was incompetent. Procopius tells us a strange tale of the doings of a Jewish magician of note, to whom Theodahat applied. He took thirty pigs—to represent unclean Gentiles, we must suppose—and penned them in three styes, ten in each. The one part he called "Goths," the second "Italians," and the third "Imperialists." He left the beasts without food or water for ten days, and bade the king visit them at the end of that time, and take augury from their condition. When Theodahat looked in he found all but two of the "Goth" pigs dead, and half of the "Italians," but the "Imperialists," though gaunt and wasted, were all, or almost all, alive. This portent the Jew expounded as meaning that at the end of the approaching war the Gothic race would be exterminated and their Italian subjects terribly thinned, while the Imperial troops would conquer, though with toil and difficult.

While Theodahat was busying himself with portents, actual war had broken out on the Illyrian frontier between the Goths and the governor of Dalmatia. There was no use in making further offers to Justinian, and the king of Italy had to face the situation as best he could.

In the summer of 535, Belisarius landed in Sicily, with an even smaller army than had been given him to conquer Africa—only 3,000 Roman troops, all Isaurians, and 4,500 barbarian auxiliaries of different sorts. Belisarius' first campaign was as fortunate as had been that which he had waged against Gelimer. All the Sicilian towns threw open their gates except Palermo, where there was a considerable Gothic garrison, and Palermo fell after a short siege. In six months the whole island was in the hands of Belisarius.

Theodahat seemed incapable of defending himself; he fell into a condition of abject helplessness, which so provoked his warlike subjects, that when the news came that Belisarius had crossed over into Italy and taken Rhegium, they rose and slew him. In his stead the army of the Goths elected as their king Witiges, a middle-aged warrior, well known for personal courage and integrity, but quite incompetent to face the impending storm.

After the fall of Rhegium, Belisarius marched rapidly on Naples, meeting no opposition; for the Goths were very thinly scattered through Southern Italy, and had not even enough men to garrison the Lucanian and Calabrian fortresses. Naples was taken by surprise, the Imperialists finding their way within the walls by crawling up a disused aqueduct. After this important conquest, Belisarius made for Rome, though his forces were reduced to a mere handful by the necessity of leaving garrisons in his late conquests. King Witiges made no effort to obstruct his approach. He had received news that the Franks were threatening an evasion of Northern Italy, and went north to oppose an imaginary danger in the Alps, when he should have been defending the line of the Tiber. Having staved off the danger of a Frankish war by ceding Provence to King Theuderic, Witiges turned back, only to learn that Rome was now in the hands of the enemy. The troops of Leudaris, the Gothic general, who had been left with 4,000 men to defend the city, had been struck with panic at the approach of Belisarius, and were cowardly and idiotic enough to evacuate it without striking a blow. Five thousand men had sufficed to seize the ancient capital of the world! [December, 536.]

Next spring King Witiges came down with the main army of the Goths—more than 100,000 strong—and laid siege to Rome. The defence of the town by Belisarius and his very inadequate garrison forms the most interesting episode in the Italian war. For more than a year the Ostrogoths lay before its walls, essaying every device to force an entry. They tried open storm; they endeavoured to bribe traitors within the city; they strove to creep along the bed of a disused aqueduct, as Belisarius had done a year before at Naples. All was in vain, though the besiegers outnumbered the garrison twenty-fold, and exposed their lives with the same recklessness that their ancestors had shown in the invasion of the empire a hundred years back. The scene best remembered in the siege was the simultaneous assault on five points in the wall, on the 21st of March, 537. Three of the attacks were beaten back with ease; but near the Prænestine Gate, at the south-east of the city, one storming party actually forced its way within the walls, and had to be beaten out by sheer hard fighting; and at the mausoleum of Hadrian, on the north-west, another spirited combat took place. Hadrian's tomb—a great quadrangular structure of white marble, 300 feet square and 85 feet high—was surmounted by one of the most magnificent collections of statuary in ancient Rome, including four great equestrian statues of emperors at its corners. The Goths, with their ladders, swarmed at the foot of the tomb in such numbers, that the arrows and darts of the defenders were insufficient to beat them back. Then, as a last resource, the Imperialists tore down the scores of statues which adorned the mausoleum, and crushed the mass of assailants beneath a rain of marble fragments. Two famous antiques, that form the pride of modern galleries—the "Dancing Faun" at Florence, and the "Barberini Faun" at Munich—were found, a thousand years later, buried in the ditch of the tomb of Hadrian, and must have been among the missiles employed against the Goths. The rough usage which they then received proved the means of preserving them for the admiration of the modern world.

A year and nine days after he had formed the siege of Rome, the unlucky Witiges had to abandon it. His army, reduced by sword and famine, had given up all hope of success, and news had just arrived that the Imperialists had launched a new army against Ravenna, the Gothic capital. Belisarius, indeed, had just received a reinforcement of 6,000 or 7,000 men, and had wisely sent a considerable force, under an officer named John, to fall on the Adriatic coast.

The scene of the war was now transported further to the north; but its character still remained the same. The Romans gained territory, the Goths lost it. Firmly fixed at Ancona and Rimini and Osimo, Belisarius gradually forced his way nearer to Ravenna, and, in A.D. 540 laid siege to it. Witiges, blockaded by Belisarius in his capital, made no such skilful defence as did his rival at Rome three years before. To add to his troubles, the Franks came down into Northern Italy, and threatened to conquer the valley of the Po, the last Gothic stronghold. Witiges then made proposals for submission; but Belisarius refused to grant any terms other than unconditional surrender, though his master Justinian was ready to acknowledge Witiges as vassal-king in Trans-Padane Italy. Famine drove Ravenna to open its gates, and the Goths, enraged at their imbecile king, and struck with admiration for the courage and generosity of Belisarius, offered to make their conqueror Emperor of the West. The loyal general refused; but bade the Goths disperse each to his home, and dwell peaceably for the future as subjects of the empire. [May, 540 A.D.] He himself, taking the great Gothic treasure-hoard from the palace of Theodoric, and the captive Witiges, sailed for Constantinople, and laid his trophies at his master's feet.

Italy now seemed even as Africa; only Pavia and Verona were still held by Gothic garrisons, and when he sailed home, Belisarius deemed his work so nearly done, that his lieutenants would suffice to crush out the last embers of the strife. He himself was required in the East, for a new Persian war with Chosroësroës, son of Kobad, was on the eve of breaking out. But things were not destined to end so. At the last moment the Goths found a king and a hero to rescue them, and the conquest of Italy was destined to be deferred for twelve years more. Two ephemeral rulers reigned for a few months at Pavia, and came to bloody ends; but their successor was Baduila,[11] the noblest character of the sixth century—"the first knight of the Middle Ages," as he has been called. When the generals of Justinian marched against him, to finish the war by the capture of Verona and Pavia, he won over them the first victory that the Goths had obtained since their enemies landed in Italy. This was followed by two more successes; the scattered armies of Witiges rallied round the banner of the new king, and at once the cities of Central and Southern Italy began to fall back into Gothic hands, with the same rapidity with which they had yielded to Belisarius. The fact was, that the war had been a cruel strain on the Italians, and that the imperial governors, and still more their fiscal agents, or "logothetes," had become unbearably oppressive. Italy had lived through the fit of enthusiasm with which it had received the armies of Justinian, and was now regretting the days of Theodoric as a long-lost golden age. Most of its cities were soon in Baduila's hands; the Imperialists retained only the districts round Rome, Naples, Otranto, and Ravenna. Of Naples they were soon deprived. [B.C. 543.] Baduila invested it, and ere long constrained it to surrender. He treated the inhabitants with a kindness and consideration which no Roman general, except Belisarius, had ever displayed. A speech which he delivered to his generals soon after this success deserves a record, as showing the character of the man. A Gothic warrior had been convicted of violating the daughter of a Roman. Baduila condemned him to death. His officers came round him to plead for the soldier's life. He answered them that they must choose that day whether they preferred to save one man's life or the life of the Gothic race. At the beginning of the war, as they knew well, the Goths had brave soldiers, famous generals, countless treasure, horses, weapons, and all the forts of Italy. And yet under Theodahat—a man who loved gold better than justice—they had so angered God by their unrighteous lives, that all the troubles of the last ten years had come upon them. Now God seemed to have avenged Himself on them enough. He had begun a new course with them, and they must begin a new course with Him, and justice was the only path. As for the present criminal being a valiant hero, let them know that the unjust man and the ravisher was never brave in fight; but that, according to a man's life, such was his luck in battle.

Such was the justice of Baduila; and it seemed as if his dream was about to come true, and that the regenerate Goths would win back all that they had lost. Ere long he was at the gates of Rome, prepared to essay, with 15,000 men, what Witiges had failed to do with 100,000. Lest all his Italian conquests should be lost, Justinian was obliged to send back Belisarius, for no one else could hold back the Goths. But Belisarius was ill-supplied with men; he had fallen into disfavour at Court, and the imperial ministers stinted him of troops and money. Unable to relieve Rome, he had to wait at Portus, by the mouth of the Tiber, watching for a chance to enter the city.

---

[11] The king's real name was Baduila, as shown on his coins, and recorded by some historians, but Imperialist writers always call him Totila, which seems to have been a nickname.

That chance he never got. The famine-stricken Romans, angry with the cruel and avaricious Bessas, who commanded the garrison, began to long for the victory of their enemy; and one night some traitors opened the Asinarian Gate, and let in Baduila and his Goths. The King thought that his troubles were over; he assembled his chiefs, and bade them observe how, in the time of Witiges, 7,000 Greeks had conquered, and robbed of kingdom and liberty, 100,000 well-armed Goths. But now that they were few, poor, and wretched, the Goths had conquered more than 20,000 of the enemy. And why? Because of old they looked to anything rather than justice: they had sinned against each other and the Romans. Therefore they must choose henceforth, and be just men and have God with them, or unjust and have God against them.

Baduila had determined to do that which no general since Hannibal had contemplated: he would destroy Rome, and with it all the traditions of the world-empire of the ancient city—to him they seemed but snares, tending to corrupt the mind of the Goths. The people he sent away unharmed—they were but a few thousand left after the horrors of the famine during the siege. But he broke down the walls, and dismantled the palaces and arsenals. For a few weeks Rome was a deserted city, given up to the wolf and the owl [A.D. 550].

For eleven unquiet years, Baduila, the brave and just, ruled Italy, holding his own against Belisarius, till the great general was called home by some wretched court intrigue. But presently Justinian gathered another army, more numerous than any that Belisarius had led, and sent it to Italy, under the command of the eunuch Narses. It was a strange choice that made the chamberlain into a general; but it succeeded. Narses marched round the head of the Adriatic, and invaded Italy from the north. Baduila went forth to meet him at Tagina, in the Apennines. For a long day the Ostrogothic knights rode again and again into the Imperialist ranks; but all their furious charges failed. At evening they reeled back broken, and their king received a mortal wound in the flight [A.D. 553].

With the death of Baduila, it was all up with the Goths; their hero's knightly courage and kingly righteousness had not sufficed to save them from the same doom which had overtaken the Vandals. The broken army made one last stand in Campania, under a chief named Teia; but he was slain in battle at Nuceria, and then the Goths surrendered. They told Narses that the hand of God was against them; they would quit Italy, and go back to dwell in the north, in the land of their fathers. So the poor remnant of the conquering Ostrogoths marched off, crossed the Po and the Alps, and passed away into oblivion in the northern darkness. The scheme of Justinian was complete. Italy was his; but an Italy so wasted and depopulated, that the traces of the ancient Roman rule had almost vanished. "The land," says a contemporary chronicler, "was reduced to primeval solitude"—war and famine had swept it bare.

ITALY & ROME
ABOUT 553 A.D.

OSTROGOTHS
A.K.A GOTHS
A K A GERMAN

DETAILS OF ST. SOPHIA.

It is strange to find that the Emperor was not tired out by waging this desperate war with the Goths; the moment it ended he began to essay another western conquest. There was civil war in Spain, and, taking advantage of it, Liberius, governor of Africa, landed in Andalusia, and rapidly took the great towns of the south of the peninsula—Cordova, Cartagena, Malaga, and Cadiz. The factious Visigoths then dropped their strife, united in arms under King Athangild, and checked the further progress of the imperial arms. But a long slip of the lost territory was not recovered by them. Justinian and his successors, down to A.D. 623, reigned over the greater part of the sea-coast of Southern Spain.

SPAIN 623 A.D.

VIII. The End Of Justinian's Reign.

The slackness with which the generals of Justinian prosecuted the Gothic war in the period between the triumph of Belisarius at Ravenna in A.D.540, and the final conquest of Italy in A.D. 553, is mainly to be explained by the fact that, just at the moment of the fall of Ravenna, the empire became involved in a new struggle with its great Eastern neighbour. Chosroës of Persia was seriously alarmed at the African and Italian conquests of Justinian, and remembered that he too, as well as the Vandals and Goths, was in possession of provinces that had formerly been Roman, and might one day be reclaimed by the Emperor. He determined to strike before Justinian had got free from his Italian war, and while the flower of the Roman army was still in the West. Using as his pretext for war some petty quarrels between two tribes of Arabs, subject respectively to Persia and the empire, he declared war in the spring of A.D. 540. Justinian, as the king had hoped, was caught unprepared: the army of the Euphrates was so weak that it never dared face the Persians in the field, and the opening of the war was fraught with such a disaster to the empire as had not been known since the battle of Adrianople, more than a hundred and sixty years before. Avoiding the fortresses of Mesopotamia, Chosroës, who led his army in person, burst into Northern Syria. His main object was to strike a blow at Antioch, the metropolis of the East, a rich city that had not seen an enemy for nearly three centuries, and was reckoned safe from all attacks owing to its distance from the frontier. Antioch had a strong garrison of 6,000 men and the "Blues" and "Greens" of its circus factions had taken arms to support the regular troops. But the commander was incompetent, and the fortifications had been somewhat neglected of late. After a sharp struggle, Chosroës took the town by assault; the garrison cut its way out, and many of the inhabitants escaped with it, but the city was sacked from cellar to garret and thousands of captives were dragged away by the Persians. Chosroës planted them by the Euphrates—as Nebuchadnezzar had done of old with the Jews—and built for them a city which he called Chosroantiocheia, blending his own name with that of their ancient abode.

This horrible disaster to the second city of the Roman East roused all Justinian's energy; neglecting the Italian war, he sent all his disposable troops to the Euphrates frontier, and named Belisarius himself as the chief commander. After this, Chosroës won no such successes as had distinguished his first campaign. Having commenced an attack on the Roman border fortresses in Colchis, far to the north, he was drawn home by the news that Belisarius had invaded Assyria and was besieging Nisibis. On the approach of the king the imperial general retired, but his manœuvre had cost the Persian the fruits of a whole summer's preparation, and the year A.D. 541 ended without serious fighting. In the next spring very similar operations followed: Belisarius defended the line of the Euphrates with success, and the invaders retired after having reduced one single Mesopotamian fortress. The war lingered for two years more, till Chosroës, disgusted at the ill-success of all his efforts since his first success at Antioch, and more especially humiliated by a bloody repulse from the walls of Edessa, consented to treat for peace [A.D. 545]. He gave up his conquests—which were of small importance—but regarded the honours of the war as being his own, because Justinian consented to pay him 2,000 lbs. of gold [£108,000] on the ratification of the treaty. One curious clause was inserted in the document—though hostilities ceased everywhere else, the rights of the two monarchs to the suzerainty of the kingdom of Lazica, on the Colchian frontier, hard by the Black Sea, were left undefined. For no less than seven years a sort of by-war was maintained in this small district, while peace prevailed on all other points of the Perso-Roman frontier. It was not till A.D. 556, after both parties had wasted much treasure and many men on the unprofitable contest, that Chosroës resigned the attempt to hold the small and rugged mountain kingdom of the Lazi, and resigned it to Justinian on the promise of an annual grant of £18,000 as compensation money.

But although Justinian had brought his second Persian war to a not unsuccessful end, the empire had come badly out of the struggle, and was by 556 falling into a condition of incipient disorder and decay. This was partly caused by the reckless financial expedients of the Emperor, who taxed the provinces with unexampled rigour while forced to maintain at once a Persian and an Italian war.

The main part of the damage, however, was wrought by other than human means. In A.D. 542 there broke out in the empire a plague such as had not been known for three hundred years—the last similar visitation had fallen in the reign of Trebonianus Gallus, far back in the third century. This pestilence was one of the epoch-making events in the history of the empire, as great a landmark as the Black Death in the history of England. The details which Procopius gives us concerning its progress and results leave no doubt that it operated more powerfully than any other factor in that weakening of the empire which is noticeable in the second half of the sixth century. When it reached Constantinople, 5,000 persons a day are said to have fallen victims to it. All customary occupations ceased in the city, and the market-place was empty save for corpse-bearers. In many houses not a single soul remained alive, and the government had to take special measures for the burial of neglected corpses. "The disease," says the chronicler, "did not attack any particular race or class of men, nor prevail in any particular region, nor confine itself to any period of the year. Summer or winter, North or South, Greek or Arabian, washed or unwashed—of such distinctions the plague took no account. A man might climb to the hill-top, and it was there; he might retire to the depths of a cavern, and it was there also." The only marked characteristic of its ravages that the chronicler could find was that, "whether by chance or providential design, it strictly spared the most wicked."[12]

Justinian himself fell ill of the plague: he recovered, but was never his old self again. Though he persevered inflexibly to his last day in his scheme for the reconquest of the empire, yet he seems to have declined in energy, and more especially to have lost that power of organization, which had been his most marked characteristic. The chroniclers complain that he had grown less hopeful and less masterful. "After achieving so much in the days of his vigour, when he entered into the last stage of his life he seemed to weary of his labours, and preferred to create

[12] Bury's "Later Roman Empire," i. 402.

discord among his foes or to mollify them with gifts, instead of trusting to his arms and facing the dangers of war. So he allowed his troops to decline in numbers, because he did not expect to require their services. And his ministers, who collected his taxes and maintained his armies were affected with the same indifference."[13]

One feature of the Emperor's later years was that he took more and more interest in theological disputes, even to the neglect of State business. The Church question of the day was the dispute on Monophysitism, the heresy which denied the existence both of a human and a divine nature in Our Lord. Justinian was not a monophysite himself, but wished to unify the sect with the main body of the Church by edicts of comprehension, which forbade the discussion of the subject, and spent much trouble in coercing prelates orthodox and heretical into a reconciliation which had no chance of permanent success. His chief difficulty was with the bishops of Rome. He forced Pope Vigilius to come to Constantinople, and kept him under constraint for many months, till he signed all that was required of him [A.D. 554]. The only result was to win Vigilius the reputation of a heretic, and to cause a growing estrangement between East and West.

The gloom of Justinian's later years was even more marked after the death of his wife; Theodora died in A.D. 548, six years after the great plague, and it may be that her loss was no less a cause of the diminished energy of his later years than was his enfeebled health. Her bold and adventurous spirit must have buoyed him up in many of the more difficult enterprises of the first half of his reign. After her death, Justinian seems to have trusted no one: his destined successor, Justinus, son of his sister, was kept in the background, and no great minister seems to have possessed his confidence. Even Belisarius, the first and most loyal soldier of the empire, does not appear to have been trusted: in the second Gothic war the Emperor stinted him of troops and hampered him with colleagues. At last he was recalled [A.D. 549] and sent into private life, from which he was only recalled on the occurrence of a sudden military crisis in A.D. 558.

This crisis was a striking example of the mismanagement of Justinian's later years. A nomad horde from the South Russian steppes, the Cotrigur Huns, had crossed the frozen Danube at mid-winter, when hostilities were least expected, and thrown themselves on the Thracian provinces. The empire had 150,000 men under arms at the moment, but they were all dispersed abroad, many in Italy, others in Africa, others in Spain, others in Colchis, some in the Thebaid, and a few on the Mesopotamian frontier. There was such a dearth of men to defend the home provinces that the barbarians rode unhindered over the whole country side from the Danube to the Propontis plundering and burning. One body, only 7,000 strong, came up to within a few miles of the city gates, and inspired such fear that the Constantinopolitans began to send their money and church-plate over to Asia. Justinian then summoned Belisarius from his retirement, and placed him in command of what troops there were available—a single regiment of 300 veterans from Italy, and the "Scholarian guards," a body of local troops 3,500 strong, raised in the city and entrusted with the charge of its gates, which inspired little confidence as its members were allowed to practice their trades and avocations and only called out in rotation for occasional service. With this undisciplined force, which had

[13] Agathias.

never seen war, at his back, Belisarius contrived to beat off the Huns. He led them to pursue him back to a carefully prepared position, where the only point that could be attacked was covered with woods and hedges on either side. The untrustworthy "Scholarians" were placed on the flanks, where they could not be seriously molested, while the 300 Italian veterans covered the one vulnerable point. The Huns attacked, were shot down from the woods and beaten off in front, and fled leaving 400 men on the field, while the Romans only lost a few wounded and not a single soldier slain. Thus the last military exploit of Belisarius preserved the suburbs of the imperial city itself from molestation; after defending Old Rome in his prime, he saved New Rome in his old age.

Even this last service did not prevent Justinian from viewing his great servant with suspicion. Four years later an obscure conspiracy against his life was discovered, and one of the conspirators named Belisarius as being privy to the plot. The old emperor affected to believe the accusation, sequestrated the general's property, and kept him under surveillance for eight months. Belisarius was then acquitted and restored to favour: he lived two years longer, and died in March, 565.[14] The ungrateful master whom he had served so well followed him to the grave nine months later.

Of Justinian as conqueror and governor we have said much. But there remain two more aspects of his life which deserve notice—his work as a builder and his codification of the laws. From the days of Diocletian the style of architecture which we call Byzantine, for want of a better name, had been slowly developing from the old classic forms, and many of the emperors of the fourth and fifth centuries had been given to building. But no previous monarch had combined in such a degree as did Justinian the will and the power to launch out into architectural experiments. He had at his disposal the hoarded treasures of Anastasius, and his tastes were as magnificent as those of the great builders of the early empire, Augustus and Nero and Hadrian. All over the empire the monuments of his wealth and taste were seen in dozens of churches, halls of justice, monasteries, forts, hospitals, and colonnades. The historian Procopius was able to compose a considerable volume entirely on the subject of Justinian's buildings, and numbers of them survive, some perfect and more in ruins, to witness to the accuracy of the work. Even in the more secluded or outlying portions of the empire, any fine building that is found is, in two cases out of three, one of the works of Justinian. Not merely great centres like Constantinople or Jerusalem, but out-of-the-way tracts in Cappadocia and Isauria, are full of his buildings. Even in the newly-conquered Ravenna his great churches of San Vitale, containing the celebrated mosaic portraits of himself and his wife, and of St. Apollinare in the suburb of Classis, outshine the older works of the fifth-century emperors and of the Goth Theodoric.

[14] It is comforting to know that the popular legend which tells how the great general lived in poverty and disgrace, begging the passer-by "dare obolum Belisario," and dying in the streets, is untrue. But the suspicious emperor's conduct was quite unpardonable.

COLUMNS IN ST. SOPHIA.

GALLERIES OF ST. SOPHIA.

Justinian's churches, indeed, are the best known of his buildings. In Oriental church-architecture his reign forms a landmark: up to his time Christian architects had still been using two patterns copied straight from Old Roman models. The first was the round domed church, whose origin can be traced back to such Roman originals as the celebrated Temple of Vesta—of such the Church of the Holy Sepulchre at Rome may serve as a type. The second was the rectangular church with apses, which was nothing more than an adaptation for ecclesiastical purposes of the Old Roman law-courts, and which had borrowed from them its name of *Basilica*. St. Paul's Outside the Walls, at Rome is a fair specimen. Justinian brought into use for the first time on a large scale the combination of a cruciform ground-plan and a very large dome. The famous Church of St. Sophia may serve as the type of this style. The great cathedral of Constantinople had already been burnt down twice, as we have had occasion to relate: the first time on the eve of the banishment of John Chrysostom, the second in the great "Nika" riot of 532. Within forty days of its destruction Justinian had commenced preparations for rebuilding it as a monument of his triumph in the civil strife. He chose as his architect Anthemius of Tralles, the greatest of Byzantine builders, and one of the few whose names have survived. The third church was different in plan from either of its predecessors, showing the new combination which we have already specified. It is a Greek cross, 241 feet long and 224 broad, having in its midst a vast dome, pierced by no less than forty windows, light and airy and soaring 180 feet above the floor. In the nave the aisles and side apses are parted from the main central spaces by magnificent colonnades of marble pillars, the majority of *verde antique*. These are not for the most part the work of Justinian's day, but were plundered from the chief pagan temples of Asia, which served as an inexhaustible quarry for the Christian builder. The whole of the interior, both roof and dome, was covered with gilding or mosaics, which the Vandalism of the Turks has covered with a coat of whitewash, to hide the representations of human forms which are offensive to the Moslems' creed. Procopius describes the church with enthusiasm, and his praises are well justified—

"It presents a most glorious spectacle, extraordinary to those who behold it, and altogether incredible to those who know it by report only. In height it rises to the very heavens, and overtops the neighbouring buildings like a ship anchored among them. It towers above the city which it adorns, and from it the whole of Constantinople can be beheld, as from a watch-tower. Its breadth and length are so judiciously chosen, that it appears both broad and long without disproportion. For it excels both in size and harmony, being more magnificent than ordinary buildings, and much more elegant than the few which approach it in size. Within it is singularly full of light and sunshine; you would declare that the place is not lighted from without, but that the rays are produced within itself, such an abundance of light is poured into it. The gilded ceiling adds glory to its interior, though the light reflected upon the gold from the marble surpasses it in beauty. Who can tell of the splendour of the columns and marbles with which the church is adorned? One would think that one had come upon a meadow full of flowers in bloom—one wonders at the purple tints of some, the green of others, the glowing red and glittering white, and those, too, which nature, like a painter, has marked with the strongest contrasts of colour. Moreover, it is impossible accurately to describe the treasures of gold and silver plate and gems which the Emperor has presented to the church: the Sanctuary alone contains forty thousand pounds weight of silver."

Justinian was almost as great a builder of forts as of churches, but his military works have for the most part disappeared. It may give some idea of his energy in fortifying the frontiers when we state that the Illyrian provinces alone were protected by 294 forts, of which Procopius gives a list, disposed in four successive lines from the Danube back to the Thessalian hills. Some were single towers, but many were elaborate fortresses with outworks, and all had to be protected by garrisons.

Thus much of Justinian as builder: space fails to enumerate a tithe of his works. Of his great legal achievement we must speak at even shorter length. The Roman law, as he received it from his predecessors was an enormous mass of precedents and decisions, in which the original basis was overlaid with the various and sometimes contradictory rescripts of five centuries of emperors. Several of his predecessors, and most especially Theodosius II., had endeavoured to codify the chaotic mass and reduce it to order. But no one of them had produced a code which sufficed to bring the law of the day into full accord with the spirit of the times. It was no mean work to bring the ancient legislation of Rome, from the days of the Twelve Tables down to the days of Justinian, into strict and logical connection with the new Christian ideas which had worked their way into predominance since the days of Constantine. Much of the old law was hopelessly obsolete, owing to the change in moral ideas which Christianity had introduced, but it is still astonishing to see how much of the old forms of the times of the early empire survived into the sixth century. Justinian employed a commission, headed by the clever but unpopular lawyer Tribonian, to draw up his new code. The work was done for ever and a day, and his "Institutes" and "Pandects" were the last revision of the Old Roman laws, and the starting-point of all systematic legal study in Europe, when, six hundred years later, the need for something more than customary folk-right began to make itself felt, as mediæval civilization evolved itself out of the chaos of the dark ages. If the Roman Empire had flourished in the century after Justinian as in that which preceded him, other revisers of the laws might have produced compilations that would have made the "Institutes" seem out of date. But, as a matter of fact, decay and chaos followed after Justinian, and succeeding emperors had neither the need nor the inclination to do his work over again. Hence it came to pass that his name is for ever associated with the last great revision of Roman law, and that he himself went down to posterity as the greatest of legislators, destined to be enthroned by Dante in one of the starry thrones of his "Paradise," and to be worshipped as the father of law by all the legists of the Renaissance.

IX. The Coming Of The Slavs.

The thirty years which followed the death of Justinian are covered by three reigns, those of Justinus II. [565-578], Tiberius Constantinus [578-582], and Maurice [582-602]. These three emperors were men of much the same character as the predecessors of Justinian; each of them was an experienced official of mature age, who was selected by the reigning emperor as his most worthy successor. Justinus was the favourite nephew of Justinian, and had served him for many years as Curopalates, or Master of the Palace. Tiberius Constantinus was "Count of the Excubiti," a high Court officer in the suite of Justinus: Maurice again served Tiberius as "Count of the Fœderati," or chief of the Barbarian auxiliaries. They were all men of capacity, and strove to do their best for the empire: historians concur in praising the justice of Justinus, the liberality and humanity of Tiberius, the piety of Maurice. Yet under them the empire was steadily going down hill: the exhausting effects of the reign of Justinian were making themselves felt more and more, and at the end of the reign of Maurice a time of chaos and disaster was impending, which came to a head under his successor.

The internal causes of the disaster of this time were the weakening of the empire by the great plague of 544 and still more by the grinding exactions of Justinian's financial system. Its external phenomena were invasions by new hordes from the north, combined with long and exhausting wars with Persia. The virtues of the emperors seem to have helped them little: Justin's justice made him feared rather than loved; Tiberius's liberality rendered him popular, but drained the treasury; Maurice, on the other hand, who was economical and endeavoured to fill the coffers which his predecessors had emptied, was therefore universally condemned as avaricious.

The troubles on the frontier which vexed the last thirty years of the sixth century were due to three separate sets of enemies—the Lombards in Italy, the Slavs and Avars in the Balkan Peninsula, and the Persians in the East.

The empire held undisputed possession of Italy for no more than fifteen years after the expulsion of the Ostrogoths in A.D. 553. Then a new enemy came in from the north, following the same path that had already served for the Visigoths of Alaric and the Ostrogoths of Theodoric. The new-comers were the race of the Lombards, who had hitherto dwelt in Hungary, on the Middle Danube, and had more frequently been found as friends than as foes of the Romans. But their warlike and ambitious King Alboin, having subdued all his nearer neighbours, began to covet the fertile plains of Italy, where he saw the emperors keeping a very inadequate garrison, now that the Ostrogoths were finally driven away. In A.D. 568 Alboin and his hordes crossed the Alps, bringing with them wife and child, and flocks and herds, while their old land on the Danube was abandoned to the Avars. The Lombards took possession of the flat country in the north of Italy, as far as the line of the Po, with very little difficulty. The region, we are told, was almost uninhabited owing to the combined effects of the great plague and the Ostrogothic war. In this once fertile and populous, but now deserted, lowland, the Lombards settled down in great numbers. There they have left their name as the permanent denomination of the plain of Lombardy. Only one city, the strong fortress of Pavia, held out against them for long; when it fell in 571, after a gallant defence of three years, Alboin made it his capital, instead of choosing one of the larger and more famous towns of Milan and Verona, the older centres of life in the land he had conquered. After subduing Lombardy the king pushed forward into Etruria, and overran the valley of the Arno. But in the midst of his wars he was cut off, if the legend tells us the truth, by the vengeance of his wife Queen Rosamund. She was the daughter of Cunimund, King of the Gepidæ, whom Alboin had slain in battle. The fallen monarch's skull was, by the victor's orders, mounted in gold and fashioned into a cup. Long years after, amid the revelry of a drinking bout, Alboin had the ghastly cup filled with wine, and bade his wife bear it around to his chosen warriors. The queen obeyed, but vowed to revenge herself by her husband's death. By the sacrifice of her honour she bribed Alboin's armour-bearer to slay his master in his bed, and then fled with him to Constantinople [A.D. 573].

But the death of Alboin did not put an end to the Lombard conquests in Italy. The kingdom, indeed, broke up for a time into several independent duchies, but the Lombard chiefs continued to win territory from the empire. Two of them founded the considerable duchies of Spoleto and Benevento, the one in Central, and the other in Southern Italy. These states survived as independent powers, but the rest of the Lombard territories were reunited by King Autharis, in 584, and he and his immediate successors completed the conquest of Northern Italy.

Thus, during the reigns of Justin, Tiberius II., and Maurice, the greater part of Justinian's Italian conquests were lost, and formed once more into Teutonic states. The emperor retained only two large stretches of territory, the one in Central Italy, where he held a broad belt of land, extending right across the peninsula, from Ravenna and Ancona on the Adriatic, to Rome on the Tyrrhenian Sea; the other comprehending the extreme south of the land—the "toe" and "heel" of the Italian boot—and comprising the territory of Bruttium and the Calabrian[15] towns of Taranto, Brindisi, and Otranto. Sardinia and Sicily were also left untouched by the Lombards, who never succeeded in building a fleet. The Roman territory which stretched across Central Italy cut the Lombards in two, the king ruling the main body of them in Tuscany and the valley of the Po; while the dukes of Spoleto and Benevento maintained an isolated existence in the south.

[15] Calabria is here used in its old sense, meaning South Apulia, and not the extreme point of Italy down by Reggio and Squillace.

CROSS OF JUSTINUS II. (*From the Vatican.*)
(*From "L'Art Byzantin," Par C. Bayet. Paris, Quantin,* 1883.)

This partition of Italy between the Lombards and the empire is worth remembering, from the fact that never again, till our own day, was the whole peninsula gathered into a single state. Not till 1870, when the kingdom of United Italy was completed by the conquest of Rome, did a time come when all the lands between the Alps and the Straits of Messina were governed by one ruler. Justinian had no successor till Victor Emmanuel.

After the Lombard conquest the imperial dominions in Italy were administered by a governor, called the Exarch, who dwelt at Ravenna, the northernmost and strongest of the imperial fortresses. All the Italian provinces were nominally beneath his control, but, as a matter of fact, he was only treated with implicit obedience by those of his subordinates who dwelt in his own neighbourhood. He found it harder to enforce his orders at Naples and Reggio, or in the distant islands of Sicily and Sardinia. But it was the bishops of Rome who profited most by his absence: although a "duke," a military officer of some importance, dwelt at Rome, he was from the first overshadowed by his spiritual neighbour. Even during the days of the Ostrogoths the Roman bishops had acquired considerable importance, as being the chief official representatives of the Italians in dealings with their Teutonic masters. But they spoke with much more freedom and weight when they had to do, not with a King of Italy dwelling quite near them, but with a mere governor fettered by orders from distant Constantinople. Gregory the Great [590-604] was the first of the popes who began to assume an independent attitude and to treat the Exarch at Ravenna with scant ceremony. He was an able and energetic man, who could not bear to see Rome suffering for want of a ruler on the spot, and readily took upon himself civil functions, in spite of the protests of his nominal superior the Exarch. In 592, for example, he made a private truce for Rome with the Lombard Duke of Spoleto, though the latter was at war with the empire. The Emperor Maurice stormed at him as foolish and disobedient, but did not venture to depose him, being too much troubled with Persian and Avaric wars to send troops against Rome. On another occasion Gregory nominated a governor for Naples, instead of leaving the appointment to the Exarch. In 599 he acted as mediator between the Lombard king and the government at Ravenna, as if he had been a neutral and independent sovereign. Although he showed no wish to sever his connection with the Roman Empire, Gregory behaved as if he considered the emperor his suzerain rather than his immediate ruler. He would never give in on disputed points, issued orders which contradicted imperial rescripts, and maintained a bitter quarrel with successive patriarchs of Constantinople, who possessed the favour of Maurice. When the patriarch John the Faster took the title of "œcumenical bishop," Gregory wrote to Maurice to tell him that the presumption of John was a sure sign that the days of Antichrist were at hand, and to urge him to repress such pretensions by the force of the civil arm. This is one of the first signs of the approach of that mediæval view of the papacy which imagined that it was the pontiff's duty to censure and advise kings and emperors on all possible topics and occasions. Gregory's immediate successors were not men of mark, or a breach with the empire might have been precipitated. The final disavowal of the supremacy of the Constantinopolitan monarch was to be still delayed for nearly two hundred years.

The wars between the Exarchs of Ravenna and the Lombard kings were little influenced by interference from the East. The emperors during the last thirty years of the sixth century were far more engrossed with their Persian and Slavonic wars. Contests with the Great king of the East occupied no less than twenty years in the reigns of Justin II., Tiberius, and Maurice. War was declared in 572, and did not cease till 592. Like the struggle between Justinian and Chosroës I., thirty years before, it was wholly indecisive. There were more plundering raids than battles, and the frontier provinces of each empire were reduced to a dreadful state of desolation and depopulation: if the Persians pushed their ravages as far as the gates of Antioch, Roman generals penetrated deep into Media and Corduene, where the imperial banner had not been seen for two hundred years. The net result of the whole twenty years of strife was that each combatant had seriously weakened and distressed his rival, without obtaining any definite superiority over him. Forced to make peace by the pressure of a civil war, Chosroës II. gave back to Maurice the two frontier cities of Dara and Martyropolis, the sole trophies of twenty campaigns, and ceded him a slice of Armenian territory. But these trivial gains were far from compensating the empire for the fearful losses caused by dozens of Persian invasions.

The Persian war was exhausting, but successful: on the northern frontier, however, the Roman army had been faring far worse, and serious losses of territory were beginning to take place. The enemies in this quarter were two new tribes, who appeared on the Danube after the Lombards had departed from it to commence their invasion of Italy. There were now no Teutons left on the northern frontier of the empire: of the incoming tribes, one was Tartar and the other Slavonic. The Avars were a nomadic race from Asia, wild horsemen of the Steppes, much like their predecessors the Huns. They had fled west to escape the Turks, who were at this time building up an empire in Central Asia, and betook themselves to the South Russian plains, not far from the mouth of the Danube. To cross the river and ravage Moesia was too tempting a prospect to be neglected, and ere long the Avaric cavalry were seen only too frequently along the Balkans and on the coast of the Black Sea. Their first raid into Roman territory fell into the year 562, just before the death of Justinian, and from that time forward they were always causing trouble. They were ready enough to make peace when money was paid them, but as they invariably broke the agreement when the money was spent, it was never long before they reappeared south of the Danube.

But the Slavs were a far more serious danger to the empire than the Avars. The latter came only to plunder, the former—like the Germans two centuries before—came pressing into the provinces to win themselves a new home. The Romans knew at first of only two tribes of them, the Slovenes and Antae, but behind these there were others who were gradually to push their way to the south and make their presence known—Croats, Servians, and many more. The Slavs were the easternmost of the Aryan peoples of Europe, and by far the most backward. They had always lain behind the Germans, and it was only when the German barrier was removed by the migration of the Goths and Lombards that they came into touch with the empire. They were rude races, far behind the Teutons in civilization; they had hardly learnt as yet the simplest arts, knew nothing of defensive armour, and could only use for boats tree-trunks hollowed out by fire—like the Australian savages of to-day. They had not learnt to live under kings or chiefs, but dwelt in village communities, governed by the patriarchs of the several families. Their abodes were mud huts, and they cultivated no grain but millet. When they went to war they could send out thousands of spearmen and bowmen, but their wild bands were not very formidable in the open field. They could resist neither cavalry nor disciplined infantry, and were only formidable in woods and defiles, where they formed ambuscades and endeavoured to take their enemy by surprise, and overwhelm him by a sudden rush. We are assured that one of their favourite devices was to conceal themselves in ponds or rivers by lying down in the water for hours together, breathing through reeds, whose points were the only things visible above the surface. Thus a thousand men might be concealed, and nothing appear except a bed of rushes. This strange stratagem would seem incredible, if we had not on record one or two occasions on which it was actually practised.

The Slavs had begun to make themselves felt early in the sixth century, but it was not till the death of Justinian that we hear of them as a pressing danger. But when the Lombards had passed away westward, they came down to the Danube and began to cross it in great numbers, in the endeavour to make permanent settlements on the Roman bank. The raids of the Slavs and the Avars were curiously complicated, for the king, or Chagan, of the Tartar tribe had made vassals of many of his Slavonic neighbours. They, on the other hand, sometimes acted in obedience to him, but more frequently tried to escape from his power by pushing forward into Roman territory. Hence it comes that we often find Slav and Avar leagued together, but at other times find them acting separately, or even in opposition to each other. A more chaotic series of campaigns it is hard to conceive.

Down to this time the inland of the Balkan peninsula had been inhabited by Thracian and Illyrian provincials, of whom the majority spoke the Latin tongue, though a few still preserved their ancient barbaric idiom.[16] They formed the only large body of subjects of the empire outside Italy, who still spoke the old ruling language, and as they were about a quarter of its population, they did much to preserve its Roman character, and to prevent it from becoming Greek or Asiatic. Their pride in their Latin tongue was very marked: Justinian, born in the heart of the district, was fond of laying special stress on the fact that Latin was his native language.

On this Latinized Thraco-Illyrian population the invasion of the Slavs and Avars fell with unexampled severity. The Goths had afflicted them before, but they, at least, had been Christian and semi-civilized, while the new-comers were in the lowest grade of savagery. It is not too much to say that between 570 and 600 the old population was almost exterminated over the greater part of the country north of the Balkans—the modern Servia and Bulgaria—and very sadly cut down even in the more sheltered Macedonian and Thracian provinces. The Latin-speaking provincials almost disappeared: the only remnants of them were the Dalmatian islanders and the "Vlachs" or Wallachians who are found in later times scattered in small bodies among the Slavs who had swept over the whole country-side. The effect of the invasion is well described by the contemporary chronicler, John of Ephesus—

"The year 581 was famous for the invasion of the accursed people called Slavonians, who overran Greece and the country by Thessalonica, and all Thrace, and captured the cities and took many forts, and devastated and burnt, and reduced the people to slavery, and made themselves masters of the whole country, and settled in it, by main force, and dwelt in it as though it had been their own. Four years have now elapsed, and still they live at their ease in the land, and spread themselves far and wide, as far as God permits them, and ravage and burn and take captive, and still they encamp and dwell there."

The open country was swept bare by the Slavs: the towns resisted better, for neither Slav nor Avar was skilled in siege operations. Relying upon the fortified towns as his base the great general Priscus, whom Maurice placed in command, was able to keep his ground along the Danube, and to perform many gallant exploits. He

[16] From them the Albanians decend: the Albanian tongue is the only relic of ancient Illyria.

even crossed the river and attacked the Slavs and Avars in their own homes beyond it; but it was to no effect that he burnt their villages and slew off their warriors. He could not protect the unarmed population in the open country within the Roman boundary, and the girdle of fortresses along the Danube soon covered nothing but a wasted region, sparsely inhabited by Slavs. The limit of Roman population had fallen back to the line of the Balkans, and even to the south of it, and the Slavs were ever slipping across the Danube in larger and larger numbers, despite the garrisons along the river which were still kept up from Singidunum [Belgrade] to Dorostolum [Silistria].

The misfortunes of the Avaric and Slavonic war were the cause of the fall of the Emperor Maurice. He had won some unpopularity by his manifest inability to stem the tide of the barbarian invasion, and more by an act of callousness, of which he was guilty in 599. The Chagan of the Avars had captured 15,000 prisoners, and offered to release them for a large ransom. Maurice—whose treasury was empty—refused to comply, and the Chagan massacred the wretched captives. But the immediate cause of the emperor's fall was his way of dealing with the army. He was unpopular with the soldiery, though an old soldier himself, and did not possess their respect or confidence. Yet he was an officer of some merit and had written a long military treatise called the “Strategicon,” which was the official handbook of the imperial armies for three hundred years.

Maurice sealed his fate when, in 602, he issued orders for the discontented army of the Danube to winter north of the river, in the waste marshes of the Slavs. The troops refused to obey the order, and chased away their generals. Then electing as their captain an obscure centurion, named Phocas, they marched on Constantinople.

Maurice armed the city factions, the “Blues” and “Greens,” and strove to defend himself. But when he saw that no one would fight for him, he fled across the Bosphorus with his wife and children, to seek refuge in the Asiatic provinces, where he was less unpopular than in Europe. Soon he was pursued by orders of Phocas, whom the army had now saluted as emperor, and caught at Chalcedon. The cruel usurper had him executed along with all his five sons, the youngest a child of only three years of age. Maurice died with a courage and piety that moved even his enemies, exclaiming with his last breath, “Thou art just, O Lord, and just are thy judgments!”

X. The Darkest Hour.

For the first time since Constantinople had become the seat of empire the throne had been won by armed rebellion and the murder of the legitimate ruler. The break in the peaceful and orderly succession which had hitherto prevailed was not only an evil precedent, but an immediate disaster. The new emperor proved a far worse governor than the unfortunate Maurice, who, in spite of his faults and his ill luck, had always been hard-working, moderate, pious, and economical. Phocas was a mere brutal soldier—cruel, ignorant, suspicious, and reckless, and in his incapable hands the empire began to fall to pieces with alarming rapidity. He opened his reign with a series of cruel executions of his predecessor's friends, and from that moment his deeds of bloodshed never ceased: probably the worst of them was the execution of Constantina, widow of Maurice and daughter of Tiberius II., whom he slew together with her three young daughters, lest their names might be used as the excuse for a conspiracy against him. But even greater horror seems to have been caused when he burnt alive the able general Narses,[17] who had won many laurels in the last Persian war. Narses had come up to the capital under safe conduct to clear himself from accusations of treason: so the Emperor not only devised a punishment which had never yet been heard of since the empire became Christian, but broke his own plighted oath.

The moment that Phocas had mounted the throne, Chosroës of Persia declared war on him, using the hypocritical pretext that he wished to revenge Maurice, for whom he professed a warm personal friendship. This war was far different from the indecisive contests in the reigns of Justinian and Justin II. In two successive years the Persians burst into North Syria and ravaged it as far as the sea; but in the third they turned north and swept over the hitherto untouched provinces of Asia Minor. In 608 their main army penetrated across Cappadocia and Galatia right up to the gates of Chalcedon. The inhabitants of Constantinople could see the blazing villages across the water on the Asiatic shore—a sight as new as it was terrifying; for although Thrace had several times been harried to within sight of the city, no enemy had ever been seen in Bithynia.

Plot after plot was formed in the capital against Phocas, but he succeeded in putting them all down, and slew the conspirators with fearful tortures. For eight years his reign continued: Constantinople was full of executions; Asia was ravaged from sea to sea; the Thracian and Illyrian provinces were overrun more and more by the Slavs, now that the army of Europe had been transferred across the Bosphorus to make head against the Persians. Yet Phocas still held on to Constantinople: the creature of a military revolt himself, it was by a military revolt alone that he was destined to be overthrown.

[17] To be carefully distinguished from his homonyn in Justinian's time.

Africa was the only portion of the Roman Empire which in the reign of Phocas was suffering neither from civil strife nor foreign invasion. It was well governed by the aged exarch Heraclius, who was so well liked in the province that the emperor had not dared to depose him. Urged by desperate entreaties from all parties in Constantinople to strike a blow against the tyrant, and deliver the empire from the yoke of a monster, Heraclius at last consented. He quietly got ready a fleet, which he placed under the orders of his son, who bore the same name as himself. This he despatched against Constantinople, while at the same time his nephew Nicetas led a large body of horse along the African shore to invade Egypt.

When Heraclius the younger arrived with his fleet at the Dardanelles, all the prominent citizens of Constantinople fled secretly to take refuge with him. As he neared the capital the troops of Phocas burst into mutiny: the tyrant's fleet was scattered after a slight engagement, and the city threw open its gates. Phocas was seized in the palace by an official whom he had cruelly wronged, and brought aboard the galley of the conqueror. "Is it thus," said Heraclius, "that you have governed the empire?" "Will you govern it any better?" sneered the desperate usurper. Heraclius spurned him away with his foot, and the sailors hewed him to pieces on the deck.

Next day the patriarch and the senate hailed Heraclius as emperor, and he was duly crowned in St. Sophia on October 5, A.D. 610.

Heraclius took over the empire in such a state of disorder and confusion that he must soon have felt that there was some truth in the dying sneer of Phocas. It seemed almost impossible to get things into better order, for resources were wanting. Save Africa and Egypt and the district immediately around the capital, all the provinces were overrun by the Persian, the Avar, and the Slav. The treasury was empty, and the army had almost disappeared owing to repeated and bloody defeats in Asia Minor.

Heraclius seems at first to have almost despaired of the possibility of evolving order out of this chaos, though he was in the prime of life and strength—"a man of middle stature, strongly built, and broad-chested, with grey eyes and yellow hair, and of a very fair complexion; he wore a bushy beard when he came to the throne, but afterwards cut it short." For the first twelve years of his reign he remained at Constantinople, endeavouring to reorganize the empire, and to defend at any rate the frontiers of Thrace and Asia Minor. The more distant provinces he hardly seems to have hoped to save, and the chronicle of his early years is filled with the catalogue of the losses of the empire. Mesopotamia and North Syria had already been lost by Phocas, but in 613, while the imperial armies were endeavouring to defend Cappadocia, the Persian general Shahrbarz turned southwards and attacked Central Syria. The great town of Damascus fell into his hands; but worse was to come. In 614 the Persian army appeared before the holy city of Jerusalem, took it after a short resistance, and occupied it with a garrison. But the populace rose and slaughtered the Persian troops when Shahrbarz had departed with his main army. This brought him back in wrath: he stormed the city and put 90,000 Christians to the sword, only sparing the Jewish inhabitants. Zacharias, Patriarch of Jerusalem, was carried into captivity, and with him went what all Christians then regarded as the most precious thing in the world—the wood of the "True Cross." Helena, the mother of Constantine, had dug the relic up, according to the well-known legend, on Mount

Moriah, and built for it a splendid shrine. Now Shahrbarz desecrated the church and took off the "True Cross" to Persia.

This loss brought the inhabitants of the East almost to despair; they thought that the luck of the empire had departed with the Holy Wood, which had served as its Palladium, and even imagined that the Last Day was at hand and that Chosroës of Persia was Antichrist. The mad language of pride and insult which the Persian in the day of his triumph used to Heraclius might also explain their belief. His blasphemous phrases seem like an echo of the letter of Sennacherib in the Second Book of Kings. The epistle ran:—

"Chosroës, greatest of gods, and master of the whole earth, to Heraclius, his vile and insensate slave. Have I not destroyed the Greeks? You say you trust in your God: why, then, has he not delivered out of my hand Caesarea, Jerusalem, and Alexandria? Shall I not also destroy Constantinople? But I will pardon all your sins if you will come to me with your wife and children; I will give you lands, vines, and olive groves, and will look upon you with a kindly aspect. Do not deceive yourself with the vain hope in that Christ, who was not even able to save himself from the Jews, who slew him by nailing him to a cross."

The horror and rage roused by the loss of the "True Cross" and the blasphemies of King Chosroës brought about the first real outburst of national feeling that we meet in the history of the Eastern Empire. It was felt that the fate of Christendom hung in the balance, and that all, from highest to lowest, were bound to make one great effort to beat back the fire-worshipping Persians from Palestine, and recover the Holy Places. The Emperor vowed that he would take the field at the head of the army—a thing most unprecedented, for since the death of Theodosius I., in 395, no Caesar had ever gone out in person to war. The Church came forward in the most noble way—at the instance of the Patriarch Sergius all the churches of Constantinople sent their treasures and ornaments to the mint to be coined down, and serve as a great loan to the state, which was to be repaid when the Persians should have been conquered. The free dole of corn which the inhabitants of the capital had been receiving ever since the days of Constantine was abolished, and the populace bore the privation without demur. It was indeed observed that this measure not only saved the treasury, but drove into the army—where they were useful—thousands of the able-bodied loiterers who were the strength of the circus factions and the pest of the city. If the dole had been continued Heraclius could not have found a penny for the war. Egypt, the granary of the empire, had been lost in 616, and the supply of government corn entirely cut off, so that the dole would have had to be provided by the treasury buying corn, a ruinously expensive task.

By the aid of the Church loan Heraclius equipped a new army and strengthened his fleet. He also provided for the garrisoning of Constantinople by an adequate force, a most necessary precaution, for in 617 the Persians had again forced their way to the Bosphorus, and this time captured Chalcedon. Heraclius would probably have taken the field next year but for troubles with the Avars. That wild race had long been working their wicked will on the almost undefended Thracian provinces, but now they promised peace. Heraclius went out, at the Chagan's pressing invitation, to meet him near Heraclea. But the conference was a snare, for the treacherous savage had planted ambushes on the way to secure the person of the Emperor, and Heraclius only escaped by the speed of his horse. He cast off his imperial mantle to ride the faster, and galloped into the capital just in time to close its gates as the vanguard of the Chagan's army came in sight. The Avars kept the Emperor engaged for some time, and it was not till 622 that he was able to take the field against the Persians.

This expedition of Heraclius was in spirit the first of the Crusades. It was the first war that the Roman Empire had ever undertaken in a spirit of religious enthusiasm, for it was to no mere political end that the Emperor and his people looked forward. The army marched out to save Christendom, to conquer the Holy Places, and to recover the "True Cross." The men were wrought up to a high pitch of enthusiasm by warlike sermons, and the Emperor carried with him, to stimulate his zeal, a holy picture—one of those *eikons* in which the Greek Church has always delighted—which was believed to be the work of no mortal hands.

Heraclius made no less than six campaigns (A.D. 622-27) in his gallant and successful attempt to save the half-ruined empire. He won great and well-deserved fame, and his name would be reckoned among the foremost of the world's warrior-kings if it had not been for the misfortunes which afterwards fell on him in his old age.

His first campaign cleared Asia Minor of the Persian hosts, not by a direct attack, but by skilful strategy. Instead of attacking the army at Chalcedon, he took ship and landed in Cilicia, in the rear of the enemy, threatening in this position both Syria and Cappadocia. As he expected, the Persians broke up from their camp opposite Constantinople, and came back to fall upon him. But after much manœuvring he completely beat the general Shahrbarz, and cleared Asia Minor of the enemy.

In his next campaigns Heraclius endeavoured to liberate the rest of the Roman Empire by a similar plan: he resolved to assail Chosroës at home, and force him to recall the armies he kept in Syria and Egypt to defend his own Persian provinces. In 623-4 the Emperor advanced across the Armenian mountains and threw himself into Media, where his army revenged the woes of Antioch and Jerusalem by burning the fire-temples of Ganzaca—the Median capital—and Thebarmes, the birthplace of the Persian prophet Zoroaster. Chosroës, as might have been expected, recalled his troops from the west, and fought two desperate battles to cover Ctesiphon. His generals were defeated in both, but the Roman army suffered severely. Winter was at hand, and Heraclius fell back on Armenia. In his next campaign he recovered Roman Mesopotamia, with its fortresses of Amida, Dara, and Martyropolis, and again defeated the general Shahrbarz.

But 626 was the decisive year of the war. The obstinate Chosroës determined on one final effort to crush Heraclius, by concerting a joint plan of operations with the Chagan of the Avars. While the main Persian army watched the emperor in Armenia, a great body under Shahrbarz slipped south of him into Asia Minor and marched on the Bosphorus. At the same moment the Chagan of the Avars, with the whole force of his tribe and of his Slavonic dependants, burst over the Balkans and beset Constantinople on the European side. The two barbarian hosts could see each other across the water, and even contrived to exchange messages, but the Roman fleet sailing incessantly up and down the strait kept them from joining forces.

In the June, July, and August of 626 the capital was thus beset: the danger appeared imminent, and the Emperor was far away on the Euphrates. But the garrison was strong, the patrician Bonus, its commander, was an able officer, the fleet was efficient, and the same crusading fervour which had inspired the Constantinopolitans in 622 still buoyed up their spirits. In the end of July 80,000 Avars and Slavs, with all sorts of siege implements, delivered simultaneous assaults along the land front of the city, but they were beaten back with great slaughter. Next the Chagan built himself rafts and tried to bring the Persians across, but the Roman galleys sunk the clumsy structures, and slew thousands of the Slavs who had come off in small boats to attack the fleet. Then the Chagan gave up the siege in disgust and retired across the Danube.

Heraclius had shown great confidence in the strength of Constantinople and the courage of its defenders. He sent a few veteran troops to aid the garrison, but did not slacken from his attack on Persia. While Shahrbarz and the Chagan were besieging his capital, he himself was wasting Media and Mesopotamia. He imitated King Chosroës in calling in Tartar allies from the north, and revenged the ravages of the Avars in Thrace by turning 40,000 Khazar horsemen loose on Northern Persia. The enemy gave way before him everywhere, and the Persians began to grow desperate.

Next year King Chosroës put into the field the last levy of Persia, under a general named Rhazates, whom he bid to go out and "conquer or die."At the same time he wrote to command Shahrbarz to evacuate Chalcedon and return home in haste. But Heraclius intercepted the despatch of recall, and Shahrbarz came not.

Near Nineveh Heraclius fell in with the Persian home army and inflicted on it a decisive defeat. He himself, charging at the head of his cavalry, rode down the general of the enemy and slew him with his lance. Chosroës could put no new army in the field, and by Christmas Heraclius had seized his palace of Dastagerd, and divided among his troops such a plunder as had never been seen since Alexander the Great captured Susa.

The Nemesis of Chosroës' insane vanity had now arrived. Ten years after he had written his vaunting letter to Heraclius he found himself in far worse plight than his adversary had ever been. After Dastagerd had fallen he retired to Ctesiphon, the capital of his empire, but even from thence he had to flee on the approach of the enemy. Then the end came: his own son Siroes and his chief nobles seized him and threw him in chains, and a few days after he died—of rage and despair according to one story, of starvation if the darker tale is true.

The new king sent the humblest messages to the victorious Roman, hailing him as his "father," and apologizing for all the woes that the ambition of Chosroës had brought upon the world. Heraclius received his ambassadors with kindness, and granted peace, on the condition that every inch of Roman territory should be evacuated, all Roman captives freed, a war indemnity paid, and the spoils of Jerusalem, including the "True Cross,"faithfully restored. Siroes consented with alacrity, and in March, 628, a glorious peace ended the twenty-six years of the Persian war.

Heraclius returned to Constantinople in the summer of the same year with his spoils, his victorious army, and his great trophy, the "Holy Wood."His entry was celebrated in the style of an old Roman triumph, and the Senate conferred on him the title of the "New Scipio." The whole of the citizens, bearing myrtle boughs, came out to meet the army, and the ceremony concluded with the exhibition of the "True Cross" before the high altar of St. Sophia. Heraclius afterwards took it back in great pomp to Jerusalem.

This was, perhaps, the greatest triumph that any emperor ever won. Heraclius had surpassed the eastern achievements of Trajan and Severus, and led his troops further east than any Roman general had ever penetrated. His task, too, had been the hardest ever imposed on an emperor; none of his predecessors had ever started to war with his very capital beleaguered and with three-fourths of his provinces in the hands of the enemy. Since Julius Caesar no one had fought so incessantly—for six years the emperor had not been out of the saddle—nor met with such uniform success.

Heraclius returned to Constantinople to spend, as he hoped, the rest of his years in peace. He had now reached the age of fifty-four, and was much worn by his incessant campaigning. But the quiet for which he yearned was to be denied him, and the end of his reign was to be almost as disastrous as the commencement.

The great Saracen invasion was at hand, and it was at the very moment of Heraclius' triumph that Mahomet sent out his famous circular letter to the kings of the earth, inviting them to embrace Islam. If the Emperor could but have known that his desolated realm, spoiled for ten long years by the Persian and the Avar, and drained of men and money, was to be invaded by a new enemy far more terrible than the old, he would have prayed that the day of his triumph might also be the day of his death.

XI. Social And Religious Life. (A.D. 320-620.)

The reign of Heraclius forms the best dividing point in the history of the empire between what may roughly be called Ancient History and the Middle Ages. There is no break at all between Constantine and Heraclius, though the area, character, social life, and religion of the empire had been greatly modified in the three hundred years that separated them. The new order of things, which commenced when Constantine established his capital on the Bosphorus, had a peaceable and orderly development. The first prominent fact that strikes the eye in the history of the three centuries is that the sceptre passed from sovereign to sovereign in quiet and undisturbed devolution. From the death of Valens onward there is no instance of a military usurper breaking the line of succession till the crowning of Phocas in 602. The emperors were either designated by their predecessors or—less frequently—chosen by the high officials and the senate. The regularity of their sequence is all the more astonishing when we realize that only in three cases in the whole period was father succeeded by son. Saving Constantine himself, Theodosius I., and Arcadius, not a single emperor left male issue; yet the hereditary instinct had grown so strong in the empire that nephews, sons-in-law, and brothers-in-law of sovereigns were gladly received as their legitimate heirs. Considering this tendency, it is extraordinary to note that the whole three hundred years did not produce a single unmitigated tyrant. Constantius II. was gloomy and sometimes cruel, Valens was stupid and avaricious, Arcadius utterly weak and inept, Justinian hard and thankless; but the general average of the emperors were men of respectable ability, and in moral character they will compare favourably with any list of sovereigns of similar length that any country can produce.

The chief modifications which must be marked in the character of the empire between 320 and 620 depend on two processes of gradual change which were going on throughout the three centuries. The first was the gradual de-Romanization (if we may coin the uncouth word) alike of the governing classes and the masses of population. In the fourth century the Roman impress was still strong in the East; the Latin language was habitually spoken by every educated man, and nearly all the machinery of the administration was worked in Latin phraseology. All law terms are habitually Latin, all titles of officers, all names of taxes and institutions. Writers born and bred in Greece or Asia still wrote in Latin as often as in the Greek which must have been more familiar to them. Ammianus Marcellinus may serve as a fair example: born in Greece, he wrote in the tongue of the ruling race rather than in his own idiom. Moreover there was still in the lands east of the Adriatic a very large body of Latin-speaking population—comprising all the inhabitants of the inland of the Balkan peninsula, for, except Greece proper, Macedonia, and a scattered line of cities along the Thracian coast, the whole land had learnt to speak the tongue of its conquerors.

By the seventh century this Roman element was rapidly vanishing. It is true that the Emperor was still hailed as the "Pius, Felix, Perpetuus, Augustus": it was not till about A.D. 800 that he dropped the old style and called himself "Ἐν Χριστῷ πιστὸς βασιλεὺς τῶν Ῥωμαίων." Nor were the old Roman official titles yet disused: men were still tribunes and patricians, counts and praetors, but little more than the names survived. Already in the sixth century a knowledge of Latin was growing unusual even among educated men. The author Johannes Lydus tells us that he owed his rise in the civil service mainly to this rare accomplishment. Procopius, the best writer of the day and a man of real merit and discernment, was absolutely ignorant of the rudiments of Latin, and blunders when he tries to translate the simplest phrase. Justinian was the last emperor who spoke Latin as his mother tongue, all his successors were better skilled in Greek.

The gradual disuse of Latin has its origin in the practical—though not formal—solution of the continuity between Rome and the East, which began with the division of the empire between the sons of Constantine and became more complete after Odoacer made himself King of Italy in 476. In the course of a century and a half the Latin element in the East, cut off from the Latin-speaking West, was bound to yield before the predominant Greek. But the process would have been slower if the Eastern provinces which spoke Latin had not been those which suffered most from the barbarians. The Visigoths and Ostrogoths harassed and decimated the Thracians, Illyrians, and Moesians, but the Slavs a century later almost exterminated them. In A.D. 400 probably a quarter of the provincials east of the Adriatic spoke Latin; in A.D. 620 not a tenth. The Romanized lands of the Balkan peninsula had now become Slavonic principalities: only the Dalmatian seaports and a few scattered survivors in the Balkans still used the old tongue. The only districts where a considerable Latin-speaking population obeyed the Emperor were Africa and the Italian Exarchate, now reunited to Constantinople by the conquests of Justinian. But they seem to have been too remote from the centre of life and government to have exercised any influence or delayed the de-Romanizing of the East. The last notable author, who being a subject of the empire wrote in Latin as his native tongue, was the poet Flavius Corippus who addressed a long panegyric to Justinus II.: as might have been expected, he was an African.

While the empire was losing its Roman characteristics, it was at the same time growing more and more Christian at heart. Under Constantine and his immediate successors the machinery of government was only just beginning to be effected by the change of the emperor's religion. Though the sovereign personally was Christian, the system remained what it had been before. Many of the high officials were still pagans, and the form and spirit of all administrative and legal business was unaltered from what it had been in the third century. It is not till forty years after Constantine's death that we find the Christian spirit fully penetrating out of the spiritual into the material sphere of life. Attempts by the State to suppress moral sin no less than legal crime begin with Theodosius I., whose crusade against sexual immorality would have been incomprehensible to even the best of the pagan emperors. The old gladiatorial shows, one of the most characteristic and repulsive features of Roman life, were abolished not long after. They survived for sixty years at Rome, though Christian Constantinople never knew them. But this was not the work of the State, but of a single individual. One day in A.D. 404 the games had begun, and the gladiators were about to engage, when the monk Telemachus leapt down into the arena and threw himself between the combatants, adjuring them not to slay their brethren. There was an angry scuffle, and the good monk was slain. But his death had the effect that his protests might have failed to bring about, and no gladiatorial show was ever given again.

GENERAL VIEW OF ST. SOPHIA.

(*From* "*L'Art Byzantin.*" *Par C. Bayet. Paris, Quantin*, 1883.)

In other provinces of social life the work of Christianity was no less marked. It put an end to the detestable practice of infanticide which pervaded the ancient world, resting on the assumption that the father had the right to decide whether or not he would rear the child he had begotten. Constantine made the State assume the charge of feeding and rearing the children of the destitute, lest their parents should be tempted to cast them forth to perish in the old fashion, and Valentinian I. in 374 assimilated infanticide to other forms of murder, and made it a capital offence.

Slavery was also profoundly affected by the teaching of the Church. The ancient world, save a few philosophers, had regarded the slave with such contempt that he was hardly reckoned a moral being or conceived to have rights or virtues. Christianity taught that he was a man with an immortal soul, no less than his own master, and bade slaves and freemen meet on terms of perfect equality around the baptismal font and before the sacred table. It was from the first taught that the man who manumitted his slaves earned the approval of heaven, and all occasions of rejoicing, public and private, were fitly commemorated by the liberation of deserving individuals. Though slavery was not extinguished for centuries, its evils were immensely modified; Justinian's legislation shows that by his time public opinion had condemned the characteristic evils of ancient slavery: he permitted the intermarriage of slaves and free persons, stipulating only for the consent of the owner of the servile partner in the wedlock. He declared the children of such mixed marriages free, and he made the prostitution of a slave by a master a criminal offence. Hereditary slavery became almost unknown, and the institution was only kept up by the introduction of barbarian captives, heathens and enemies, whose position did not appeal so keenly to the mind of their captors.

SLAVERY

The improvement of the condition of all the unhappy classes of which we have been speaking—women, infants, slaves, gladiators—can be directly traced back to a single fundamental Christian truth. It was the belief in the importance of the individual human soul in the eyes of God that led the converted Roman to realize his responsibility, and change his attitude towards the helpless beings whom he had before despised and neglected. It is only fair to add that the realization of this central truth did not always operate for good in the Roman world of the fifth and sixth centuries. Some of the developments of the new idea were harmful and even dangerous to the State. They took the form of laying such exclusive stress on the relations between the individual soul and heaven, that the duties of man to the State were half forgotten. Chief among these developments was the ascetic monasticism which, starting from Egypt, spread rapidly all over the empire, more especially over its eastern provinces. When men retire from their duties as citizens, intent on nothing but on saving their own souls, take up a position outside the State, and cease to be of the slightest use to society, the result may be harmless so long as their numbers are small. But at this time the monastic impulse was working on such a large scale that its development was positively dangerous. It was by thousands and ten thousands that the men who ought to have been bearing the burdens of the State, stepped aside into the monastery or the hermit's cave. The ascetics of the fifth century had neither of the justifications which made monasticism precious in a later age, they were neither missionaries nor men of learning. The monastery did not devote itself either to sending out preachers and teachers, or to storing up and cherishing the literary treasures of the ancient world. The first abbot to whom it occurred to turn the vast leisure of his monks to good account by setting them systematically to work at copying manuscripts was Cassiodorus, the ex-secretary to King Theodoric the Goth [A.D. 530-40]. Before his time monks and books had no special connection with each other.

When a State contains masses of men who devote their whole energies to a repulsively selfish attempt to save their own individual souls, while letting the world around them slide on as best it may, then the body politic is diseased. The Roman Empire in its fight with the barbarians was in no small degree hampered by this attitude of so many of its subjects. The ascetic took the barbarian invasions as judgments from heaven rightly inflicted upon a wicked world, and not as national calamities which called on every citizen to join in the attempt to repel them. Many men complacently interpreted the troubles of the fifth century as the tribulations predicted in the Apocalypse, and watched them develop with something like joy, since they must portend the close approach of the Second Advent of our Lord.

This apathetic attitude of many Christians during the afflictions of the empire was maddening to the heathen minority which still survived among the educated classes. They roundly accused Christianity of being the ruin of the State by its anti-social teaching which led men to neglect every duty of the citizen. The Christian author Orosius felt himself compelled to write a lengthy history to confute this view, aiming his work at the pagan Symmachus whose book had been devoted to tracing all the calamities of the world to the conversion of Constantine.

It was fortunate for the empire that its governing classes continued to preserve the old traditions of Roman state-craft, and fought on doggedly against all the ills of their time—barbarian invasion, famine, and pestilence, instead of bowing to the yoke and recognizing in every calamity the righteous judgment of heaven and the indication of the approaching end of the world.

Paganism had practically disappeared by the end of the fifth century as an active force; none save a few philosophers made an open profession of it, and in 529 Justinian put a formal end to their teaching, by closing the schools of Athens, the last refuge of the professors of the expiring religion. But if open heathenism was dead, a large measure of indifferentism prevailed among the educated classes: many men who in the fifth century would have been pagans were Christians in name in the sixth, but little affected by Christianity in their lives. This type was extremely common among the literary and official classes. There are plenty of sixth-century authors—Procopius may serve as an example—whose works show no trace of Christian thought, though the writer was undoubtedly a professing member of the Church. Similar examples could be quoted by the dozen from among the administrators, lawyers, and statesmen of the day, but all were now nominally Christian. As time went on, such men grew rarer, and the old stern, non-religious Roman character passed away into the emotional and superstitious mediæval type of mind. The survival of pre-Christian feeling, which appeared as indifferentism among the educated classes, took a very different shape among the lower strata of society. It revealed itself in a crowd of gross superstitions connected with magic, witchcraft, fortune-telling, charms, and trivial or obscene ceremonies practised in secret. The State highly disapproved of such practices, treated them as impious or heretical, and imposed punishment on those who employed them: but nevertheless these contemptible survivals of heathenism persisted down to the latest days of the empire.

It has been usual to include all the Eastern Romans of all the centuries between Constantine I. and Constantine XIV. in one sweeping condemnation, as cowardly, corrupt, and effete. The ordinary view of Byzantine life may be summed up in Mr. Lecky's irritating statement[18] that"the universal verdict of history is that it constitutes the most base and despicable form that civilization ever assumed, and that there has been no other enduring civilization so absolutely destitute of all the forms and elements of greatness, none to which the epithet *mean* may be so emphatically applied. It is a monstrous story of the intrigues of priests, eunuchs, and women; of poisoning, conspiracies, uniform ingratitude, perpetual fratricide." How Mr. Lecky obtained his universal verdict of history, it is hard to see: certainly that verdict can not have been arrived at after a study of the evidence bearing on the life of the persons accused. It sounds like a cheap echo of the second-hand historians of fifty years ago, whose staple commodity was Gibbon-and-water.

[18] "History of European Morals," ii. p. 13.

ILLUMINATED INITIALS. (*From Byzantine MSS.*)
(*From "L'Art Byzantin." Par C. Bayet. Paris, Quantin*, 1883.)

If we must sum up the characteristics of the East Romans and their civilization, the conclusion at which we arrive will be very different. It is only fair to acknowledge that they had their faults: what else could be expected when we know that the foundations of the Eastern Empire were laid upon the Oriental provinces of the old Roman world, among races that had long been stigmatized by their masters as hopelessly effete and corrupt—Syrians, Egyptians, and Hellenized Asiatics, whom even the degenerate Romans of the third century had been wont to despise. The Byzantine Empire displayed from its very cradle a taint of weakness derived from this Oriental origin. It showed features particularly obnoxious to the modern mind of the nineteenth century—such as the practice of a degrading and grovelling court etiquette, full of prostrations and genuflexions, the introduction of eunuchs and slaves into high offices of State, the wholesale and deliberate use of treachery and lying in matters of diplomacy.

But remembering its origins we shall, on the whole, wonder at the good points in Byzantine civilization rather than at its faults. It may fairly be said that Christianity raised the Roman East to a better moral position than it had known for a thousand years. With all their faults the monks and hermits of the fifth century are a good substitute for the priests of Cybele and Mithras of the second. It was something that the Government and the public opinion of the day had concurred to sweep away the orgies of Daphne and Canopus. Church and State united in the reign of Justinian to punish with spiritual and bodily death the unnatural crimes which had been the open practice of emperors themselves in the first centuries of the empire.

The vices of which the East Romans have most commonly been accused are cowardice, frivolity, and treachery. On each of these points they have been grossly wronged. Cowardice was certainly not the chief characteristic of the centuries that produced emperors like Theodosius I. and Heraclius, prelates like Athanasius and Chrysostom, public servants like Belisarius and Priscus. It is not for cowardice that we note the Byzantine populace which routed Gainas and his mercenaries, and raised the *Nika* sedition, but for turbulence. If military virtue was wanting to the East-Roman armies, how came the Ostrogoth and Vandal to be conquered, the Persian and the Hun to be driven off, how, above all, was the desperate struggle against the fanatical Saracen protracted for four hundred years, till at last the Caliphate broke up?

Frivolity and luxury are an accusation easy to bring against any age. Every moralist, from Jeremiah to Juvenal, and from Juvenal to Mr. Ruskin, has believed his own generation to be the most obnoxious and contemptible in the world's history. We have numerous tirades against the manners of Constantinople preserved in Byzantine literature, and may judge from them something of the faults of the time. It would seem that there was much of the sort of luxury to which ascetic preachers take exception—much splendour of raiment, much ostentatious display of plate and furniture, of horses and chariots. Luxury and evil living often go together, but when we examine all the enormities laid to the charge of the Byzantines, there is less alleged than we might expect. When Chrysostom raged against the contemporaries of Arcadius, his anathemas fell on such crimes as the use of cosmetics and dyes by fashionable dames, on the gambling propensities of their husbands, on the immoral tendencies of the theatre, on the drunken orgies at popular festivals—accusations to which any age—our own included—might plead guilty. The races of the Circus played a disproportionate part in social life, and attracted the enthusiastic attention of thousands of votaries; but it is surely hard that our own age, with all its sporting and athletic interests, should cast a stone at the sixth century. We have not to look far around us to discover classes for whom horse-racing still presents an inexplicable attraction. When we remember that the Constantinopolitans were excitable Orientals, and had no other form of sport to distract their attention from the Circus, we can easily realize the genesis of the famous riots of the Blues and Greens.

From the darker forms of vice great cities have never been free, and there is no reason to think that Constantinople in the sixth century differed from London in the nineteenth. It is fair to point out that Christian public opinion and the Government strove their best to put down sexual immorality. Theodosius and Justinian are recorded to have entered upon the herculean task of endeavouring to suppress all disorderly houses: the latter made exile the penalty for panders and procuresses, and inflicted death on those guilty of the worst extremes of immorality. We must remember, too, that if Constantinople showed much vice, it also displayed shining examples of the social virtues. The Empress Flaccilla was wont to frequent the hospitals, and tend the beds of the sick. Of the monastic severity which the Empress Pulcheria displayed in the palace we have spoken already.

After cowardice and light morals, it is treachery that is popularly cited as the most prominent vice of the Eastern Empire. There have been other states and epochs more given to plots and revolts, but it is still true that there was too much intrigue at Constantinople. The reason is not far to seek: the "*carrière ouverte aux talents*" practically existed there, and the army and the civil service were full of poor, able, and ambitious men of all races and classes mixed together. The converted Goth or the renegade Persian, the half-civilized mountaineer from Isauria, the Copt and Syrian and Armenian were all welcomed in the army or civil service, if only they had ability. Both the bureaucracy and the army therefore had elements which lacked patriotism, conscience, and stability, and were prone to seek advancement either by intrigue or military revolt. This being granted, it is perhaps astonishing to have to record that between 350 and 600 the empire never once saw its legitimate ruler dethroned, either by palace intrigue or military revolt. The fact that all the plots—and there were many in the period—failed hopelessly, is, on the whole, a proof that if there was much treachery there was much loyalty among the East Romans. There have certainly been periods in more recent times which show a much worse record.[19] A single instance may suffice—Mediæval Italy from the thirteenth to the fifteenth century could produce far more shocking examples of conscienceless and unjustifiable plotting than the Byzantine Empire in the whole thousand years of its existence.

[19] Mr. Lecky speaks of the "perpetual fratricide" of the Byzantine emperors. It may be interesting to point out that from 340 to 1453 there was not a single emperor murdered by a brother, and only one dethroned by a brother. Two were dethroned by sons, but not murdered.

XII. The Coming Of The Saracens.

After the peace of 628 the Roman and the Persian Empires, drained of men and money, and ravaged from end to end by each other's marauding armies, sank down in exhaustion to heal them of their deadly wounds. Never before had either power dealt its neighbour such fearful blows as in this last struggle: in previous wars the contest had been waged around border fortresses, and the prize had been the conquest of some small slice of marchland. But Chosroës and Heraclius had struck deadly blows at the heart of each other's empire, and harried the inmost provinces up to the gates of each other's capitals. The Persian had turned the wild hordes of the Avars loose on Thrace, and the Roman had guided the yet wilder Chazars up to the walls of Ctesiphon. Hence it came to pass that at the end of the war the two powers were each weaker than they had ever been before. They were bleeding at every pore, utterly wearied and exhausted, and desirous of nothing but a long interval of peace to recover their lost strength.

Precisely at this moment a new and terrible enemy fell upon the two war-worn combatants, and delivered an attack so vehement that it was destined to destroy the ancient kingdom of Persia and to shear away half the provinces of the Roman Empire.

The politics of Arabia had up to this time been of little moment either to Roman or Persian. Each of them had allies among the Arab tribes, and had sometimes sent an expedition or an embassy southward, into the land beyond the Syrian desert. But neither of them dreamed that the scattered and disunited tribes of Arabia would ever combine or become a serious danger.

But while Heraclius and Chosroës were harrying each other's realms events of world-wide importance had been taking place in the Arabian peninsula. For the first and last time in history there had arisen among the Arabs one of those world-compelling minds that are destined to turn aside the current of events into new channels, and change the face of whole continents.

Mahomet, that strangest of moral enigmas, prophet and seer, fanatic and impostor, was developing his career all through the years of the Persian war. By an extraordinary mixture of genuine enthusiasm and vulgar cunning, of self-deception and deliberate imposture, of benevolence and cruelty, of austerity and licence, he had worked himself and his creed to the front. The turbulent polytheists of Arabia had by him been converted into a compact band of fanatics, burning to carry all over the world by the force of their swords their new war-cry, that "God was God, and Mahomet His prophet."

In 628, the last year of the great war, the Arab sent his summons to Heraclius and Chosroës, bidding them embrace Islam. The Persian replied with the threat that he would put the Prophet in chains when he had leisure. The Roman made no direct reply, but sent Mahomet some small presents, neglecting the theological bent of his message, and only thinking of enlisting a possible political ally. Both answers were regarded as equally unsatisfactory by the Prophet, and he doomed the two empires to a similar destruction. Next year [629] the first collision between the East-Romans and the Arabs took place, a band of Moslems having pushed a raid up to Muta, near the Dead Sea. But it was not till three years later, when Mahomet himself was already dead, that the storm fell on the Roman Empire. In obedience to the injunctions of his deceased master, the Caliph Abu Bekr prepared two armies, and launched the one against Palestine and the other against Persia.

Till the last seven or eight years English writers have been inclined to underrate the force and fury of an army of Mahometan fanatics in the first flush of their enthusiasm. Now that we have witnessed in our own day the scenes of Tamaai and Abu Klea we do so no longer. The rush that can break into a British square bristling with Martini-Henry rifles is not a thing to be despised. For the future we shall not treat lightly the armies of the early Caliphs, nor scoff with Gibbon at the feebleness of the troops who were routed by them. If the soldiers of Queen Victoria, armed with modern rifles and artillery, found the fanatical Arab a formidable foe, let us not blame the soldiers of Heraclius who faced the same enemy with pike and sword alone. In the early engagements between the East-Romans and the Saracens the superior discipline and more regular arms of the one were not a sufficient counterpoise to put against the mad recklessness of the other. The Moslem wanted to get killed, that he might reap the fruits of martyrdom in the other world, and cared not how he died, if he had first slain an enemy. The Roman fought well enough; but he did not, like his adversary, yearn to become a martyr, and the odds were on the man who held his life the cheapest.

The moment of the Saracen invasion was chosen most unhappily for Heraclius. He had just paid off the enormous debt that he had contracted to the Church, and to do so had not only drained the treasury but imposed some new and unwise taxes on the harassed provincials, and disbanded many of his veterans for the sake of economy. Syria and Egypt, after spending twelve and ten years respectively under the Persian yoke, had not yet got back into their old organization. Both countries were much distracted with religious troubles; the heretical sects of the Monophysites and Jacobites who swarmed within their boundaries had lifted up their heads under the Persian rule, being relieved from the governmental repression that had hitherto been their lot. They seem to have constituted an actual majority of the population, and bitterly resented the endeavours of Heraclius to enforce orthodoxy in the reconquered provinces. Their discontent was so bitter that during the Saracen invasion they stood aside and refused to help the imperial armies, or even on occasion aided the alien enemy.

The details of the Arab conquest of Syria have not been preserved by the East-Roman historians, who seem to have hated the idea of recording the disasters of Christendom. The Moslems, on the other hand, had not yet commenced to write, and ere historians arose among them, the tale of the invasion had been intertwined with a whole cycle of romantic legends, fitter for the "Arabian Nights" than the sober pages of a chronicle.

But the main lines of the war can be reconstructed with accuracy. The Saracen horde under Abu Obeida emerged from the desert in the spring of 634 and captured Bostra, the frontier city of Syria to the east, by the aid of treachery from within. The Romans collected an army to drive them off, but in July it was defeated at Aijnadin

[Gabatha] in Ituraea. Thoroughly roused by this disaster Heraclius set all the legions of the East marching, and sixty thousand men crossed the Jordan and advanced to recover Bostra. The Arabs met them at the fords of the Hieromax, an Eastern tributary of the Jordan, and a fierce battle raged all day. The Romans drove the enemy back to the very gates of their camp, but a last charge, headed by the fierce warrior Khaled, broke their firm array when a victory seemed almost assured. All the mailed horsemen of Heraclius, his Armenian and Isaurian archers, his solid phalanx of infantry, were insufficient to resist the wild rush of the Arabs. Urged on by the cry of their general, "Paradise is before you, the devil and hell-fire behind," the fanatical Orientals threw themselves on regiment after regiment and drove it off the field.

All Syria east of Jordan was lost in this fatal battle. Damascus, its great stronghold, resisted desperately but fell early in 635. Most of its population were massacred. This disaster drew Heraclius into the field, though he was now over sixty, and was beginning to fail in health. He could do nothing; Emesa and Heliopolis were sacked before his eyes, and after an inglorious campaign he hurried to Jerusalem, took the "True Cross" from its sanctuary, where he had replaced it in triumph five years before, and retired to Constantinople. Hardly had he reached it when the news arrived that his discontented and demoralized troops had proclaimed a rebel emperor, though the enemy was before them. The rebel—his name was Baanes—was put down, but meanwhile Antioch, Chalcis, and all Northern Syria fell into the hands of the Arabs.

Worse yet was to follow. In the next year, 637, Jerusalem fell, after a desperate resistance, protracted for more than twelve months. The inhabitants refused to surrender except to the Caliph in person, and the aged Omar came over the desert, proud to take possession of the city which Mahomet had reckoned the holiest site on earth save Mecca alone. The Patriarch Sophronius was commanded to guide the conqueror around the city, and when he saw the rude Arab standing by the altar of the Church of the Holy Sepulchre, cried aloud, "Now is the Abomination of Desolation, which was spoken of by Daniel the prophet, truly in the Holy Place." The Caliph did not confiscate any of the great Christian sanctuaries, but he took the site of Solomon's Temple, and erected on it a magnificent Mosque, known ever since as the Mosque of Omar.

The tale of the last years of Heraclius is most melancholy. The Emperor lay at Constantinople slowly dying of dropsy, and his eldest son Constantine had to take the field in his stead. But the young prince received a crushing defeat in 638, when he attempted to recover North Syria, and next year the Arabs, under Amrou, pressed eastward across the Isthmus of Suez, and threw themselves upon Egypt. Two years more of fighting sufficed to conquer the granary of the Roman Empire; and in February, 641, when Heraclius died, the single port of Alexandria was the sole remaining possession of the Romans in Egypt.

The ten years' war which had torn Syria and Egypt from the hands of the unfortunate Heraclius had been even more fatal to his Eastern neighbour. The Arabs had attacked the Persian kingdom at the same moment that they fell on Syria: two great battles at Kadesia [636] and Yalulah [637] sufficed to place all Western Persia in the hands of the Moslems. King Isdigerd, the last of the Sassanian line, raised his last army in 641, and saw it cut to pieces at the decisive field of Nehauend. He fled away to dwell as an exile among the Turks, and all his kingdom as far as the borders of India became the prey of the conquerors.

Heraclius had married twice; by his first wife, Eudocia, he left a single son, Constantine, who should have been his sole heir. But he had taken a second wife, and this wife was his own niece Martina. The incestuous choice had provoked much scandal, and was the one grave offence which could be brought against Heraclius, whose life was in other respects blameless. Martina, an ambitious and intriguing woman, prevailed on her aged husband to make her eldest son, Heracleonas, joint-heir with his half brother Constantine.

This arrangement, as might have been expected, worked very badly. The court and army was at once split up between the adherents of the two young Emperors, and while the defence of the empire against the Saracens should have been the sole care of the East-Romans, they found themselves distracted by fierce Court intrigues. Armed strife between the Emperors seemed destined to break out, but after reigning only a few months Constantine III. died. It was rumoured far and wide that his step-mother had poisoned him, to make the way clear for her own son Heracleonas, who immediately proclaimed himself sole emperor. The senate and the Byzantine populace were both highly indignant at this usurpation, for the deceased Constantine left a young son named Constans, who was thus excluded from the throne to which he was the natural heir. Heracleonas had reigned alone no more than a few weeks when the army of the East and the mob of Constantinople were heard demanding in angry tones that Constans should be crowned as his uncle's colleague. Heracleonas was frightened into compliance, but his submission only saved him for a year. In the summer of 642 the senate decreed his deposition, and he was seized by the adherents of Constans and sent into exile, along with his mother Martina. The victorious faction very cruelly ordered the tongue of the mother and the nose of the son to be slit—the first instance of that hateful Oriental practice being applied to members of the royal house, but not the last.

Constans II. was sole emperor from 642 to 668, and his son and successor, Constantine IV., reigned from 668 to 685. They were both strong, hard-headed warrior princes, fit descendants of the gallant Heraclius. Their main credit lies in the fact that they fought unceasingly against the Saracen, and preserved as a permanent possession of the empire nearly every province that they had still remained Roman at the death of Heraclius. During the minority indeed of Constans II., Alexandria[20] a nd Aradus, the two last ports preserved by the Romans in Egypt and Syria were lost. But the Saracens advanced no further by land; the sands of the African desert and the passes of Taurus were destined to hold them back for many years. The times, however, were still dangerous till the murder of the Caliph Othman in 656, after which the outbreak of the first civil war among the Moslems—the contest of Ali and Moawiah for the Caliphate—gave the empire a respite. Moawiah, who held the lands on the Roman frontier—his rival's power lying further to the east—secured a free hand against Ali, by making peace with Constans. He even consented to pay him a small annual subsidy so long as the truce should last. This agreement was invaluable to the empire. After twenty-seven years of incessant war the mangled

[20] To the credit of Amrou and his Saracens it must be recorded that the great Alexandrian Library was not burt by them in sheer fanatical wantonness as the legends tell. It has perished long before.

realm at last obtained an interval of repose. It was something, too, that the Saracens were induced to pause, and saw that the extension of their conquests was not destined to spread at once over the whole world. When they realized that their victories were not to go on for ever, they lost the first keenness of the fanatical courage which had made them so terrible.

Freed from the Saracen war, which had threatened not merely to curtail, but to extinguish the empire, Constans was at liberty to turn his attention to other matters. It seems probable that it was at this moment that the reorganization of the provinces of the empire took place, which we find in existence in the second half of the seventh century. The old Roman names and boundaries, which had endured since Diocletian's time, now disappear, and the empire is found divided into new provinces with strange denominations. They were military in their origin, and each consisted of the district covered by a large unit of soldiery—what we should call an army corps. "Theme" meant both the corps and the district which it defended, and the corps-commander was also the provincial governor. There were six corps in Asia, called the Armeniac, Anatolic, Thracesian, Bucellarian, Cibyrrhæot, and Obsequian themes. Of these the first two explain themselves, they were the "army of Armenia" and the "army of the East"; the Obsequian theme, quartered along the Propontis, was so called because it was a kind of personal guard for the Emperor and the home districts. The Thracesians were the "Army of Thrace," who in the stress of the war had been drafted across to Asia to reinforce the Eastern troops. The Bucellarii seem to have been corps composed of natives and barbarian auxiliaries mixed; they are heard of long before Constans, and he probably did no more than unite them and localize them in a single district. The Cibyrrhæot theme alone gets its name from a town, the port of Cibyra in Pamphylia, which must have been the original headquarters of the South-Western Army Corps. Its commander had a fleet always in his charge, and his troops were often employed as marines.[21]

The western half of the empire seems to have had six "Themes" also; they bear however old and familiar names—Thrace, Hellas, Thessalonica, Ravenna, Sicily, and Africa, and their names explain their boundaries. In both halves of the empire there were, beside the great themes, smaller districts under the command of military governors, who had charge of outlying posts, such as the passes of Taurus, or the islands of Cyprus and Sardinia. Some of these afterwards grew into independent themes.

Thus came to an end the old imperial system of dividing military authority and civil jurisdiction, which Augustus had invented and Diocletian perpetuated. Under stress of the fearful Saracenic invasion the civil governors disappear, and for the future a commander chosen for his military capacity has also to discharge civil functions.

Constans II., when once he had made peace with Moawiah, would have done well to turn to the Balkan Peninsula, and evict the Slavs from the districts south of Haemus into which they had penetrated during the reign of Heraclius. But he chose instead to do no more than compel the Slavs to pay homage to him and give tribute, and set out to turn westward, and endeavour to drive the Lombards out of Italy.

[21] Mr. Bury's excellent chapter on "Themes," in vol. ii. of his "Later Roman Empire," is most convincing as to these very puzzling provinces and their origin.

Falling on the Duchy of Benevento, he took many towns, and even laid siege to the capital. But he failed to take it, and passed on to Rome, which had not seen the face of an emperor for two hundred years. When an emperor did appear he brought no luck, for Constans signalized his visit by taking down the bronze tiles of the Pantheon and sending them off to Constantinople [664].

The Emperor lingered no less than five years in the West, busied with the affairs of Italy and Africa, till the Constantinopolitans began to fear that he would make Rome or Syracuse his capital. But in 668 he was assassinated in a most strange manner. "As he bathed in the baths called Daphne, Andreas his bathing attendant smote him on the head with his soap-box, and fled away." The blow was fatal, Constans died, and Constantine his son reigned in his stead.

Constantine IV., known as Pogonatus, "the Bearded," reigned for seventeen years, of which more than half were spent in one long struggle with the Saracens. Moawiah, the first of the Ommeyades, had now made himself sole Caliph; the civil wars of the Arabs were now over, and once more they fell on the empire. Constantine's reign opened disastrously, with simultaneous attacks by the armies and fleets of Moawiah on Africa, Sicily, and Asia Minor. But this was only the prelude; in 673 the Caliph made ready an expedition, the like of which had never yet been undertaken by the Saracens. A great fleet and land army started from Syria to undertake the siege of Constantinople itself, an enterprise which the Moslems had not yet attempted. It was headed by the general Abderrahman, and accompanied by Yezid, the Caliph's son and heir. The fleet beat the imperial navy off the sea, forced the passage of the Dardanelles, and took Cyzicus. Using that city as its base, it proceeded to blockade the Bosphorus.

The great glory of Constantine IV. is that he withstood, defeated, and drove away the mighty armament of Moawiah. For four years the investment of Constantinople lingered on, and the stubborn resistance of the garrison seemed unable to do more than stave off the evil day. But the happy invention of fire-tubes for squirting inflammable liquids (probably the famous "Greek-fire" of which we first hear at this time), gave the Emperor's fleet the superiority in a decisive naval battle. At the same time a great victory was won on land and thirty thousand Arabs slain. Abderrahman had fallen during the siege, and his successors had to lead back the mere wrecks of a fleet and army to the disheartened Caliph.

It is a thousand pities that the details of this, the second great siege of Constantinople, are not better known. But there is no good contemporary historian to give us the desired information. If he had but met with his "sacred bard," Constantine IV. might have gone down to posterity in company with Heraclius and Leo the Isaurian, as the third great hero of the East-Roman Empire.

The year after the raising of the great siege, Moawiah sued for peace, restored all his conquests, and offered a huge war indemnity, promising to pay 3000 lbs. of gold per annum for thirty years. The report of the triumph of Constantine went all over the world, and ambassadors came even from the distant Franks and Khazars to congratulate him on the victory which had saved Eastern Christendom from the Arab.

While Constantine was defending his capital from the Eastern enemy, the wild tribes of his northern border took the opportunity of swooping down on the European provinces, whose troops had been drawn off to resist the Arabs. The Slavs came down from the inland, and laid siege for two years to Thessalonica, which was only relieved from their attacks when Constantine had finished his war with Moawiah. But a far more dangerous attack was made by another enemy in the eastern part of the Balkan Peninsula. The Bulgarians, a nomad tribe of Finnish blood, who dwelt in the region of the Pruth and Dniester, came over the Danube, subdued the Slavs of Moesia, and settled between the Danube and the Eastern Balkans, where they have left their name till this day. They united the scattered Slavonic tribes of the region into a single strong state, and the new Bulgarian kingdom was long destined to be a troublesome neighbour to the empire. The date 679 counts as the first year of the reign of Isperich first king of Bulgaria. Constantine IV. was too exhausted by his long war with Moawiah to make any serious attempt to drive the Bulgarians back over the Danube, and acquiesced in the new settlement.

The last six years of Constantine's reign were spent in peace. The only notable event that took place in them was the meeting at Constantinople of the Sixth Oecumenical Council in 680-1. At this Synod, the doctrine of the Monothelites, who attributed but one will to Our Lord, was solemnly condemned by the united Churches of the East and West. The holders of Monothelite doctrines, dead and alive, were solemnly anathematised, among them Pope Honorius of Rome, who in a previous generation had consented to the heresy.

Constantine IV. died in 685, before he had reached his thirty-sixth year, leaving his throne to his eldest son Justinian, a lad of sixteen.

XIII. The First Anarchy.

Justinian II., the last of the house of Heraclius, was a sovereign of a different type from any emperor that we have yet encountered in the annals of the Eastern Empire. He was a bold, reckless, callous, and selfish young man, with a firm determination to assert his own individuality and have his own way,—he was, in short, of the stuff of which tyrants are made. Justinian was but seventeen when he came to the throne, but he soon showed that he intended to rule the empire after his own good pleasure long before he had begun to learn the lessons of state-craft.

Ere he had reached his twenty-first year Justinian had plunged into war with the Bulgarians. He attacked them suddenly, inflicted several defeats on their king, and took no less than thirty thousand prisoners, whom he sent over to Asia, and forced to enlist in the army of Armenia. He next picked a quarrel with the Saracen Caliph on the most frivolous grounds. The annual tribute due by the treaty of 679 had hitherto been paid in Roman *solidi*, but in 692 Abdalmalik tendered it in new gold coins of his own mintage, bearing verses of the Koran. Justinian refused to receive them, and declared war.

His second venture in the field was disastrous: his unwilling recruits from Bulgaria deserted to the enemy, when he met the Saracens at Sebastopolis in Cilicia, and the Roman army was routed with great slaughter. The two subsequent campaigns were equally unsuccessful, and the troops of the Caliph harried Cappadocia far and wide.

Justinian's wars depleted his treasury; yet he persisted in plunging into expensive schemes of building at the same time, and was driven to collect money by the most reckless extortion. He employed two unscrupulous ministers, Theodotus, the accountant general—an ex-abbot who had deserted his monastery—and the eunuch Stephanus, the keeper of the privy purse. These men were to Justinian what Ralph Flambard was to William Rufus, or Empson and Dudley to Henry VII: they raised him funds by flagrant extortion and illegal stretching of the law. Both were violent and cruel: Theodotus is said to have hung recalcitrant tax-payers up by ropes above smoky fires till they were nearly stifled. Stephanus thrashed and stoned every one who fell into his hands; he is reported to have actually administered a whipping to the empress-dowager during the absence of her son, and Justinian did not punish him when he returned.

While the emperor's financial expedients were making him hated by the moneyed classes, he was rendering himself no less unpopular in the army.

After his ill-success in the Saracen war, he began to execute or imprison his officers, and to decimate his beaten troops: to be employed by him in high command was almost as dangerous as it was to be appointed a general-in-chief during the dictatorship of Robespierre.

In 695 the cup of Justinian's iniquities was full. An officer named Leontius being appointed, to his great dismay, general of the "theme" of Hellas, was about to set out to assume his command. As he parted from his friends he exclaimed that his days were numbered, and that he should be expecting the order for his execution to arrive at any moment. Then a certain monk named Paul stood forth, and bade him save himself by a bold stroke; if he would aim a blow at Justinian he would find the people and the army ready to follow him.

Leontius took the monk's counsel, and rushing to the state prison, at the head of a few friends, broke it open and liberated some hundreds of political prisoners. A mob joined him, he seized the Cathedral of St. Sophia, and then marched on the palace. No one would fight for Justinian, who was caught and brought before the rebel leader in company with his two odious ministers. Leontius bade his nose be slit, and banished him to Cherson. Theodotus and Stephanus he handed over to the mob, who dragged them round the city and burnt them alive.

Twenty years of anarchy followed the usurpation of Leontius. The new emperor was not a man of capacity, and had been driven into rebellion by his fears rather than his ambition. He held the throne barely three years, amid constant revolts at home and defeats abroad. The Asiatic frontier was ravaged by the armies of Abdalmalik, and at the same time a great disaster befel the western half of the empire. A Saracen army from Egypt forced its way into Africa, where the Romans had still maintained themselves by hard fighting while the emperors of the house of Heraclius reigned. They reduced all its fortresses one after the other, and finally took Carthage in 697—a hundred and sixty-five years after it had been restored to the empire by Belisarius.

CHURCH OF THE TWELVE APOSTLES AT THESSALONICA.
(*From "L'Art Byzantin." Par Charles Bayet. Paris, Quantin*, 1883.)

The larger part of the army of Africa escaped by sea from Carthage when the city fell. The officers in command sailed for Constantinople, and during their voyage plotted to dethrone Leontius. They enlisted in their scheme Tiberius Apsimarus, who commanded the imperial fleet in the Aegean, and proclaimed him emperor when he joined them with his galleys. The troops of Leontius betrayed the gates of the capital to the followers of the rebel admiral, and Apsimarus seized Constantinople. He proclaimed himself emperor by the title of Tiberius, third of that name, and condemned his captive rival to the same fate that he himself had inflicted on Justinian II. Accordingly the nose of Leontius was slit, and he was placed in confinement in a monastery.

Tiberius III. was more fortunate in his reign than his predecessor: his troops gained several victories over the Saracens, recovered the frontier districts which Justinian II. and Leontius had lost, and even invaded Northern Syria. But these successes did not save Tiberius from suffering the same doom which had fallen on Justinian and Leontius. The people and army were out of hand, the ephemeral emperor could count on no loyalty, and any shock was sufficient to upset his precarious throne.

We must now turn to the banished Justinian, who had been sent into exile with his nose mutilated. He had been transported to Cherson, the Greek town in the Crimea, close to the modern Sebastopol, which formed the northernmost outpost of civilization, and enjoyed municipal liberty under the suzerainty of the empire. Justinian displayed in his day of adversity a degree of capacity which astonished his contemporaries. He fled from Cherson and took refuge with the Khan of the Khazars, the Tartar tribe who dwelt east of the Sea of Azof. With this prince the exile so ingratiated himself that he received in marriage his sister, who was baptized and christened Theodora. But Tiberius III. sent great sums of money to the Khazar to induce him to surrender Justinian, and the treacherous barbarian determined to accept the bribe, and sent secret orders to two of his officers to seize his brother-in-law. The emperor learnt of the plot through his wife, and saved himself by the bold expedient of going at once to one of the two Khazar chiefs and asking for a secret interview. When they were alone he fell on him and strangled him, and then calling on the second Khazar served him in the same fashion, before the Khan's orders had been divulged to any one.

This gave him time to escape, and he fled in a fishing boat out into the Euxine with a few friends and servants who had followed him into exile. While they were out at sea a storm arose, and the boat began to fill. One of his companions cried to Justinian to make his peace with God, and pardon his enemies ere he died. But the Emperor's stern soul was not bent by the tempest. "May God drown me here," he answered, "if I spare a single one of my enemies if ever I get to land!" The boat weathered the storm, and Justinian survived to carry out his cruel oath. He came ashore in the land of the Bulgarians, and soon won favour with their king Terbel, who wanted a good excuse for invading the empire, and found it in the pretence of supporting the exiled monarch. With a Bulgarian army at his back Justinian appeared before Constantinople, and obtained an entrance at night near the gate of Blachernæ. There was no fighting, for the adherents of Tiberius were as unready to strike a blow for their master as the followers of Leontius had been [705 A.D.]

So Justinian recovered his throne without fighting, for the people had by this time half forgotten his tyranny, and regretted the rule of the house of Heraclius. But they were soon to find out that they had erred in submitting to the exile, and should have resisted him at all hazards. Justinian came back in a relentless mood, bent on nothing but revenging his mutilated nose and his ten years of exile. His first act was to send for the two usurpers who had sat on his throne: Leontius was brought out from his monastery, and Tiberius caught as he tried to flee into Asia. Justinian had them led round the city in chains, and then bound them side by side before his throne in the Cathisma, the imperial box at the Hippodrome. There he sat in state, using their prostrate bodies as a footstool, while his adherents chanted the verse from the ninety-first Psalm, "Thou shalt tread on the lion and asp: the young lion and dragon shalt thou trample under thy feet." The allusion was to the names of the usurpers, the Lion and Asp being Leontius and Apsimarus!

After this strange exhibition the two ex-emperors were beheaded. Their execution began a reign of terror, for Justinian had his oath to keep, and was set on wreaking vengeance on every one who had been concerned in his deposition. He hanged all the chief officers and courtiers of Leontius, and put out the eyes of the patriarch who had crowned him. Then he set to work to hunt out meaner victims:

many prominent citizens of Constantinople were sown up in sacks and drowned in the Bosphorus. Soldiers were picked out by the dozen and beheaded. A special expedition was sent by sea to sack Cherson, the city of the Emperor's exile, because he had a grudge against its citizens. The chief men were caught and sent to the capital, where Justinian had them bound to spits and roasted.

These atrocities were mere samples of the general conduct of Justinian. In a few years he had made himself so much detested that it might be said that he had been comparatively popular in the days of his first reign.

The end came into 711, when a general named Philippicus took arms, and seized Constantinople while Justinian was absent at Sinope. The army of the tyrant laid down their arms when Philippicus approached, and he was led forth and beheaded without further delay—an end too good for such a monster. The conqueror also sought out and slew his little son Tiberius, whom the sister of the Khan of the Khazars had borne to him during his exile. So ended the house of Heraclius, after it had sat for five generations and one hundred and one years on the throne of Constantinople.

The six years which followed were purely anarchical. Justinian's wild and wicked freaks had completed the demoralization which had already set in before his restoration. Everything in the army and the state was completely disorganized and out of gear. It required a hero to restore the machinery of government and evolve order out of chaos. But the hero was not at once forthcoming, and the confusion went on increasing.

To replace Justinian by Philippicus was only to substitute King Log for King Stork. The new emperor was a mere man of pleasure, and spent his time in personal enjoyment, letting affairs of state slide on as best they might. In less than two years he was upset by a conspiracy which placed on the throne Artemius Anastasius, his own chief secretary. Philippicus was blinded, and compelled to exchange the pleasures of the palace for the rigours of a monastery. But the Court intrigue which dethroned Philippicus did not please the army, and within two years Anastasius was overthrown by the soldiers of the Obsequian theme, who gave the imperial crown to Theodosius of Adrammytium, a respectable but obscure commissioner of taxes. More merciful than any of his ephemeral predecessors, Theodosius III. dismissed Anastasius unharmed, after compelling him to take holy orders.

Meanwhile the organization of the empire was visibly breaking up. "The affairs both of the realm and the city were neglected and decaying, civil education was disappearing, and military discipline dissolved." The Bulgarian and Saracen commenced once more to ravage the frontier provinces, and every year their ravages penetrated further inland. The Caliph Welid was so impressed with the opportunity offered to him, that he commenced to equip a great armament in the ports of Syria with the express purpose of laying siege to Constantinople. No one hindered him, for the army raised to serve against him turned aside to engage in the civil war between Anastasius and Theodosius. The landmarks of the Saracens' conquests by land are found in the falls of the great cities of Tyana [710], Amasia [712], and Antioch-in-Pisidia [713]. They had penetrated into Phrygia by 716, and were besieging the fortress of Amorium with every expectation of success, when at last there appeared the man who was destined to save the East-Roman Empire from a premature dismemberment.

This was Leo the Isaurian, one of the few military officers who had made a great reputation amid the fearful disasters of the last ten years. He was now general of the "Anatolic" theme, the province which included the old Cappadocia and Lycaonia. After inducing the Saracens, more by craft than force, to raise the siege of Amorium, Leo disowned his allegiance to the incapable Theodosius and marched toward the Bosphorus.

The unfortunate emperor, who had not coveted the throne he occupied, nor much desired to retain it, allowed his army to risk one engagement with the troops of Leo. When it was beaten he summoned the Patriarch, the Senate, and the chief officers of the court, pointed out to them that a great Saracen invasion was impending, that civil war had begun, and that he himself did not wish to remain responsible for the conduct of affairs. With his consent the assembly resolved to offer the crown to Leo, who formally accepted it early in the spring of 717.

Theodosius retired unharmed to Ephesus, where he lived for many years. When he died the single word ΥΓΙΕΙΑ, "Health," was inscribed on his tomb according to his last directions.

XIV. The Saracens Turned Back.

By dethroning Theodosius III. on the very eve of the great Saracen invasion, Leo the Isaurian took upon himself the gravest of responsibilities. With a demoralized army, which of late had been more accustomed to revolt than to fight, a depleted treasury, and a disorganized civil service, he had to face an attack even more dangerous than that which Constantine IV. had beaten off thirty years before. Constantine too, the fourth of a race of hereditary rulers, had a secure throne and a loyal army, while Leo was a mere adventurer who had seized the crown only a few months before he was put to the test of the sword.

The reigning Caliph was now Suleiman, the seventh of the house of the Ommeyades. He had strained all the resources of his wide empire to provide a fleet and army adequate to the great enterprise which he had taken in hand. The chief command of the expedition was given to his brother Moslemah, who led an army of eighty thousand men from Tarsus across the centre of Asia Minor, and marched on the Hellespont, taking the strong city of Pergamus on his way. Meanwhile a fleet of eighteen hundred sail under the vizier Suleiman, namesake of his master the Caliph, sailed from Syria for the Aegean, carrying a force no less than that which marched by land. Fleet and army met at Abydos on the Hellespont without mishap, for Leo had drawn back all his resources, naval and military, to guard his capital.

In August, 717, only five months after his coronation, the Isaurian saw the vessels of the Saracens sailing up the Propontis, while their army had crossed into Thrace and was approaching the city from the western side. Moslemah caused his troops to build a line of circumvallation from the sea to the Golden Horn, cutting Constantinople off from all communication with Thrace, while Suleiman blocked the southern exit of the Bosphorus, and tried to close it on the northern side also, so as to prevent any supplies coming by water from the Euxine. Leo, however, sallied forth from the Golden Horn with his galleys and fire-vessels bearing the dreaded Greek fire, and did so much harm to the detachment of Saracen ships which had gone northward up the strait, that the blockade was never properly established on that side.

The Saracens relied more on starving out the city than on taking it by storm: they had come provided with everything necessary for a blockade of many months, and sat down as if intending to remain before the walls for an indefinite time. But Constantinople had been provisioned on an even more lavish scale; each family had been bidden to lay in a stock of corn for no less a period than two years, and famine appeared in the camp of the besiegers long ere it was felt in the houses of the besieged. Nor had Moslemah and Suleiman reckoned with the climate. Hard winters occasionally occur by the Black Sea, as our own army learnt to its cost in the Crimean War. But the Saracens were served even worse by the winter of 717-18, when the frost never ceased for twelve weeks. Leo might have boasted, like Czar Nicholas, that December, January, and February were his best generals—for these months wrought fearful havoc in the Saracen host. The lightly clad Orientals could not stand the weather, and died off like flies of dysentery and cold. The vizier Suleiman was among those who perished. Meanwhile the Byzantines suffered little, being covered by roofs all the winter.

When next spring came round Moslemah would have had to raise the siege if he had not been heavily reinforced both by sea and land. A fleet of reserve arrived from Egypt, and a large army came up from Tarsus and occupied the Asiatic shores of the Bosphorus.

But Leo did not despair, and took the offensive in the summer. His fire-ships stole out and burnt the Egyptian squadron as it lay at anchor. A body of troops landing on the Bithynian coast, surprised and cut to pieces the Saracen army which watched the other side of the strait. Soon, too, famine began to assail the enemy; their stores of provisions were now giving out, and they had harried the neighbourhood so fiercely that no more food could be got from near at hand, while if they sent foraging parties too far from their lines they were cut off by the peasantry. At last Moslemah suffered a disaster which compelled him to abandon his task. The Bulgarians came down over the Balkans, and routed the covering army which observed Adrianople and protected the siege on the western side. No less than twenty thousand Saracens fell, by the testimony of the Arab historians themselves, and the survivors were so cowed that Moslemah gave the order to retire. The fleet ferried the land army back into Asia, and both forces started homeward. Moslemah got back to Tarsus with only thirty thousand men at his back, out of more than a hundred thousand who had started with him or come to him as reinforcements. The fleet fared even worse: it was caught by a tempest in the Aegean, and so fearfully shattered that it is said that only five vessels out of the whole Armada got back to Syria unharmed.

Thus ended the last great endeavour of the Saracen to destroy Constantinople. The task was never essayed again, though for three hundred and fifty years more wars were constantly breaking out between the Emperor and the Caliph. In the future they were always to be border struggles, not desperate attempts to strike at the heart of the empire, and conquer Europe for Islam. To Leo, far more than to his contemporary the Frank Charles Martel, is the delivery of Christendom from the Moslem danger to be attributed. Charles turned back a plundering horde sent out from an outlying province of the Caliphate. Leo repulsed the grand-army of the Saracens, raised from the whole of their eastern realms, and commanded by the brother of their monarch. Such a defeat was well calculated to impress on their fatalistic minds the idea that Constantinople was not destined by providence to fall into their hands. They were by this time far removed from the frantic fanaticism which had inspired their grandfathers, and the crushing disaster they had now sustained deterred them from any repetition of the attempt. Life and power had grown so pleasant to them that martyrdom was no longer an "end in itself"; they preferred, if checked, to live and fight another day.

Leo was, however, by no means entirely freed from the Saracens by his victory of 718. At several epochs in the latter part of his reign he was troubled by invasions of his border provinces. None of them, however, were really dangerous, and after a victory won over the main army of the raiders in 739 at Acroinon in Phrygia, Asia Minor was finally freed from their presence.

XV. The Iconoclasts. (A.D. 720-802.)

If Leo the Isaurian had died on the day on which the army of the Caliph raised the siege of Constantinople it would have been well for his reputation in history. Unhappily for himself, though happily enough for the East-Roman realm, he survived yet twenty years to carry through a series of measures which were in his eyes not less important than the repulse of the Moslems from his capital. Historians have given to the scheme of reform which he took in hand the name of the Iconoclastic movement, because of the opposition to the worship of images which formed one of the most prominent features of his action.

For the last hundred years the empire had been declining in culture and civilization; literature and art seemed likely to perish in the never-ending clash of arms: the old-Roman jurisprudence was being forgotten, the race of educated civil servants was showing signs of extinction, the governors of provinces were now without exception rough soldiers, not members of that old bureaucracy whose Roman traditions had so long kept the empire together. Not least among the signs of a decaying civilization were the gross superstitions which had grown up of late in the religious world. Christianity had begun to be permeated by those strange mediæval fancies which would have been as inexplicable to the old-Roman mind of four centuries before as they are to the mind of the nineteenth century. A rich crop of puerile legends, rites, and observances had grown up of late around the central truths of religion, unnoticed and unguarded against by theologians, who devoted all their energies to the barren Monothelite and Monophysite controversies. Image-worship and relic-worship in particular had developed with strange rapidity, and assumed the shape of mere Fetishism. Every ancient picture or statue was now announced as both miraculously produced and endued with miraculous powers. These wonder-working pictures and statues were now adored as things in themselves divine: the possession of one of them made the fortune of a church or monastery, and the tangible object of worship seems to have been regarded with quite as much respect as the saint whose memory it recalled. The freaks to which image-worship led were in some cases purely grotesque; it was, for example, not unusual to select a picture as the godfather of a child in baptism, and to scrape off a little of its paint and produce it at the ceremony to represent the saint. Even patriarchs and bishops ventured to assert that the hand of a celebrated representation of the Virgin distilled fragrant balsam. The success of the Emperor Heraclius in his Persian campaign was ascribed by the vulgar not so much to his military talent as to the fact that he carried with him a small picture of the Virgin, which had fallen from heaven!

BISHOPS, MONKS, KINGS, LAYMEN, AND WOMEN, ADORING THE MADONNA. (*From a Byzantine MS.*)
(*From "L'Art Byzantin." Par Charles Bayet. Paris, Quantin,* 1883.)

All these vain beliefs, inculcated by the clergy and eagerly believed by the mob, were repulsive to the educated laymen of the higher classes. Their dislike for vain superstitions was emphasized by the influence of Mahometanism on their minds. For a hundred years the inhabitants of the Asiatic provinces of the empire had been in touch with a religion of which the noblest feature was its emphatic denunciation of idolatry under every shape and form. An East-Roman, when taunted by his Moslem neighbour for clinging to a faith which had grown corrupt and idolatrous, could not but confess that there was too much ground for the accusation, when he looked round on the daily practice of his countrymen.

Hence there had grown up among the stronger minds of the day a vigorous reaction against the prevailing superstitions. It was more visible among the laity than among the clergy, and far more widespread in Asia than in Europe. In Leo the Isaurian this tendency stood incarnate in its most militant form, and he left the legacy of his enthusiasm to his descendants. Seven years after the relief of Constantinople he commenced his crusade against superstition. The chief practices which he attacked were the worship of images and the ascription of divine honours to saints—more especially in the form of Mariolatry. His son Constantine, more bold and drastic than his father, endeavoured to suppress monasticism also, because he found the monks the most ardent defenders of images; but Leo's own measures went no further than a determined attempt to put down image-worship.

The struggle which he inaugurated began in A.D. 725, when he ordered the removal of all the images in the capital. Rioting broke out at once, and the officials who were taking down the great figure of Christ Crucified, over the palace-gate, were torn to pieces by a mob. The Emperor replied by a series of executions, and carried out his policy all over the empire by the aid of armed force.

The populace, headed by the monks, opposed a bitter resistance to the Emperor's doings, more especially in the European provinces. They set the wildest rumours afloat concerning his intentions; it was currently reported that the Jews had bought his consent to image-breaking, and that the Caliph Yezid had secretly converted him to Mahometanism. Though Leo's orthodoxy in matters doctrinal was unquestioned, and though he had no objection to the representation of the cross, as distinguished from the crucifix, he was accused of a design to undermine the foundations of Christianity. Arianism was the least offensive fault laid to his account. The Emperor's enemies did not confine themselves to passive resistance to his crusade against images. Dangerous revolts broke out in Greece and Italy, and were not put down without much fighting. In Italy, indeed, the imperial authority was shaken to its foundations, and never thoroughly re-established. The Popes consistently opposed the Iconoclastic movement, and by their denunciation of it placed themselves at the head of the anti-imperial party, nor did they shrink from allying themselves with the Lombards, who were now, as always, endeavouring to drive the East-Roman garrisons from Ravenna and Naples.

The hatred which Leo provoked might have been fatal to him had he not possessed the full confidence of the army. But his great victory over the Saracens had won him such popularity in the camp, that he was able to despise the wrath of the populace, and carry out his schemes to their end. Beside instituting ecclesiastical reforms he was a busy worker in all the various departments of the administration. He published a new code of laws, the first since Justinian, written in Greek instead of Latin, as the latter language was now quite extinct in the Balkan Peninsula. He reorganized the finances of the empire, which had fallen into hopeless confusion in the anarchy between 695 and 717. The army had much of his care, but it was more especially in the civil administration of the empire that he seems to have left his mark. From Leo's day the gradual process of decay which had been observable since the time of Justinian seems to come to an end, and for three hundred years the reorganized East-Roman state developed a power and energy which appear most surprising after the disasters of the unhappy seventh century. Having once lived down the Saracen danger, the empire reasserted its ancient mastery in the East, until the coming of the Turks in the eleventh century. We should be glad to have the details of Leo's reforms, but most unhappily the monkish chroniclers who described his reign have slurred over all his good deeds, in order to enlarge to more effect on the iniquities of his crusade against image-worship. The

LEO - IMAGES

GREEK

effects of his work are to be traced mainly by noting the improved and well-ordered state of the empire after his death, and comparing it with the anarchy that had preceded his accession.

REPRESENTATION OF THE MADONNA ENTHRONED.
(*From a Byzantine Ivory.*)
(*From "L'Art Byzantin." Par Charles Bayet. Paris, Quantin,* 1883.)

Leo died in 740, leaving the throne to his son, Constantine V., whom he had brought up to follow in his own footsteps. The new emperor was a good soldier and a capable man of business, but his main interest in life centred in the struggle against image-worship. Where Leo had chastised the adherents of superstition with whips Constantine chastised them with scorpions. He was a true persecutor, and executed not only rioters and traitors, as his father had done, but all prominent opponents of his policy who provoked his wrath. Hence he incurred an amount of hatred even greater than that which encompassed Leo III., and his very name has been handed down to history with the insulting byword *Copronymus* tacked on to it.

Though strong and clever, Constantine was far below his father in ability, and his reign was marked by one or two disasters, though its general tenor was successful enough. Two defeats in Bulgaria were comparatively unimportant, but a noteworthy though not a dangerous loss was suffered when Ravenna and all the other East-Roman possessions in Central Italy were captured by the Lombards in A.D. 750. At this time Pope Stephen, when attacked by the same enemy, sent for aid to Pipin the Frank, instead of calling on the Emperor, and for the future the papacy was for all practical purposes dependent on the Franks and not on the empire. The loss of the distant exarchate of Ravenna seemed a small thing, however, when placed by the side of Constantine's successes against the Saracens, Slavs, and Bulgarians, all of whom he beat back with great slaughter on the numerous occasions when they invaded the empire.

But in the minds both of Constantine himself and of his contemporaries, his dealings with things religious were the main feature of his reign. He collected a council of 338 bishops at Constantinople in 761, at which image-worship was declared contrary to all Christian doctrine, and after obtaining this condemnation, attacked it everywhere as a heresy and not merely a superstition. In the following year, finding the monks the strongest supporters of the images, he commenced a crusade against monasticism. He first forbade the reception of any novices, and shortly afterwards begun to close monasteries wholesale. We are told that he compelled many of their inmates to marry by force of threats; others were exiled to Cyprus by the hundred; not a few were flogged and imprisoned, and a certain number of prominent men were put to death. These unwise measures had the natural effect: the monks were everywhere regarded as martyrs, and the image-worship which they supported grew more than ever popular with the masses.

IMAGES

While still in the full vigour of his persecuting enthusiasm, Constantine Copronymus died in 775, leaving the throne to his son, Leo IV., an Iconoclast, like all his race, but one who imitated the milder measures of his grandfather rather than the more violent methods of his father. Leo was consumptive and died young, after a reign of little more than four years, in which nothing occurred of importance save a great victory over the Saracens in 776. His crown fell to his son, Constantine VI., a child of ten, while the Empress-Dowager Irene became sole regent, and her name was associated with that of her son in all acts of state.

The Isaurian dynasty was destined to end in a fearful and unnatural tragedy. The Empress Irene was clever, domineering, and popular. The irresponsible power of her office of regent filled her with overweening ambition. She courted the favour of the populace and clergy by stopping the persecution of the image-worshippers, and filled all offices, civil and military, with creatures of her own. For ten years she ruled undisturbed, and grew so full of pride and self-confidence that she looked forward with dismay to the prospect of her son's attaining his majority and claiming his inheritance. Even when he had reached the age of manhood she kept him still excluded from state affairs, and compelled him to marry, against his will, a favourite of her own. Constantine was neither precocious nor unfilial, but in his twenty-second year he rebelled against his mother's dictation, and took his place at the helm of the state. Irene had actually striven to oppose him by armed force, but he pardoned her, and after secluding her for a short time, restored her to her former dignity. The unnatural mother was far from acquiescing in her son's elevation, and still dreamed of reasserting herself. She took advantage of the evil repute which Constantine won by a disastrous war with Bulgaria, and an unhappy quarrel with the Church, on the question of his divorce from the wife who had been forced upon him. More especially, however, she relied on her popularity with the multitude, which had been won by stopping the persecution of the image-worshippers during her regency, for Constantine had resumed the policy of his ancestors and developed strong Iconoclastic tendencies when he came to his own.

In 797 Irene imagined that things were ripe for attacking her son, and conspirators, acting by her orders, seized the young emperor, blinded him, and immured him in a monastery before any of his adherents were able to come to his aid. Thus ended the rule of the Isaurian dynasty. Constantine himself, however, survived many years as a blind monk, and lived to see the ends of no less than five of his successors.

The wicked Irene sat on her ill-gained throne for some five troublous years, much vexed by rebellion abroad and palace intrigues at home. It is astonishing that her reign lasted so long, but it would seem that her religious orthodoxy atoned in the eyes of many of her subjects for the monstrous crime of her usurpation. The end did not come till 802, when Nicephorus, her grand treasurer, having gained over some of the eunuchs and other courtiers about her person, quietly seized her and immured her in a monastery in the island of Chalke. No blow was struck by any one in the cause of the wicked empress, and Nicephorus quietly ascended the throne.

DETAILS OF ST. SOPHIA.

Though containing little that is memorable in itself, the reign of Irene must be noted as the severing-point of that connection between Rome and Constantinople, which had endured since the first days of empire. In the year 800 Pope Leo III. crowned Karl, King of the Franks, as Roman Emperor, and transferred to him the nominal allegiance which he had hitherto paid to Constantinople. Since the Italian rebellion in the time of Constantine Copronymus, that allegiance had been a mere shadow, and the papacy had been in reality under Frankish influence. But it was not till 800 that the final breach took place. The Iconoclastic controversy had prepared the way for it, while the fact that a woman sat on the imperial throne served as a good excuse for the Pope's action. Leo declared that a female reign was an anomaly and an abomination, and took upon himself the onus of ending it, so far as Italy was concerned, by creating a new emperor of the West. There was, of course, no legality in the act, and Karl the Great was in no real sense the successor of Honorius and Romulus Augustulus, but he ruled a group of kingdoms which embraced the larger half of the old Western Empire, and formed a fair equipoise to the realm now ruled by Irene. From 800, then, onward we have once more a West-Roman empire in existence as well as the East-Roman, and it will be convenient for many purposes to use the adjective Byzantine instead of the adjective Roman, when we are dealing with the remaining history of the realm that centred at Constantinople.

XVI. The End Of The Iconoclasts. (A.D. 802-886.)

The Iconoclastic controversy was far from being extinguished with the fall of the house of Leo the Isaurian. It was destined to continue in a milder form for more than half a century after the dethronement of Constantine VI. The lines on which it was fought out were still the same—the official hierarchy and the Asiatic provinces favoured Iconoclasm, the clergy and the European provinces were "Iconodules."[22] Hence it is interesting to note that through the greater part of the ninth century, while emperors of Eastern birth sat on the throne, the views of Leo the Isaurian were still in vogue, and that the eventual triumph of the image-worshippers only came about when a royal house sprung from one of the European themes—the family of Basil the Macedonian—gained possession of the crown.

The treasurer, Nicephorus, who overthrew Irene, and so easily obtained possession of the empire, was of Oriental extraction. His ancestor had been a Christian Arab prince, expelled from his country at the time of the rise of Mahomet, and his family had always dwelt in Asia Minor. Hence we are not surprised to find that Nicephorus was an Iconoclast, and refused to follow in the steps of Irene in the direction of restoring image-worship. He did not persecute the "Iconodules," as the Isaurians had done, but he gave them no personal encouragement. This being so, it is natural that we should find his character described in the blackest terms by the monkish chroniclers of the succeeding century. He was, we are told, a hypocrite, an oppresser, and a miser; but we cannot find any very distinct traces of the operation of such vices in his conduct during the nine years of his reign. He was not, however, a very fortunate ruler; though he put down with ease several insurrections of discontented generals, he was unlucky with his foreign wars. The Caliph Haroun-al-Raschid did much harm to the Asiatic provinces, ravaging the whole country as far as Ancyra, nor could Nicephorus get rid of him without signing a rather ignominious peace, and paying a large war-indemnity. A yet greater disaster concluded another war. Nicephorus invaded Bulgaria in 811, to punish King Crumn for ravaging Thrace. The Byzantine army won a battle and sacked the palace and capital of the Bulgarian king; but a few days later Nicephorus allowed himself to be surprised by a night attack on his camp. In the panic and confusion the emperor fell, and his son and heir, Stauracius, was desperately wounded. The routed army did not stay its flight till Adrianople, and left the body of the Emperor in the hands of the Bulgarians, who cut off his head, and made the skull into a drinking-cup, just as the Lombards had dealt with the skull of King Cunimund three hundred years before.

Stauracius, the only son of Nicephorus, was proclaimed emperor, but it soon became evident that his wound was mortal, and Michael Rhangabe, his brother-in-law, who had married the eldest daughter of Nicephorus, took his place on the throne before the breath was out of the dying emperor's body.

---

[22] "Slaves to images"; a term of contempt not unfairly applied to the image-worshippers.

Michael I. was a weak, good-natured man, who owed his elevation to the mere chance of his marriage. He was a devoted servant and admirer of monks, and began to undo the work of his father-in-law, and remove all Iconoclasts from office. This provoked the wrath of that powerful party, and led to conspiracies against Michael, but he might have held his own if it had not been for the disgracefully incompetent way in which he conducted the Bulgarian war. He allowed an enemy whom the East-Romans had hitherto despised, not only to ravage the open country in Thrace, but to storm the fortresses of Mesembria and Anchialus, and to push their invasions up to the gates of Constantinople. The discontent of the army found vent in a mutiny, and Leo the Armenian, an officer of merit and capacity, was proclaimed emperor in the camp. Michael I. made no resistance, and retired into a monastery after only two years of reign. [811-13.]

Leo the Armenian proved himself worthy of the confidence of the army. When the Bulgarians appeared in front of the walls of Constantinople they were repulsed, but Leo tarnished the glory of his success by a treacherous attempt to assassinate King Crumn at a conference—a crime as unnecessary as it was unsuccessful, for the Emperor might, as the event proved, have trusted to the sword instead of the dagger. In the next spring he took the offensive himself, marched out to Mesembria, and inflicted on the enemy such a sanguinary defeat that hardly a man escaped his sword, and Bulgaria was so weakened that it gave no further trouble for more than fifty years.

Almost the moment that he was freed from the Bulgarian war, Leo became involved in the fatal Iconoclastic controversy. Being a native of an Oriental theme, he was naturally imbued with the views of his great namesake, the Isaurian, and inclined to reverse the policy of the monk-loving Michael I. But being moderate and wary he tried to introduce, without the use of force, a middle policy between image-breaking and image-worship—a fruitless attempt, which only brought him the nickname of "the Chameleon." Leo's idea was the quaint device of permitting the use of images, but of hanging them so high from the ground that the public should not be able to touch or kiss them! This pleased nobody; on the one side, the patriarch and his monks inveighed against the moving of the images, while, on the other, tumultuous companies of Asiatic soldiery broke into churches and mutilated all the pictures and figures they could find. The seven years of Leo's reign were full of ecclesiastical bickerings, but it should be remembered to his credit that no single person suffered death for his conscience' sake in the whole period. The most violent of the opponents of the Emperor were merely interned in remote monasteries, when they ventured to set their will against his. Long ere the end of his reign, Leo had been compelled to leave his half measures and prohibit all use of images. Like Constantine Copronymus, he called a council to endorse his action, and a majority of the Eastern bishops resolved that Iconolatry was a dangerous heresy, and anathematized the patriarch Nicephorus and all other defenders of the images.

Leo's reign was prosperous in all save the matter of his religious troubles. But he was not destined to die in peace in his bed. Michael the Amorian, the best general in the empire, was detected in a conspiracy against his master. Leo cast him into prison, but delayed his punishment, and left his accomplices at large. Michael had many friends in the palace who determined to strike a blow ere the Emperor should have discovered their guilt. They resolved to slay Leo in his private chapel, as he attended matins on Christmas Day, for he was accustomed to come unarmed and unguarded to the early communion. Accordingly, the conspirators attended the service, and attacked the Emperor in the midst of the Eucharistic hymn. Leo snatched the heavy metal cross off the altar and struck down some of his assailants, but numbers were too many for him, and he was cut down and slain at the very foot of the holy table. [Christmas Day, 820.]

Michael the Amorian was dragged out of his dungeon, saluted as emperor, and crowned, even before the fetters were off his feet. It was not till the ceremony had been performed that time was found to send for a smith to strike away the rings.

Michael was by birth a mere peasant, but had raised himself to high rank in the army by his courage and ability. He is sometimes styled "the Amorian," from his birth-place, Amorium in Phrygia, but more often mentioned by his nickname of "the Stammerer." He had been the friend and adviser of Leo the Armenian at the time of the latter's elevation to the throne, and his conspiracy must be reckoned a gross piece of ingratitude, even though we acknowledge that he was not personally responsible for his master's murder.

Though rough and uncultured, Michael was a man of very considerable ability. He strengthened his title to the crown by a marriage with the last scion of the Isaurian house, the princess Euphrosyne, daughter of the blind Constantine VI. The religious difficulties of the day he endeavoured to treat in an absolutely impartial way, so as to offend neither Iconoclasts nor Iconodules. He recalled from exile the image-worshipping monks whom Leo the Armenian had sent to distant monasteries, and proclaimed that for the future every subject of the empire should enjoy complete liberty of conscience on the disputed question. This was far from satisfying the image-worshippers, who wished Michael to restore their idols to their ancient places: but the Amorian would not consent to this, and obtained but a very qualified measure of approval from the monastic party.

It was not to be expected that the reign of a military usurper, with no title to the throne whatever, would be untroubled by revolts. Michael had his share of such afflictions, and though he finally slew Thomas and Euphemius, the two pretenders who laid claim to his crown, yet by their means he lost two not inconsiderable provinces of his empire. While the rebellion of Thomas was in progress, an army of Saracens from Alexandria threw themselves on the island of Crete, and conquered it from end to end. When Michael's hands were free he sent two great armaments to expel the intruders, but both failed, and Crete was destined to remain for a whole century in Moslem hands. Its hundred harbours became the haunts of innumerable Corsairs, who grew to be the bane of commerce in the Levant, and were a serious danger to the empire whenever its fleet fell into bad hands and failed to keep the police of the seas.

A similar rising in Sicily under a rebel named Euphemius led to the invasion of that island by an army of Moors from Africa, who landed in 827, and maintained a foothold in spite of all efforts to expel them. At first their gains were not rapid, but in the time of Michael's successors they gradually won for themselves the whole of the island.

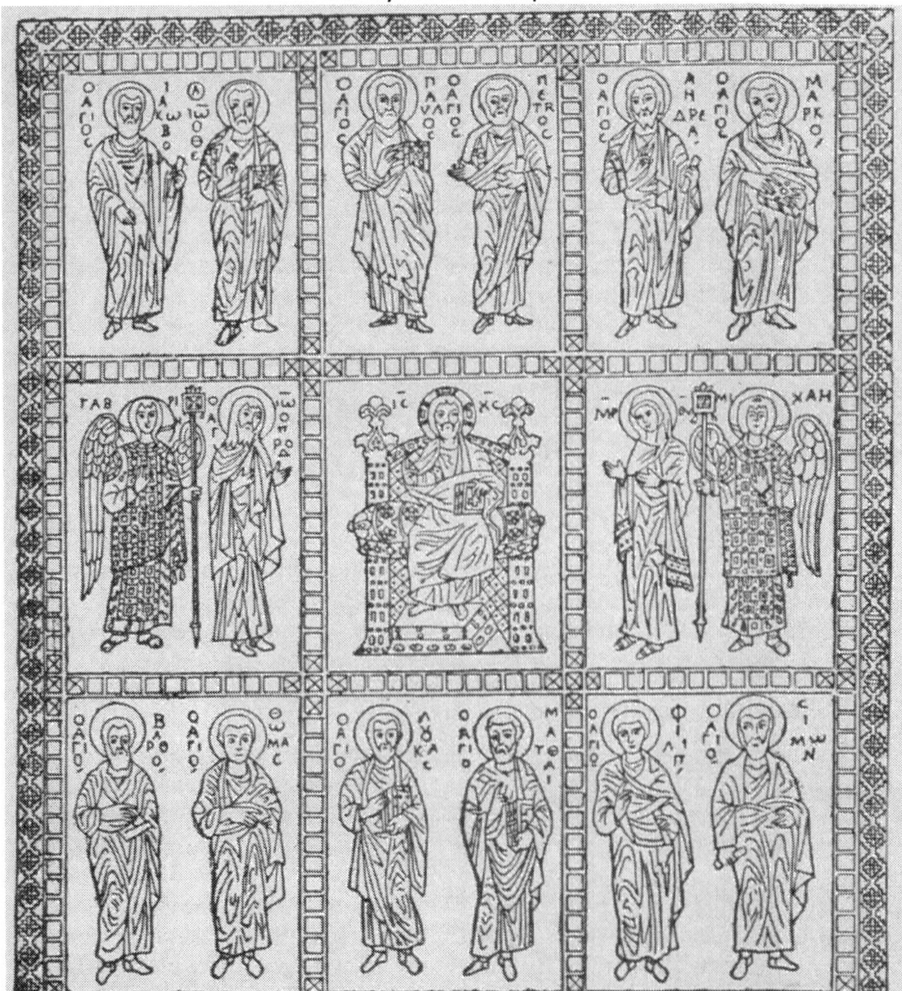

BYZANTINE METAL WORK (Our Lord and the Twelve Apostles).
(*From "L'Art Byzantin." Par Charles Bayet. Paris, Quantin.* 1883.)

After nine years of reign the Amorian died a natural death, still wearing the crown he had won. It was just fifty years since any ruler of the empire had met such a peaceful end. He was succeeded by his son Theophilus, a vehement Iconoclast, whose persecuting tendencies had been with difficulty restrained in his father's life-time. His accession was the signal for a new campaign against image-worship; he induced the patriarch John the Grammarian, a strong Iconoclast like himself, to excommunicate as idolaters all who differed from him, and began to flog, banish, and imprison their leading men. His persecution would have been almost as vehement as that of Constantine Copronymus, but for the fact that he did not ever inflict the punishment of death; branding and mutilation however he did not disdain.

The Iconodules saw the vengeance of heaven for the misdeeds of Theophilus in the disasters which he suffered in war from the Saracens. He fell out with the Caliph Motassem, and in the first campaign took and burnt the town of Zapetra, for which the Commander of the Faithful had great regard.[23] This roused Motassem to furious wrath; he swore that he would destroy in revenge the town which Theophilus held most dear; he collected the largest Saracen army that had been seen since Moslemah beleaguered Constantinople in 717, and marched out of Tarsus with 130,000 men, each of whom (if legend speaks true) had the word Amorium painted on his shield. For it was Amorium, the birth-place of the Emperor, and the home of his ancestors that Motassem had sworn to sack. While one division of the Caliph's army defeated Theophilus, who had taken the field in person, another headed by Motassem himself marched straight on Amorium, and took it after a brave defence of fifty-five days. Thirty thousand of its inhabitants were massacred, and the town was burnt, but the Caliph then turned home satisfied with his revenge, and the empire suffered nothing more from this most dangerous invasion. The Saracen war dragged on in an indecisive way, but no further disaster was encountered.

There are other things to be recorded of Theophilus beside his persecution of image-worshippers and his war with the Caliph. He was long remembered for his taste for gorgeous display; of all the East-Roman emperors he seems to have delighted the most in gold and silver work, gems and embroidery. His golden plane-tree was the talk of the East, and the golden lions at the foot of his throne, which rose and roared by the means of ingenious machinery within, were remembered for generations.

Nor should the curious tale of his second marriage be left untold. When left a widower he bade the Empress-dowager Euphrosyne assemble at her levée all the most beautiful of the daughters of the East-Roman aristocracy, and came among them to choose a wife, carrying like Paris a golden apple in his hand. His glance was first fixed on the fair Eikasia, but approaching her he found no better topic to commence a conversation than the awkward statement that "most of the evil had come into the world by means of women." The lady retorted that surely most of the good had also come into the world by their means, a reply which apparently discomposed Theophilus, for he walked on and without a further word gave the golden apple to Theodora, a rival beauty. The choice was hasty and unhappy, for Theodora was a devoted Iconodule, and used all her influence against her husband's religious opinions.

Theophilus died in 842, while still a young man, leaving the throne to his only son Michael, a child of three years, and the regency to the young empress. The moment that her husband's grave was closed Theodora set to work to undo his policy. Amid the applause of the monks and the populace of Constantinople she proclaimed the end of the persecution, sent for the banished image-worshippers from their places of exile, and deposed John the Grammarian, the Iconoclastic patriarch who had served Theophilus. Within thirty days of the commencement of the new reign the images had appeared once more on the walls of all the churches of Constantinople. The Iconoclasts seem to have been taken by surprise, and made no

[23] It is said to have been either his birth-place or that of his mother.

resistance to the revolution: however the empress did not take any measures to persecute them; it was only power and not security for life and limb that they lost. The sole permanent result of the long struggle which they had kept up was a curious compromise in the Eastern Church on the subject of representation of the human figure. Statues were never again erected in places of worship, but only paintings and mosaics. It was apparently believed that the actual image savoured too much of the heathen idol, but that no offence could possibly be given by the picture, which served as a pious remembrance of the holy personage it represented, but could be nothing more. Nevertheless the veneration of the Byzantines for their holy "Eikons" became almost as grotesque as idol-worship, and led to many quaint and curious forms of superstition.

Theodora, engrossed in things religious, handed over the education of her young son to her brother Bardas, who became her co-regent and was afterwards made Caesar. He brought up the young Michael in the most reckless and unconscientious manner, teaching him his own vices of drunkenness and debauchery. Michael was an apt pupil, and ere he reached the age of twenty-one had become a confirmed dipsomaniac. History knows him by the dishonourable nickname of "Michael the Drunkard." Some years after his majority he grew discontented with his uncle, and slew him, in order that he might reign alone. His profligacy and intemperance became still more unbearable after Bardas was dead, and had it not been for the splendid organization of the Byzantine civil service the administration of the empire must have gone to pieces. Presently Michael grew tired of spending on state affairs any time that he could spare from his orgies, and appointed as Caesar and colleague his boon companion Basil the Macedonian. Basil had reached the position of grand chamberlain purely by the Emperor's favour; he rose from the lowest ranks and is said to have first entered Michael's service in the humble position of a groom. His practical ability, combined with a head hard enough to withstand the effect of even the longest debauch, won Michael's admiration, and so he came to be first chamberlain and then Caesar. Under the mask of a roisterer Basil concealed the most devouring ambition, and when he knew that his drunken benefactor had won the contempt of all the East-Roman world, had the impudence and ingratitude to plan his murder. Michael was stabbed while sleeping off the effects of one of his orgies, and his low-born colleague seized the palace and proclaimed himself emperor.

It might have been expected that the East-Roman world would have refused to receive as its lord a man who owed his elevation to the freak of a drunkard, and had then become the assassin of his benefactor. But strangely enough Basil was destined to found the longest dynasty that ever sat upon the Constantinopolitan throne. He turned out a far better ruler than might have been expected from his disgraceful antecedents, being one of those fortunate men who are able to utilize the work of others when their own powers and knowledge fall short.

Basil is mainly remembered for his codification of the laws of the empire, which superseded the *Ecloga* of Leo the Isaurian, even as Leo's compilation had superseded the more solid and thorough work of Justinian. The *Basilika* of Basil with the additions made by his son Leo VI. formed the code of the Byzantine Empire down to its last days, no further rearrangement being ever made.

Basil, being of European birth and not an Asiatic like the preceding emperors, was naturally an orthodox image-worshipper. He showed his bigotry by a fierce persecution of the Paulicians, an Asiatic sect of heretics accused of Manicheanism, whom the Iconoclast emperors had been wont to tolerate. Basil's oppression drove many of them over the Saracen frontier, where they took refuge with the Moslems and maintained themselves by plundering the borders of the empire.

Among the other transactions of his nineteen years of reign [867-886], the only one deserving notice is the final loss of Sicily. The Saracens of Africa, who had held a footing in the island ever since the time of Michael II., now finished their work by storming Syracuse in 878.

XVII. The Literary Emperors And Their Time. (A.D. 886-963.)

The eighty years which followed the death of Basil the Macedonian were the most uneventful and monotonous in the whole history of the empire. They are entirely taken up by the two long reigns of Leo the Wise and Constantine Porphyrogenitus,[24] the son and grandson of the founder of the dynasty. Basil had been a mere adventurer, an ignorant and uneducated but capable upstart. His successors—strange issue from such a stock—were a pair of mild, easy-going, and inoffensive men of literature. They wrote no annals with their sword, though the times were not unpropitious for military enterprise, but devoted themselves to the pen, and have left behind them some of the most useful and interesting works in Byzantine literature.

If the times had been harder it is doubtful whether Leo VI. and Constantine VII. would have been strong enough to protect their throne. But the period 880-960 was less troubled by foreign wars than any other corresponding period in the history of the East-Roman state. The empire of the Caliphs was breaking up in the East—the empire of Charles the Great had already broken up in the West—the Bulgarians and other neighbours of the realm on the north were being converted to Christianity, and settling down into quiet. The only troubles to which the East-Roman realm was exposed were piratical raids of the Russians on the north and the Saracens of Africa on the south. These were vexatious, but not dangerous. An active and warlike emperor would probably have found the time propitious for conquest from his neighbours, but Leo and Constantine were quiet, unenterprising men, who dwelt contentedly in the palace, and seldom or never took the field.

Leo's reign of twenty-six years was only diversified by an unfortunate invasion of Bulgaria, which failed through the mismanagement of the generals, and for a great raid of Saracen pirates on Thessalonica in 904. The capture of the second city of the empire by a fleet of African adventurers was an incident disgraceful to the administration of Leo, and caused much outcry and sensation. But it is fair to say that it was taken almost by surprise, and stormed from the side of the sea where no attack had been expected. The armies and fleet of the empire would have availed to rescue the town if only its fall had been delayed a few weeks. When they had taken it the Saracens fled with their booty, and made no attempt to hold its walls.

Constantine Porphyrogenitus, the offspring of the fourth wife of Leo the Wise, and the child of his old age, was only seven when his heritage fell to him. For many years he was under the tutelage of guardians; first his father's brother Alexander ruled as his colleague, and became emperor-regent. Some years after Alexander had died an ambitious admiral named Romanus Lecapenus usurped the same position, declared himself emperor, and administered the realm. The life of Romanus was

[24] This name was given him because he was born in the Purple Chamber, the room in the palace set aside for the Empress. Emperors born in their father's reign had been scarce of late, Constantine VI. and Michael the Drunkard were the only two in the 110 years before Constantine VII.

protracted into extreme old age, long after Constantine had reached his majority; but the ambitious veteran held tight to the sceptre, and kept the rightful heir in the background. Constantine consoled himself by writing books and painting pictures; it was not till he was nearly forty that he came to his own. Even then his success was not owing to his own energy; the sons of the aged Romanus had resolved to succeed their parent on the throne, in despite of the rights of Constantine. But when they declared themselves emperors and made their old father abdicate, an outburst of popular wrath was provoked. The mob and the guards joined to sweep away the presumptuous Stephen Lecapenus and his brother. They were immured in monasteries, and Constantine emerged from his seclusion to administer the empire for twenty years. He was somewhat weak and ineffective, but neither obstinate nor tyrannical; many abler men made worse rulers.

The chief achievements of both Leo and Constantine were their books. Those of Leo consist of a manual on the Art of War, some theological treatises, and a book of prophecies, a collection of political enigmas, which were long the puzzle and admiration of the East.[25] The first-named work is most valuable and interesting, bringing down the history of military organization, tactics, and strategy to Leo's own time, and giving us a perfect picture of the Byzantine army and its tactics, as well as incidental sketches of all the enemies with which it had to contend. The backbone of the force was still the "themes" or "turmæ" of heavy cavalry, of which every province had one. The number of the provinces had been much increased since the days of the emperors of the house of Heraclius, and this implied a corresponding increase in the troops. They were raised from subjects of the empire and officered by the Byzantine nobility, for as Leo observed, "There was no difficulty in obtaining officers of good birth and private means, whose origin made them respected by the soldiery, while their money enabled them to win the good graces of their men by many gifts of small creature comforts, over and above their pay." The names of some of the great noble houses are found for generation after generation in the imperial muster rolls, such as those of Ducas, Phocas, Comnenus, Bryennius, Kerkuas, Diogenes, and many more. The pages of Leo's work breathe an entire confidence in the power of the army to deal with any foe; against Saracen, Turk, Hungarian, and Slav, instant and decisive action is advised; when caught, they should be fought and beaten. It is only when dealing with the men of the West, the Franks and Lombards, that Leo recommends caution and deprecates any rash engagement in a general action, preferring to wear the enemy down by cutting off his supplies and harassing his marches. We gather a very favourable impression of the Byzantine army from Leo's book; it was organized, armed, and supplied in a manner that has no parallel till modern times. Each regiment possessed its special uniform, and was equipped with regularity. There was none of that variety in arms and organizations which was the bane of mediæval armies. The regiments had each attached to them an elaborate military train, a small body of engineers, and a provision of surgeons and ambulances. To encourage the saving of wounded men, Leo tells us that the bearer company was given a gold piccc for every disabled

[25] There is a splendid copy of this book in the Bodleian Library, made as late as 1560, whree all the prophecies are applied to the Turks and Venetians.

soldier whom it brought off the field after a lost battle. It would be hard to find any similar care shown for the wounded till the days of our own century.

The Byzantine fleet, as Leo describes it, had for its chief object the maintenance of the police of the seas in the Aegean, Levant, and South Italian waters. Its enemies were the Saracens of the Syrian and African coasts, and more especially the troublesome Corsairs of Crete, who were often beaten but never subdued till Nicephorus Phocas exterminated them in 961. The empire maintained three fleets, small ones in the Black Sea and in Western waters; but the largest in the Aegean. This was composed of sixty "dromonds," or war-vessels of the largest rating; their great depôt was in the arsenal at Constantinople, but they could also be refitted at Samos, Thessalonica, and several other ports. Owing to their superior size, and still more to their employment of the celebrated Greek fire, the imperial fleets generally had the better of the Saracen, but though they checked his larger squadrons, they could never suppress the petty piracy by isolated sea-robbers, which rendered all mediæval commerce so dangerous.

The works of Constantine Porphyrogenitus are even more interesting than those of his father. His treatise called "On the Themes" is invaluable to the historian, as it gives a complete list of the Themes, their boundaries, inhabitants, characteristics, and resources, with some other incidental notices of value. Still more important is the book, "On the Administration of the Empire," which contains directions for the foreign policy of the realm, and sketches the condition and resources of the various nations with whom the Constantinopolitan government had dealings. Constantine also wrote a biography of his grandfather, Basil the Macedonian, couched in terms of respect which that hardy usurper was far from deserving. But his longest and most ambitious work was on Court Ceremonies, a manual of etiquette and precedence, describing the official hierarchy of the empire, its duties and privileges, and containing elaborate directions for the conduct of state ceremonials and the interior economy of the royal household. On this comparatively trifling topic Constantine spent far more pains than on the works of larger interest which he composed. His books show him to have been a man of no great originative faculty, but gifted with the powers of a careful and methodical compiler, who loved details and never shirked trouble. His care for court pageants was very characteristic of the peaceful emperor, who had long been kept at home by his guardian, and forced to compensate himself by ceremonial for the want of real power.

The fact that two successive emperors devoted themselves to literary work is a sufficient sign that by the end of the ninth century the times of intellectual dearth and destitution which had so long prevailed were now at an end. From the death of Justinian to the end of the Heraclian dynasty matters grew gradually worse; from the rise of Leo the Isaurian onward they began slowly to improve. The darkest age in Byzantine literary history was from about 600 to 750, a period in which we have hardly any contemporary annalists, no poetry save the lost Heracliad of George of Pisidia, and very little even of theology. Literature seemed absolutely dead at the accession of the Isaurians, but the quickening influence of the reforms of the great Leo seems to have been felt in that province as in every other. By the end of the eighth century writers were far more numerous, though many of them were only anti-Iconoclastic controversialists, like Theodore Studita. By the ninth century we can trace the existence of a much larger literary class, and find a few really first-rate authors, such as the patriarch Photius (857-69), whose learning and width of culture was astonishing, and whose library-catalogue is the envy of modern scholars.

Perhaps the most interesting development of Byzantine literature were the epics, or Romances of Chivalry as we feel more inclined to call them, which were written toward the end of the times of the Macedonian dynasty. The epic of Digenes Akritas, a work of the end of the tenth century, celebrating the praises of a hero who lived in the reigns of Nicephorus Phocas and John Zimisces [963-80], may serve as a type of the class. It tells of the adventures in love and war of Basil Digenes Akritas, warden of the Cilician Marches, or "Clissurarch of Taurus," as his official title would have run. He was a mighty hunter, both of bears and of Saracens, put down the Apelates (or moss-troopers, to use a modern analogy) who infested the border, and led many a foray into Syria. He is even credited with the slaying of an occasional dragon by his admiring bard. But perhaps the most interesting episode is the story of his elopement with the fair Eudocia Ducas, daughter of the general of the Cappadocian theme, whom he carried off in despite of her father and seven brethren. Pursued by the irate family, he rode them down one by one at vantage points in the passes, but spared their lives, and was reconciled to them at the intercession of his bride. "Digenes Akritas" is the best as well as the earliest of the class which it represents.

A WARRIOR-SAINT (ST. LEONTIUS).

(From a Byzantine Fresco.)

(From "L'Art Byzantin." Par Charles Bayet. Paris, Quantin. 1883.)

Art followed much the same course as literature in the period 600-900. It was in a state of decay for the first century and a half, and the surviving works of that time are often grotesquely rude. For sheer bad drawing and bad execution nothing can be worse than a coin of Constans II. or Constantine V.; a Frankish or Visigoth piece could not be much more unsightly. The few manuscripts which survive from that period display a corresponding, though not an equally great, decline in art. Mosaic work perhaps showed less decline than other branches of the decoration, but even here seventh and eighth century work is very rare.

In the ninth century everything improves wonderfully. It is most astonishing to see how the old classical tradition of painting revive in the best manuscript illumination of the period; many of them might have been executed in the fifth or even the fourth century, so closely do they reproduce the old Roman style. It seems that the Iconoclastic controversy stimulated painting; persecuted by the emperors, the art of sacred portraiture became respected above all others by the multitude. Several of the most prominent "Iconodule" martyrs were painters, of whom it is recorded that their works were no less beautiful than edifying: those of Lazarus, whom the Emperor Theophilus tortured, are especially cited as triumphs of art as well as sanctity.

Though a persecutor of painters, Theophilus deserves a word of mention as the first great builder since Justinian, and as a patron of the minor arts of jewellery, silver work, and mosaic. There is good evidence that these were all in a very flourishing condition in his time. [829-42.]

There is one more point in the history of the empire in the ninth century to which attention must be called. This is the unique commercial importance of Constantinople during this and the two succeeding centuries. All other commerce than that of the empire had been swept off the seas by the Saracen pirates in the preceding hundred years, and the only touch between Eastern and Western Christendom was kept up under the protection of the imperial navy. The Eastern products which found their way to Italy or France were all passed through the warehouses of the Bosphorus. It was East-Roman ships that carried all the trade; save a few Italian ports, such as Amalphi and the new city of Venice, no place seems even to have possessed merchant ships. This monopoly of the commerce of Europe was one of the greatest elements in the strength of the empire. So much money and goods passed through it that a rather harsh and unwise system of taxation did no permanent harm.

XVIII. Military Glory.

While Constantine Porphyrogenitus had been dragging out the monotonous years of his long reign, events which completely changed the aspect of affairs in the Moslem East had been following each other in quick succession on the Asiatic frontier of his realm. Ever since it first came into existence the Byzantine Empire had been faced in Asia by a single powerful enemy; first by the Sassanian kingdom of Persia, then by the Caliphate under the two dynasties of the Ommeyades and the Abbasides. Now, however, the Caliphate had at last broken up, and the descendants of Abdallah-es-Saffah and Haroun-al-Raschid had become the vassals of a rebellious subject, and preserved a mere nominal sovereignty which did not extend beyond the walls of their palace in Bagdad.

The crisis had come in 951 A.D., when the armies of the Buhawid prince Imad-ud-din, who had seized on the sovereignty of Persia, broke into Bagdad and made the Caliph a prisoner in his own royal residence. For the future the Caliphs were no more than puppets, and the Buhawid rulers used their names as a mere form and pretence. But the conquerors did not gain possession of the whole of the Caliphate; only Persia and the Lower Euphrates Valley obeyed them. Other dynasties rose and fought for the more western provinces of the old Moslem realm. The Emirs of Aleppo and Mosul, who ruled respectively in North Syria and in Mesopotamia, became the immediate neighbours of the East-Roman Empire, while the lands beyond them, Egypt and South Syria, formed the dominions of the house of the Ikshides.

Thus the Byzantines found on their eastern frontier no longer one great centralized power, but the comparatively weak Emirates of Aleppo and Mosul, with the Buhawid and Ikshidite kingdoms in their rear. The four Moslem states were all new and precarious creations of the sword, and were generally at war with each other. An unparalleled opportunity had arrived for the empire to take its revenge on its ancient enemies and to move back the Mahometan boundaries from the line along the Taurus where they had so long been fixed.

Fortunately it was not only the hour that had arrived, but also the man. The empire had at its disposal at this moment the best soldier that it had possessed since the death of Leo the Isaurian. Nicephorus Phocas was the head of one of those great landholding families of Asia Minor who formed the flower of the Byzantine aristocracy; he owned broad lands in Cappadocia, along the Mahometan frontier. His father and grandfather before him had been distinguished officers, for the whole race lived by the sword, but Nicephorus far surpassed them. He was not only a practical soldier, but a military author: his book, Περὶ Παραδρόμης πολέμου, dealing with the organization of armies, still survives to testify to his capacity.

It was on Nicephorus then that Romanus II., the son and heir of Constantine VII., fixed his choice, when he resolved to commence an attack on the Mahometan powers. The point selected for assault was the island of Crete, the dangerous haunt of Corsairs which lay across the mouth of the Aegean, and sheltered the pestilent galleys that preyed on the trade of the empire with the West. Several expeditions against it had failed during the last half-century, but this one was fitted out on the largest scale. The vessels are said to have been numbered by the thousand, and the land force was chosen from the flower of the Asiatic "themes." Complete success followed the arms of Nicephorus. He drove the Saracens into their chief town Chandax (Candia), stormed that city, and took an enormous booty—the hoarded wealth of a century of piracy. The whole island then submitted, and Nicephorus sailed back to Constantinople to present to his sovereign, in bonds, Kurup the captive Emir of Crete, and all the best of the booty of the island [961 A.D.].

Nicephorus was duly honoured for his feat of arms, and given command of an army destined to open a campaign in the next year against the great frontier strongholds of the Saracens in Asia Minor. Descending by the passes of the Central Taurus into Cilicia, Phocas stormed Anazarbus, and then forced Mount Amanus, and marched into Northern Syria. There he took the great town of Hierapolis, and laid siege to Aleppo, the capital of the Emir Seyf-ud-dowleh, who ruled from Mount Lebanon to the Euphrates. The Emir was routed, the walls of his capital were stormed, and Aleppo, with all its wealth, fell into the hands of the Byzantine general. But the citadel still held out, and its protracted resistance gave time for the Moslems of South Syria and Mesopotamia to combine for the relief of their northern compatriots. So great an army appeared before the walls of Aleppo that Phocas determined not to risk a battle, and retreated with his booty and his numerous prisoners into the defiles of Taurus [962 A.D.]. Sixty captured forts and castles in Cilicia and North Syria were the permanent fruits of his campaign.

The next year the emperor Romanus II. died, very unexpectedly, ere he had reached his twenty-sixth year. He left a young wife, and two little boys, Basil, aged seven, and Constantine, who was only two. There followed the form of regency that custom had made usual. Nicephorus, the most powerful and popular subject of the empire, claimed the guardianship of the two young Caesars, and had himself crowned as their colleague. To secure his place he married their mother, the young and beautiful empress-dowager Theophano.

The joint reign of Nicephorus Phocas and his wards, Basil II. and Constantine VIII. lasted six years, 963-969. The regent behaved with scrupulous loyalty to the young princes, and made no attempt to encroach on their rights, or to supplant them by any of his numerous nephews, who had looked forward to his accession as likely to lead to their own promotion to imperial power.

Nicephorus was an indefatigable soldier, and spent more of his reign in the field than in the palace. His end in life was to complete, as emperor, the conquest of Cilicia and North Syria, which he had commenced as general. The years 964 and 965 were spent in achieving the former object: three long sieges made him master of the great Cilician frontier fortresses, Adana, Mopsuestia, and Tarsus. Their rich bronze gates were sent as trophies to Constantinople, and set up again in the archways of the imperial palace. A few months later the tale of victories was completed by the news that Cyprus also had fallen back into Byzantine hands, after having passed seventy-seven years in the power of the Saracens.

For two years after this Phocas was employed at home, where his administration was less popular than in the camp. The stern old soldier was not a friend of either priests or courtiers. He had several quarrels with the patriarch Polyeuctus, which made him detested by the clergy, and in his public life he displayed a dislike for pomp and ceremony which led the Byzantine populace to style him a niggard and an extortioner. He suppressed shows and sports, and turned all the public revenues into the war budget, which lay nearest his heart. When he left the city in 968 for a new campaign against the Saracens, he was a much less popular ruler than when he had entered it in triumph in 966 after the conquest of Cilicia.

In the camp, however, Nicephorus was as well loved and as successful as ever. His last Syrian expedition was no less glorious than his earlier campaign in the same quarter six years before. All the North Syrian cities fell into his hands—Emesa, Hierapolis, Laodicea, and with them Aleppo, the residence of the Emir: Damascus bought off the invader by a great tribute. Only Antioch, the ancient capital of the land, held out, and Antioch also was taken in the winter by escalade, through the daring of an officer named Burtzes. The story of its fall is curious. The Emperor had left a blockading army before it under a general named Peter, with orders not to risk an assault. Burtzes, the second in command, disobeyed orders and stormed a corner tower on a snowy night at the head of a small band of 300 men. Peter, in fear of the Emperor's orders, refused to send him aid, and for more than two days Burtzes maintained himself unaided in the tower he had won. At last, however, the main body entered, and the Saracens fled from the town. Nicephorus dismissed both his generals from the service—Burtzes for having acted against orders, Peter for having obeyed them too slavishly, and allowing an important advantage to be imperilled.

Nicephorus returned to Constantinople in the following year, to meet his death at the hands of those who should have been his nearest and dearest. His wife, Theophano had learnt to hate her grim and stern husband, who, though he possessed all the virtues, displayed none of the graces. She had cast her eyes in love on the Emperor's favourite nephew, John Zimisces, a young cavalry officer, who had greatly distinguished himself in the Syrian war. Zimisces listened to her tempting, but he was not swayed by lust, but by ambition: he had hoped that his uncle would make him heir to the throne, to the detriment of the young emperor Basil. The loyal old soldier had no idea of wronging his wards, and his nephew resolved to gain by murder what he could not gain by favour.

RETURN OF A VICTORIOUS EMPEROR.
(From an Embroidered Robe.)
(From "L'Art Byzantin." Par Charles Bayet. Paris, Quantin, 1883.)

So John and Theophano conspired against their best friend, and basely murdered him in the palace one December night in 969. The Emperor was awakened from sleep to find a dozen of the assassins forcing his door. John threw him to the ground, and the others stabbed him, while he cried in his death-agony, "Oh, God! grant me Thy mercy!"

Thus ended the brave and virtuous Nicephorus Phocas. His murderers succeeded in their end, for John Zimisces was able to seduce the guards, overawe the ministers, and force the patriarch to crown him emperor. He showed some contrition for the base slaughter of his uncle, giving away half his private fortune to found hospitals for lepers, and the other half to be distributed among the poor of the city. He did not wed the partner of his guilt, the empress Theophano, but refused to see her face, and ultimately sent her to a monastery.

If the manner of his accession could but be forgiven John might pass for a favourable specimen of an emperor. He respected the rights of the young emperors Basil and Constantine as scrupulously as his uncle had done, and proved that as an administrator and a soldier he was not unworthy to sit in the seat of Phocas. But the Nemesis of the murder of his uncle rested upon him in the shape of a long civil war. His cousin Bardas Phocas took arms to revenge the death of the old Nicephorus, and stirred up troubles among his Cappadocian countrymen for several years, till at last he was captured and immured in a monastery.

The chief feat for which John Zimisces is remembered is his splendid victory over the Russians, whose great invasion of the Balkan Peninsula falls within the limits of his reign. We have not yet had much occasion to mention the Russian tribes, who for many centuries had been dwelling in obscurity and barbarism, by the waters of the Dnieper and the Duna, in a land of forest and marsh, far remote from the boundaries of the empire. Nor should we hear of them now, but for the fact that their scattered tribes had been of late unified into a single horde by a power from without, and urged forward into a career of conquest by a race of ambitious princes. Into the land of the Russians there had come some hundred years before the reign of John Zimisces [862 A.D.], a Viking band from Sweden, headed by Rurik, the ancestor of all the princes and Tzars of Russia. The descendants of these adventurers from the north had gradually conquered and subdued all the Slavonic tribes of the great forest-land, and formed them into a single powerful kingdom. Its capital lay at Kief on the Dnieper, and it had proved a formidable neighbour to all the barbarous tribes around. The Viking blood of the new Russian princes drove them seaward, and ere many generations had passed they had forced their way down the Dnieper into the Euxine, and begun to vex the northern borders of the Byzantine Empire with raids and ravages like those which the Danes inflicted on Western Europe. Twice already, within the tenth century, had large fleets of light Russia row-boats—they were copies on a smaller scale of the Viking ships of the North—stolen down from the Dnieper mouth to the shores of Thrace, and landed their plundering crews within a few miles of the Bosphorus, for a hurried raid on the rich suburban provinces. On the first occasion in 907, the Russians had returned home laden with plunder, but on the second, which fell in 941, the Byzantine fleet had caught them at sea, and revenged the harrying of Thrace by sinking scores of their light boats, which could not resist for a moment the impact of the heavy war-galley urged by its hundred oars.

ARABESQUE DESIGN FROM A BYZANTINE MS.

(*From "L'Art Byzantin." Par Charles Bayet. Paris, Quantin,* 1883.)

But the attack which John Zimisces had to meet in 970 was far more formidable than either of those which had preceded it. Swiatoslaf, king of the Russians, had come down the Dnieper with no less than 60,000 men, and had thrown himself on to the kingdom of Bulgaria, which was at the moment distracted by civil war. He conquered the whole country, and soon his marauders were crossing the Balkans and showing themselves in the plain of Thrace. They even sacked the considerable town of Philippopolis before the imperial troops came to its aid. This roused Zimisces, who had been absent in Asia Minor, and in the early spring of 971 an imperial army of 30,000 men set out to cross the Balkans and drive the Russians into the Danube. The struggle which ensued was one of the most desperate which East-Roman history records. The Russians all fought on foot, in great square columns, armed with spear and axe: they wore mail shirts and peaked helmets, just like the Normans of Western Europe, to whom their princes were akin. The shock of their columns was terrible, and their constancy in standing firm almost incredible. Against these warriors of the North Zimisces led the mailed horsemen of the Asiatic themes, and the bowmen and slingers who were the flower of the Byzantine infantry. The tale of John's two great battles with the Russians at Presthlava and Silistria reads much like the tale of the battle of Hastings. In Bulgaria, as in Sussex, the sturdy axeman long beat off the desperate cavalry charges of their opponents. But they could not resist the hail of arrows to which they had no missile weapons to oppose, and when once the archers had thinned their ranks, the Byzantine cavalry burst in, and made a fearful slaughter in the broken phalanx. More fortunate than Harold Godwineson at the field of Senlac, King Swiatoslaf escaped with his life and the relics of his army. But he was beleaguered within the walls of Silistria, and forced to yield himself, on the terms that he and his men might take their way homeward, on swearing never to molest the empire again. The Russian swore the oath and took a solemn farewell of Zimisces. The contrast between the two monarchs struck Leo the Deacon, a chronicler who seems to have been present at the scene, and caused him to describe the meeting with some vigour. We learn how the Emperor, a small alert fair-haired man, sat on his great war-horse by the river bank, in his golden armour with his guards about him, while the burly Viking rowed to meet him in a boat, clad in nothing but a white shirt, and with his long moustache floating in the wind. They bade each other adieu, and the Russian departed, only to fall in battle ere the year was out, at the hands of the Patzinak Tartars of the Southern Steppes. Soon after Swiatoslaf's death the majority of the Russians became Christians, and ere long ceased to trouble the empire by their raids. They became faithful adherents of the Eastern Church, and drew their learning, their civilization, even their names and titles from Constantinople. The Tzars are but Caesars misspelt, and the list of their names—Michael, Alexander, Nicholas, John, Peter, Alexis—sufficiently witnesses to their Byzantine godparents. Russian mercenaries were ere long enlisted in the imperial army, and formed the nucleus of the "Varangian guard," in which at a later day, Danes, English, and Norsemen of all sorts were incorporated.

RUSSIAN ARCHITECTURE FROM BYZANTINE MODEL.
(*Church at Vladimir.*)
(*From "L'Art Byzantin." Par Charles Bayet. Paris, Quantin,* 1883.)

John Zimisces survived his great victory at Silistria for five years, and won, ere he died, more territory in Northern Syria from the Saracens. The border which his uncle Nicephorus had pushed forward to Antioch and Aleppo was advanced by him as far as Amida and Edessa in Mesopotamia. But in the midst of his conquests Zimisces was cut off by death, while still in the flower of his age. Report whispered that he had been poisoned by one of his ministers, whom he had threatened to displace. But the tale cannot be verified, and all that is certain is that John died after a short illness, leaving the throne to his young ward Basil II., who had now attained the age of twenty years [976 A.D.].

XIX. The End Of The Macedonian Dynasty.

Basil II., who now sat in his own right on the throne which his warlike guardians Nicephorus and John had so long protected, was by no means unworthy to succeed them. Unlike his ancestors of the Macedonian house, he showed from the first a love for war and adventure. Probably the deeds of John and Nicephorus excited him to emulation: at any rate his long reign from 976 till 1025, is one continuous record of wars, and almost entirely of wars brought to a successful termination. Basil seemed to have modelled himself on the elder of his two guardians, the stern Nicephorus Phocas. His earliest years on the throne, indeed, were spent in the pursuit of pleasure, but ere he reached the age of thirty a sudden transformation was visible in him. He gave himself up entirely to war and religion: he took a vow of chastity, and always wore the garb of a monk under his armour and his imperial robes. His piety was exaggerated into bigotry and fanaticism, but it was undoubtedly real, though it did not keep him from the commission of many deeds of shocking cruelty in the course of his wars. His justice was equally renowned, but it often degenerated into mere harshness and indifference to suffering. No one could have been more unlike his gay pleasure-loving father, or his mild literary grandfather, than the grim emperor who won from posterity the title of Bulgaroktonos, "the Slayer of the Bulgarians."

Basil's life-work was the moving back of the East-Roman border in the Balkan Peninsula as far as the Danube, a line which it had not touched since the Slavonic immigration in the days of Heraclius, three hundred and fifty years before. In the first years of his reign, indeed, he accomplished little, being much harassed by two rebellions of great Asiatic nobles—Bardas Phocas, the nephew of Nicephorus II., and Bardas Skleros, the general of the Armeniac theme. But after Phocas had died and Skleros had surrendered, Basil reserved all his energies for war in Europe, paying comparatively little attention to the Eastern conquests which had engrossed Nicephorus Phocas and John Zimisces.

The whole interior of the Balkan Peninsula formed at this period part of the dominions of Samuel King of the Bulgarians, who reigned over Bulgaria, Servia, inland Macedonia, and other districts around them. It was a strong and compact kingdom, administered by an able man, who had won his way to the throne by sheer strength and ability, for the old royal house had ceased out of the land during Swiatoslaf's invasion of Bulgaria ten years before. The main power of Samuel lay not in the land between Balkan and Danube, which gave his kingdom its name, but in the Slavonic districts further West and South. The centre of his realm was the fortress of Ochrida, which he had chosen as his capital—a strong town situated on a lake among the Macedonian hills. There Samuel mustered his armies, and from thence he started forth to attach either Thessalonica or Adrianople, as the opportunity might come to him.

The duel between Basil and Samuel lasted no less than thirty-four years, till the Bulgarian king died a beaten man in 1014. This long and unremitting struggle taxed all the energies of the empire, for Samuel was not a foe to be despised; he was no mere barbarian, but had learnt the art of war from his Byzantine neighbours, and had specially studied fortification. It was the desperate defences of his numerous hill-castles that made Basil's task such a long one. The details of the struggle are too long to follow out: suffice it to say that after some defeats in his earlier years, Basil accomplished the conquest of Bulgaria proper, as far as the Danube, in 1002, the year in which Widdin, the last of Samuel's strongholds in the North surrendered to him. For twelve years more the enemy held out in the Central Balkans, in his Macedonian strongholds, about Ochrida and Uskup. But at last, Basil's constant victories in the field, and his relentless slaughter of captives after the day was won, broke the force of the Bulgarian king. In 1014 the Emperor gained a crowning victory, after which he took 15,000 prisoners: he put out the eyes of all save one man in each hundred, and sent the poor wretches with their guides to seek King Samuel in his capital. The old Bulgarian was so overcome at the horrible sight that he was seized with a fit, and died on the spot, of rage and grief. His successors Gabriel and Ladislas could make no head against the stern and relentless emperor, and in 1018 the last fortress of the kingdom of Ochrida surrendered at discretion. Contrary to his habit, Basil treated the vanquished foe with mildness, indulged in no massacres, and contented himself with repairing the old Roman roads and fortresses of the Central Balkans, without attempting to exterminate the Slavonic tribes that had so often defied him. His conquests rounded off the empire on its northern frontier, and made it touch the Magyar kingdom of Hungary, for Servia no less than Bulgaria and Macedonia formed part of his conquests. The Byzantine border now ran from Belgrade to the Danube mouth, a line which it was destined to preserve for nearly two hundred years, till the great rebellion of Bulgaria against Isaac Angelus in the year 1086.

Having justly earned his grim title of "the Slayer of the Bulgarians" by his long series of victories in Europe, Basil turned in his old age to continue the work of John Zimisces on the Eastern frontier. There the Moslem states were still weak and divided; though a new power, the Fatimite dynasty in Egypt, had come to the front, and acquired an ascendency over its neighbours. Basil's last campaigns, in 1021-2, were directed against the princes of Armenia, and the Iberians and Abasgians who dwelt beyond them to the north. His arms were entirely successful, and he added many Armenian districts to his Eastern provinces; but it may be questioned whether these conquests were beneficial to the empire. A strong Armenian kingdom was a useful neighbour to the Byzantine realm; being a Christian state it was usually friendly to the empire, and acted as a barrier against Moslem attacks from Persia. Basil broke up the Armenian power, but did not annex the whole country, or establish in it any adequate provision against the ultimate danger of attacks from the East by the Mahometan powers.

Basil died in 1025 at the age of sixty-eight, just as he was preparing to send forth an expedition to rescue Sicily from the hands of the Saracens. He had won more provinces for the empire than any general since the days of the great Belisarius, and at his death the Byzantine borders had reached the furthest extension which they ever knew. His successors were to be unworthy of his throne, and were destined to lose provinces with as constant regularity as he himself had shown in gaining them. There was to be no one after him who could boast that he had fought thirty campaigns in the open field with harness on his back, and had never turned aside from any enterprise that he had ever taken in hand.

Basil's brother Constantine had been his colleague in name all through the half century of his reign. No one could have been more unlike the ascetic and indefatigable "Slayer of the Bulgarians." Constantine was a mere worldling, a man of pleasure, a votary of the table and the wine cup, whose only redeeming tastes were a devotion to music and literature. He had dwelt in his corner of the palace surrounded by a little court of eunuchs and flatterers, and excluded by the stern Basil from all share and lot in the administration of the empire. Now Constantine found himself the heir of his childless brother, and was forced at the age of sixty to take up the responsibilities of empire. He proved an idle and incompetent, but not an actively mischievous sovereign. His worst act was to hand over the administration of the chief offices of state to six of his old courtiers—all eunuchs—whose elevation was a cause of wild anger to the great noble families, and whose inexperience led to much weak and futile government during his short reign.

Constantine died in 1028, after a very brief taste of empire. He was the last male of the Macedonian house, and left no heirs save his elderly unmarried daughters—whose education and moral training he had grossly neglected. Zoe, the eldest, was more than forty years of age, but her father had never found her a husband. On his death-bed, however, he sent for a middle-aged noble named Romanus Argyrus, and forced him, at an hour's notice, to wed the princess. Only two days later Romanus found himself left, by his father-in-law's death, titular head of the empire. But Zoe, a clever, obstinate, and unscrupulous woman, kept the reins of authority in her own hands, and gave her unwilling spouse many an evil hour. She was inordinately vain, and pretended, like Queen Elizabeth of England, to be the mistress of all hearts long after she was well advanced in middle age. Her husband let her go her own way, and devoted himself to such affairs of state as he was allowed to manage. His interference with warlike matters was most unhappy. Venturing a campaign in Syria, he led his army to defeat, and saw several towns on the border fall into the hands of the Emir of Aleppo. After a reign of six years Romanus died of a lingering disease, and Zoe was left a widow. Almost before the breath was out of her husband's body, the volatile empress—she was now over fifty—had chosen and wedded another partner. The new emperor was Michael the Paphlagonian, a young courtier who had been Gentleman of the Bedchamber to Romanus: he was twenty-eight years of age and noted as the most handsome man in Constantinople. His good looks had won Zoe's fancy, and to his own surprise he found himself seated on the throne by his elderly admirer [1034].

The object of Zoe's anile affection was a capable man, and justified his rather humiliating elevation by good service to the empire. He beat back the Saracens from Syria and put down a Bulgarian rebellion with success. But in his last years he saw Servia, one of the conquests of Basil II., burst out into revolt, and could not quell it. He also failed in a project to reconquer Sicily from the Moors, though he sent against the island George Maniakes, the best general of the day, who won many towns and defeated the Moslems in two pitched battles. The attempt to subdue the whole island failed, and the conquests of Maniakes were lost one after the other.

Michael IV., though still a young man, was fearfully afflicted with epileptic fits, which sapped his health, and so enfeebled him that he died a hopeless invalid ere he reached the age of thirty-six. The irrepressible Zoe, now again a widow, took a few days to decide whether she would adopt a son, or marry a third husband. She first tried the former alternative, and crowned as her colleague her late spouse's nephew and namesake Michael V. But the young man proved ungrateful, and strove to deprive the aged empress of the control of affairs. When he announced his intention of removing her from the capital, the city mob, who loved the Macedonian house, and laughed at rather than reprobated the foibles of Zoe, took arms to defend their mistress. In a fierce fight between the rioters and the guards of Michael V., 3,000 lives were lost: but the insurgents had the upper hand, routed the soldiery, and caught and blinded Michael.

Zoe, once more at the head of the state, now made her third marriage, at the age of sixty-two. She chose as her partner Constantine Monomachus, an old debauchee who had been her lover thirty years ago. Their joint reign was unhappy both at home and abroad. Frequent rebellions broke out both in Asia Minor and in the Balkan Peninsula. The Patzinaks sent forays across the Danube, while a new enemy, the Normans of South Italy, conquered the "theme of Langobardia," the last Byzantine possession to the West of the Adriatic, and established in its stead the duchy of Apulia [1055]. A still more dangerous foe began also to be heard of along the Eastern frontier. The Seljouk Turks were now commencing a career of conquest in Persia and the lands on the Oxus. In 1048 the advance guard of their hordes began to ravage the Armenian frontier of the empire. But this danger was not yet a pressing one.

When Zoe and Constantine IX. were dead, the sole remaining scion of the Macedonian house was saluted as ruler of the empire. This was Theodora, the younger sister of Zoe, an old woman of seventy, who had spent the best part of her days in a nunnery. She was as sour and ascetic as her sister had been vain and amorous; but she does not seem to have been the worst of the rulers of Byzantium, and her two years of power were not troubled by rebellions or vexed by foreign war. Her austere virtues won her some respect from the people, and the fact that she was the last of her house, and that with its extinction the troubles of a disputed succession were doomed to come upon the empire, seems to have sobered her subjects, and led them to let the last days of the Basilian dynasty pass away in peace.

Theodora died on the 30th of August, 1057, having on her death-bed declared that she adopted Michael Stratioticus as her successor. Then commenced the reign of trouble, the "third anarchy" in the history of the Byzantine Empire.

XX. Manzikert. (1057-1081.)

The moment that the last of the Macedonian dynasty was gone, the elements of discord seemed unchained, and the double scourge of civil war and foreign invasion began to afflict the empire. In the twenty-four years between 1057 and 1081 were pressed more disasters than had been seen in any other period of East-Roman history, save perhaps the reign of Heraclius. For now came the second cutting-short of the empire, the blow that was destined to shear away half its strength, and leave it maimed beyond any possibility of ultimate recovery.

Domestic troubles were the first inevitable consequence of the extinction of the Macedonian dynasty. The aged Theodora had named as her successor on the throne Michael Stratioticus, a contemporary of her own who had been an able soldier twenty-five years back. But Michael VI. was grown aged and incompetent, and the empire was full of ambitious generals, who would not tolerate a dotard on the throne. Before a year had passed a band of great Asiatic nobles entered into a conspiracy to overturn Michael, and replace him by Isaac Comnenus, the chief of one of the ancient Cappadocian houses, and the most popular general of the East.

Isaac Comnenus and his friends took arms, and dispossessed the aged Michael of his throne with little difficulty. But a curse seemed to rest upon the usurpation; Isaac was stricken down by disease when he had been little more than a year on the throne, and retired to a monastery to die. His crown was transferred to Constantine Ducas, another Cappadocian noble, who was supposed to be second only to Isaac in competence and popularity. Constantine reigned for seven troubled years, and disappointed all his supporters, for he proved but a sorry administrator. His mind was set on nothing but finance, and in the endeavour to build up again the imperial treasure, which had been sorely wasted since the death of Basil II., he neglected all the other departments of state. To save money he disbanded no inconsiderable portion of the army, and cut down the pay of the rest. This was sheer madness, when there was impending over the empire the most terrible military danger that had been seen for four centuries. The safety of the realm was entirely in the hands of its well-paid and well-disciplined national army, and anything that impaired the efficiency of the army was fraught with the deadliest peril.

The Seljouk Turks were now drawing near. Pressing on from the Oxus lands, their hordes had overrun Persia and extinguished the dynasty of the Buhawides. In 1050, they had penetrated to Bagdad, and their great chief, Togrul Beg, had declared himself "defender of the faith and protector of the Caliph." Armenia had next been overrun, and those portions of it which had not been annexed to the empire, and still obeyed independent princes, had been conquered by 1064. In that year fell Ani, the ancient Armenian capital, and the bulwark which protected the Byzantine Empire from Eastern invasions.

The reign of Constantine Ducas was troubled by countless Seljouk invasions of the Armeniac, Anatolic, and Cappadocian themes. Sometimes the invaders were driven back, sometimes they eluded the imperial troops and escaped with their booty. But whether successful or unsuccessful, they displayed a reckless cruelty, far surpassing anything that the Saracens had ever shown. Wherever they passed they not merely plundered to right and left, but slew off the whole population. Meanwhile, Constantine X., with his reduced army, proved incompetent to hold them back; all the more so that his operations were distracted by an invasion of the Uzes, a Tartar tribe from the Euxine shore, who had burst into Bulgaria.

Ducas died in 1067, leaving the throne to his son, Michael, a boy of fourteen years. The usual result followed. To secure her son's life and throne, the Empress-dowager Eudocia took a new husband, and made him guardian of the young Michael. The new Emperor-regent was Romanus Diogenes, an Asiatic noble, whose brilliant courage displayed in the Seljouk wars had dazzled the world, and caused it to forget that caution and ability are far more regal virtues than headlong valour. Romanus took in hand with the greatest vigour the task of repelling the Turks, which his predecessor had so grievously neglected. He led into the field every man that could be collected from the European or Asiatic themes, and for three successive years was incessantly marching and counter-marching in Armenia, Cappadocia, and Syria, in the endeavour to hunt down the marauding bands of the Seljouks.

The operations of Romanus were not entirely unsuccessful. Alp Arslan, the Sultan of the Seljouks, contented himself at first with dispersing his hordes in scattered bands, and attacking many points of the frontier at once. Hence the Emperor was not unfrequently able to catch and slay off one of the minor divisions of the Turkish army. But some of them always contrived to elude him; his heavy cavalry could not come up with the light Seljouk horse bowmen, who generally escaped and rode back home by a long detour, burning and murdering as they went. Cappadocia was already desolated from end to end, and the Turkish raids had reached as far as Amorium, in Phrygia.

In 1071 came the final disaster. In pursuing the Seljouk plunderers, Romanus was drawn far eastward, to Manzikert, on the Armenian frontier. There he found himself confronted, not by a flying foe, but by the whole force of the Seljouk sultanate, with Alp Arslan himself at its head. Though his army was harassed by long marches, and though two large divisions were absent, the Emperor was eager to fight. The Turks had never before offered him a fair field, and he relied implicitly on the power of his cuirassiers to ride down any number, however great, of the light Turkish horse.

OUR LORD BLESSING ROMANUS DIOGENES AND EUDOCIA.

(From an Ivory at Paris.)

(From "L'Art Byzantin." Par Charles Bayet. Paris, Quantin, 1883.)

The decisive battle of Manzikert, which it is not too much to call the turning-point of the whole course of Byzantine history, was fought in the early summer of 1071. For a long day the Byzantine horsemen continued to roll back and break through the lines of Turkish horse bowmen. But fresh hordes kept coming on, and in the evening the fight was still undecided. As the night was approaching, Romanus prepared to draw his troops back to the camp, but an unhappy misconception of orders broke up the line, and the Seljouks edged in between the two halves of the army. Either from treachery or cowardice Andronicus Ducas, the officer who commanded the reserve, led his men off without fighting. The Emperor's division was beset on all sides by the enemy, and broke up in the dusk. Romanus himself was wounded, thrown from his horse, and made prisoner. The greater part of his men were cut to pieces.

NICEPHORUS BOTANIATES SITTING IN STATE.
(*From a contemporary MS.*)
(*From "L'Art Byzantin." Par Charles Bayet. Paris, Quantin*, 1883.)

Alp Arslan showed himself more forbearing to his prisoner than might have been expected. It is true that Romanus was led after his capture to the tent of the Sultan, and laid prostrate before him, that, after the Turkish custom, the conqueror might place his foot on the neck of his vanquished foe. But after this humiliating ceremony the Emperor was treated with kindness, and allowed after some months to ransom himself and return home. He would have fared better, however, if he had remained the prisoner of the Turk. During his captivity the conduct of affairs had fallen into the hands of John Ducas, uncle of the young emperor Michael. The unscrupulous regent was determined that Romanus should not supersede him and mount the throne again. When the released captive reappeared, John had him seized and blinded. The cruel work was so roughly done that the unfortunate Romanus died a few days later.

After this fearful disaster Asia Minor was lost; there was no chief to take the place of Romanus, and the Seljouk hordes spread westward almost unopposed. The next ten years were a time of chaos and disaster. While the Seljouks were carving their way deeper and deeper into the vitals of the empire, the wrecks of the Byzantine army were employed not in resisting them, but in carrying on a desperate series of civil wars. After the death of Romanus, every general in the empire seemed to think that the time had come for him to assume the purple buskins and proclaim himself emperor. History records the names of no less than six pretenders to the throne during the next nine years, besides several rebels who took up arms without assuming the imperial title. The young emperor, Michael Ducas, proved, when he came of age, to be a vicious nonentity; he is remembered in Byzantine history only by his nickname of Para-pinakes, the "peck-filcher," given him because in a year of famine he sold the measure of wheat to his subjects a fourth short of its proper contents. His name and that of Nicephorus Botaniates, the rebel who overthrew him, cover in the list of emperors a space of ten years that would better be represented by a blank; for the authority of the nominal ruler scarcely extended beyond the walls of the capital, and the themes that were not overrun by the Turks were in the hands of governors who each did what was right in his own eyes. At last a man of ability worked himself up to the surface. This was Alexius Comnenus, nephew of the emperor Isaac Comnenus, whose short reign we related in the opening paragraph of this chapter.

Alexius was a man of courage and ability, but he displayed one of the worst types of Byzantine character. Indeed, he was the first emperor to whom the epithet "Byzantine," in its common and opprobrious sense could be applied. He was the most accomplished liar of his age, and, while winning and defending the imperial throne, committed enough acts of mean treachery, and swore enough false oaths to startle even the courtiers of Constantinople. He could fight when necessary, but he preferred to win by treason and perjury. Yet as a ruler he had many virtues, and it will always be remembered to his credit that he dragged the empire out of the deepest slough of degradation and ruin that it had ever sunk into. Though false, he was not cruel, and seven ex-emperors and usurpers, living unharmed in Constantinople under his sceptre, bore witness to the mildness of his rule. The tale of his reign sufficiently bears witness to the strange mixture of moral obliquity and practical ability in his character.

XXI. The Comneni And The Crusades.

Alexius Comnenus found himself, in 1081, placed in a position almost as difficult and perilous as that which Leo the Isaurian faced in 716. Like Leo, he was a usurper without prestige or hereditary claims, seated on an unsteady throne, and forced to face imminent danger from the Moslem enemy without, and from rival adventurers within. It may be added that the Isaurian, grievously threatened as he was by the enemy from the East, had no peril impending from the West. Alexius had to face at one and the same time the assault of the Seljouks on Asia Minor, and the attack of a new and formidable foe in his western provinces. We have already mentioned the manner in which the Byzantine dominion in Italy had come to an end. Now the same Norman adventurers who had stripped the empire of Calabria and Apulia were preparing to cross the straits of Otranto, and seek out the Emperor in the central provinces of his realm. The forces of the Italian and Sicilian Normans were united under their great chief Robert Guiscard, the hardy and unscrupulous Duke of Apulia. Just ten years before he had captured Bari, the last Byzantine fortress on his own side of the straits; now he was resolved to take advantage of the anarchy which had prevailed in the empire ever since the day of Manzikert, and to build up new Norman principalities to the east of the Adriatic. There seemed to be nothing presumptuous in the scheme to those who remembered how a few hundred Norman adventurers had conquered all Southern Italy and Sicily, and swelled into a victorious army fifty thousand strong. Nor could the invaders fail to remember how, but fifteen years before, another Norman duke had crossed another strait in the far West, and won by his strong right hand the great kingdom of England. Alexius Comnenus sat like Harold Godwinson on a lately-acquired and unsteady throne, and Duke Robert thought to deal with him much as Duke William had dealt with the Englishman.

In June, 1081, the Normans landed, thirty thousand strong, and laid siege to Durazzo, the maritime fortress that guarded the Epirot coast. The Emperor at once flew to its succour. Always active, hopeful, and versatile, he trusted that he might be able to beat off the new invaders, whose military worth he was far from appreciating at its true value. He patched up a hasty pacification with Suleiman, Sultan of the Seljouks, by surrendering to him all the territory of which the Turk was in actual possession, a tract which now extended as far as the waters of the Propontis, and actually included the city of Nicaea, close to the Bithynian shore, and only seventy miles from Constantinople.

The army with which Alexius had to face the Normans was the mere wreck and shadow of that which Romanus IV. had led against the Turks ten years before. The military organization of the empire had gone to pieces, and we no longer hear of the old "Themes" of heavy cavalry which had formed its backbone. The new army contained quite a small proportion of national troops. Its core was the imperial guard of Varangians—the Russian, Danish, and English mercenaries, whose courage had won the confidence of so many emperors. With them marched many Turkish, Frankish, Servian, and South-Slavonic auxiliaries; the native element comprised the regulars of the three provinces of Thrace, Macedonia, and Thessaly, all that now remained in Alexius' hands of the ancient East-Roman realm.

Alexius brought Robert Guiscard to battle in front of Durazzo, and suffered a crushing defeat at his hands. The Emperor's bad tactics were the main cause of his failure: his army came upon the ground in successive detachments, and the van was cut to pieces before the main body had reached the field. The brunt of the battle was borne by the Varangians: carried away by their fiery courage, they charged the Normans before the rest of Alexius's troops had formed their line of battle. Rushing on the wing of Robert's army, commanded by the Count of Bari, they drove it horse and foot into the sea. Their success, however, disordered their ranks, and the Norman duke was able to turn his whole force against them ere the Emperor was near enough to give them aid. A fierce cavalry charge cut off the greater part of the Varangians; the rest collected on a mound by the sea-shore, and for some time beat off the Normans with their axes, as King Harold's men had done at Senlac on the last occasion when English and Norman had met. But Robert shot them down with his archers, and then sent more cavalry against them. They fell, save a small remnant who defended themselves in a ruined chapel, which Guiscard had finally to burn before he could make an end of its obstinate defenders.

The rest of Alexius's army only came into action when the Varangians had been destroyed. It was cowed by the loss of its best corps, fought badly, and fled in haste. Alexius himself, who lingered last upon the field, was surrounded, and only escaped by the speed of his horse and the strength of his sword-arm. Durazzo fell, and in the next year the Normans overran all Epirus and descended into Thessaly. Alexius risked two more engagements with them, but his inexperienced troops were defeated in both. Disaster taught him to avoid pitched battles, and at last, in 1083, after a more cautious campaign, his patience was rewarded by the dispersion of the Norman army. Catching it while divided, the Emperor inflicted on it a severe defeat at Larissa, and forced it back into Epirus. After this the war slackened, and when Robert Guiscard died in 1085 the Norman danger passed away.

Thus one foe was removed, but Alexius was not destined to win peace. Constant rebellions at home, and wars with the Patzinaks, the Slavs, and the Seljouks filled the next ten years. Alexius, however, was never discouraged: "eking out the lion's skin with the fox's hide," he fought and intrigued, lied and negotiated, and at the end of the time had held his own and lost no more territory, while his throne was growing more secure.

But in the fifteenth year of his reign a new cloud began to arise in the west, which was destined to exercise unsuspected influence, both for good and evil, on the empire. The Crusades were on the eve of their commencement. Ever since the Seljouks had taken Jerusalem in 1075, four years after Manzikert, the western pilgrims to the Holy Land had been suffering grievous things at the hands of the barbarians. But all thc wrath that their ill-treatment provoked would have been fruitless, if the way to Syria had not been opened of late to the nations of Western Christendom. Two series of events had made free communication between East and West possible in the end of the eleventh century, in a measure which had never before been seen.

START

COMMUNICATION BETWEEN EAST & WEST

The first of these was the conversion of Hungary, begun by St. Stephen in 1000, and completed about 1050. For the future there lay between the Byzantine Empire and Germany not a barbarous pagan state, but a semi-civilized Christian kingdom, which had taken its place among the other nations of the Roman Catholic faith. Communication down the Danube, between Vienna and the Byzantine outposts in Bulgaria, became for the first time possible, and ere long the route grew popular. The second phenomenon which made the Crusades possible was the destruction of the Saracen naval power in the Central Mediterranean. This was carried out first by the Pisans and Genoese, whose fleets conquered Corsica and Sardinia from the Moslems, and then by the Normans, whose occupation of Sicily made the voyage from Marseilles and Genoa to the East safe and sure. Four new maritime powers—the Genoese, Pisans, and Normans in the open sea, and the Venetians in the Adriatic—had developed themselves into importance, and now their fleets swept the waters where no Christian war-galleys save those of Byzantium, had ever been seen before.

It was the fact that free access to the East was now to be gained, both by land and sea, as it had never been before, that made the Crusades feasible. Of the preaching of Peter the Hermit and the efforts of Pope Urban we need not speak. Suffice it to say, that in 1095 news came to the Emperor Alexius that the nations of the West were mustering by myriads, and directing their march towards his frontiers, with the expressed intention of driving the Moslems from Palestine. The Emperor had little confidence in the purity of the zeal of the Crusaders; his wily mind could not comprehend their enthusiasm, and he dreaded that some unforeseen circumstance might turn their arms against himself. When the hordes of armed Frankish pilgrims began to arrive, his fears were justified: the new-comers pillaged his country right and left upon their way, and were drawn into many bloody fights with the peasantry and the imperial garrisons, which might have ended in open war. But Alexius set himself to work to smooth matters down; all his tact and patience were needed, and there was ample scope for his talent for intrigue and insincere diplomacy. He had resolved to induce the crusading chiefs to do him homage, and to swear to restore to him all the old dominions of the empire which they might reconquer from the Turks. After long and tedious negotiations he had his way: the leaders of the Crusade, from Godfrey of Bouillon and Hugh of Vermandois down to the smallest barons, were induced to swear him allegiance. Some he flattered, others he bribed, others he strove to frighten into compliance. The pages of the history written by his daughter, Anna Comnena, who regarded his powers of cajolery with greater respect than any other part of his character, are full of tales of the ingenious shifts by which he brought the stupid and arrogant Franks to reason. At length they went on their way, with Alexius's gold in their pockets, and encouraged by his promise that he would aid them with his troops, continue to supply them with provisions, and never abandon them till the Holy City was reconquered.

In the spring of 1097 the Crusaders began to cross the Bosphorus, and in two marches found themselves within Turkish territory. They at once laid siege to Nicaea, the frontier fortress of the Seljouk Sultan. Encompassed by so great a host the Turkish garrison soon lost heart and surrendered, not to the Franks, but to Alexius, whose troops they secretly admitted within the walls. This nearly led to strife between the Emperor and the Crusaders, who had been reckoning on the plunder of the town; but Alexius appeased them with further stores of money, and the pilgrim host rolled forward once more into the interior of Asia Minor.

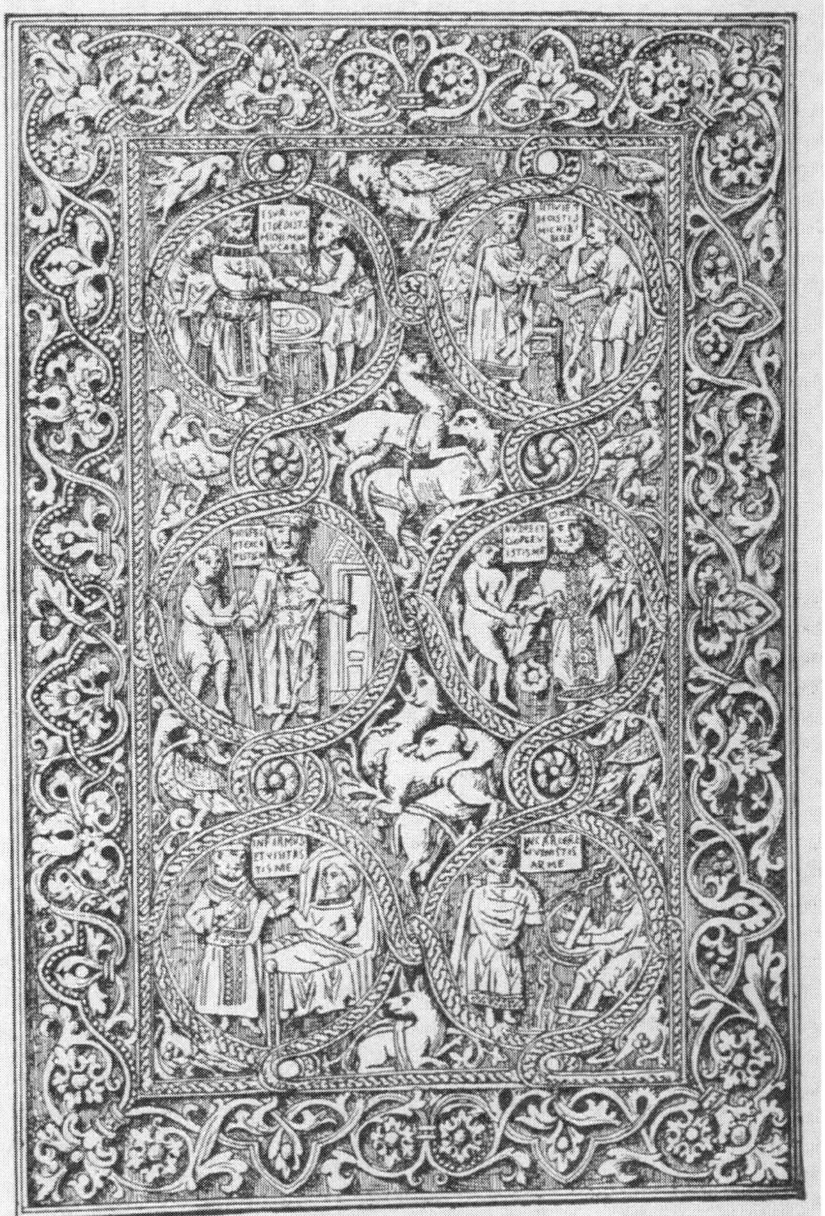

BYZANTINE IVORY-CARVING OF THE TWELFTH CENTURY.
(*From the British Museum.*)
(*From "L'Art Byzantin." Par Charles Bayet. Paris, Quantin,* 1883.)

In 1097 the Crusaders forced their way through Phrygia and Cappadocia, beating back the Seljouks at every encounter, till they reached North Syria, where they laid siege to Antioch. Alexius had undertaken to help them in their campaign, but he was set on playing an easier game. When they were crushing the Turks he followed in their rear at a safe distance, like the jackal behind the lion, picking up the spoil which they left. While the Sultan was engaged with them Alexius despoiled him of Smyrna, Ephesus, and Sardis, reconquering Western Asia Minor almost without a blow, since the Seljouk hordes were drawn away eastward. It was the same in the next year; when the Crusaders were fighting hard round Antioch against the princes of Mesopotamia, and sent to ask for instant help, Alexius despatched no troops to Syria, but gathered in a number of Lydian and Phrygian fortresses which lay nearer to his hand. Hence there resulted a bitter quarrel between the Emperor and the Franks, for since he gave them no help they refused to hand over to him Antioch and their other Syrian conquests. Each party, in fact, broke the compact signed at Constantinople, and accused the other of treachery. Hence it resulted that the Crusade ended not in the re-establishment of the Byzantine power in Syria, but in the foundation of new Frankish states, the principalities of Edessa, Antioch, and Tripoli, and the more important kingdom of Jerusalem.

That he did not recover Syria was no real loss to Alexius; he would not have been strong enough to hold it, had it been handed over to him. The actual profit which he made by the Crusade was enough to content him: the Franks had rolled back the Turkish frontier in Asia not less than two hundred miles: instead of the Seljouk lying at Nicaea, he was now chased back behind the Bithynian hills, and the empire had recovered all Lydia and Caria with much of the Phrygian inland. The Seljouks were hard hit, and for well-nigh a century were reduced to fight on the defensive.

Owing, then, to the fearful blow inflicted by the Crusades on the Moslem powers of Asia Minor and Syria, the later years of Alexius were free from the danger which had overshadowed the beginning of his reign. He was able, between 1100 and 1118, to strengthen his position at home and abroad; the constant rebellions which had vexed his early years ceased, and when the Normans, under Bohemund of Tarentum, tried to repeat, in 1107, the feats which Robert Guiscard had accomplished in 1082, they were beaten off with ease, and forced to conclude a disadvantageous peace.

The reign of Alexius might have been counted a period of success and prosperity if it had not been for two considerations. The first was the rapid decline of Constantinople as a commercial centre, which was brought about by the Crusades. When the Genoese and Venetians succeeded in establishing themselves in the seaports of Syria, they began to visit Constantinople far less than before. It paid them much better to conduct their business at Acre or Tyre than on the Bosphorus. The king of Jerusalem, the weakest of feudal sovereigns, could be more easily bullied and defrauded than the powerful ruler of Constantinople. In his own seaports he possessed hardly a shadow of authority: the Italians traded there on such conditions as they chose. Hence the commerce of the West with Persia, Egypt, Syria, and India, ceased to pass through the Bosphorus. Genoa and Venice became the marts at which France, Italy, and Germany, sought their Eastern goods. It is probable that the trade of Constantinople fell off by a third or even a half in the fifty years that followed the first Crusade. The effect of this decline on the coffers of the state was deplorable, for it was ultimately on its commercial wealth that the Byzantine state based its prosperity. All through the reigns of Alexius and his two successors the complaints about the rapid fall in the imperial revenue grew more and more noticeable.

This dangerous decay in the finances of the empire was rendered still more fatal by the political devices of Alexius, who began to bestow excessive commercial privileges to the Italian republics, in return for their aid in war. This system commenced in 1081, when the Emperor, then in the full stress of his first Norman war, granted the Venetians the free access to most of the ports of his empire without the payment of any customs dues. To give to foreigners a boon denied to his own subjects was the height of economic lunacy; the native merchants complained that the Venetians were enabled to undersell them in every market, owing to this exemption from import and export duties. Matters were made yet worse in 1111, when Alexius bestowed a similar, though less extensive, grant of immunities on the Pisans.

When John II., the son of Alexius, succeeded in 1118 to the empire which his father had saved, the fabric was less strong than it appeared to the outward eye. Territorial extension seemed to imply increased strength, and the rapid falling off in the financial resources of the realm attracted little attention. John however was one of those prudent and economical princes who stave off for years the inevitable day of distress. Of all the rulers who ever sat upon the Byzantine throne, he is the only one of whom no detractor has ever said an evil word. When we remember that he was his father's son, it is astonishing to find that his honesty and good faith were no less notable than his courage and generosity. His subjects named him "John the Good," and their appreciation of his virtues was sufficiently marked by the fact that no single rebellion[26] marred the internal peace of his long reign. [1118-1143.]

John was a good soldier, and during his rule the frontier of the empire in Asia continued to advance, at the expense of the Turks. But his strategy would seem to have been at fault since he preferred to reconquer the coast districts of Northern and Southern Asia Minor, rather than to strike at the heart of the Seljouk power on the central table-land. When he had reduced all Cilicia, Pisidia, and Pontus, his dominions became a narrow fringe of coast, surrounding on three sides the realm of the Sultan, who still retained all the Cappadocian and Lycaonian plateau. It should then have been John's task to finish the reconquest of Asia Minor, but he preferred to plunge into Syria, where he forced the Frank prince of Antioch and the Turkish Emir of Aleppo to pay him tribute, but left no permanent monument of his conquests. He was preparing a formidable expedition against the Franks of the kingdom of Jerusalem, when he perished by accident while on a hunting expedition.[27]

John the Good was succeeded by his son Manuel, whose strength and weakness combined to give a deathblow to the empire. Manuel was a mere knight-errant, who loved fighting for fighting's sake, and allowed his passion for excitement and adventure to be his only guide. His whole reign was one long series

[26] There were two place intrigues against him, both headed by members of his own family. Neither of them won any support from people of army.

[27] He pierced himself by misadventure with one of his own poisoned arrows, and died of the wound.

of wars, entered into and abandoned with equal levity. Yet for the most part they were successful wars, for Manuel was a good cavalry officer if he was but a reckless statesman, and his fiery courage and untiring energy made him the idol of his troops. At the head of the veteran squadrons of mercenary horsemen that formed the backbone of his army, he swept off the field every enemy that ever dared to face him. He overran Servia, invaded Hungary, to whose king he dictated terms of peace, and beat off with success an invasion of Greece by the Normans of Sicily. His most desperate struggle, however, was a naval war with Venice, in which his fleet was successful enough, and drove the Doge and his galleys out of the Ægean. But the damage done to the trade of Constantinople by the Venetian privateers, who swarmed in the Levant after their main fleet had been chased away, was so appalling that the Emperor concluded peace in 1174, restoring to the enemy all the disastrous commercial privileges which his grandfather Alexius had granted them eight years before.

HUNTERS

(*From a Byzantine MS.*)

(*From "L'Art Byzantin."* *Par Charles Bayet* *Paris, Quantin,* 1883.)

The main fault of Manuel's wars was that they were conducted in the most reckless disregard of all financial considerations. With a realm which was slowly growing poorer, and with a constantly dwindling revenue, he persisted in piling war on war, and on devoting every bezant that could be screwed out of his subjects to the support of the army alone. The civil service fell into grave disorder, the administration of justice was impaired, roads and bridges went to decay, docks and harbours were neglected, while the money which should have supported them was wasted on unprofitable expeditions to Egypt, Syria, or Italy. So long as the ranks of his mercenaries were full and their pay forthcoming, the Emperor cared not how his realm might fare.

Of all Manuel's wars only one went ill, but that was the most important of them all, the one necessary struggle to which he should have devoted all his energies. This was the contest with the Seljouks, which ended in 1176 by a disastrous defeat at Myriokephalon in Phrygia, brought about by the inexcusable carelessness of Manuel himself, who allowed his army to be caught in a defile from which there was no exit, and routed piecemeal by an enemy who could have made no stand on the open plains. Manuel then made peace, and left the Seljouks alone for the rest of his reign.

In 1180 Manuel died, and with him died the good fortune of the House of Comnenus. His son and heir, Alexius, was a boy of thirteen, and the inevitable contest for the regency, which always accompanied a minority, ensued. After two troubled years Andronicus Comnenus, a first cousin of the Emperor Manuel, was proclaimed Caesar, and took over the guardianship of the young Alexius. Andronicus was an unscrupulous ruffian, whose past life should have been sufficient warning against putting any trust in his professions. He had once attempted to assassinate Manuel, and twice deserted to the Turks. But he was a consummate hypocrite, and won his way to the throne by professions of piety and austere virtue. No sooner was he seated by the side of Alexius II., and felt himself secure, than he seized and strangled his young relative [1183].

But, like our own Richard III., Andronicus found that the moment of his accession to sole power was the moment of the commencement of his troubles. Rebels rose in arms all over the empire to avenge the murdered Alexius, and the Normans of Sicily seized the opportunity of invading Macedonia. Conspiracies were rife in the capital, and the executions which followed their detection were so numerous and bloody that a perfect reign of terror set in. The Emperor plunged into the most reckless cruelty, till men almost began to believe that his mind was affected. Ere long the end came. An inoffensive nobleman named Isaac Angelus, being accused of treason, was arrested at his own door by the emissaries of the tyrant. Instead of surrendering himself, Isaac drew his sword and cut down the official who laid hands on him. A mob came to his aid, and met no immediate opposition, for Andronicus was absent from the capital. The mob swelled into a multitude, the guards would not fight, and when the Emperor returned in haste, he was seized and torn to pieces without a sword being drawn in his cause. Isaac Angelus reigned in his stead.

XXII. The Latin Conquest Of Constantinople.

The state which had been drained of its resources by the energetic but wasteful Manuel, and disorganized by the rash and wicked Andronicus, now passed into the hands of the two most feeble and despicable creatures who ever sat upon the imperial throne—the brothers Isaac and Alexius Angelus, whose reigns cover the years 1185-1204.

Among all the periods which we have hitherto described in the tale of the East-Roman Empire, that covered by the reign of the two wretched Angeli may be pronounced the most shameful. The peculiar disgrace of the period lies in the fact that the condition of the empire was not hopeless at the time. With ordinary courage and prudence it might have been held together, for the attacks directed against it were not more formidable than others which had been beaten off with ease. If the blow had fallen when a hero like Leo III., or even a statesman like Alexius I. was on the throne, there is no reason to doubt that it would have been parried. But it fell in the times of two incompetent triflers, who conducted the state on the principle of, "Let us eat and drink, for tomorrow we die." Isaac and Alexius felt in themselves no power of redeeming the empire from the evil day, and resignedly fell back on personal enjoyment. Isaac's taste lay in the direction of gorgeous raiment and the collecting of miraculous "eikons." Alexius preferred the pleasures of the table. Considered as sovereigns there was little to choose between them. Each was competent to ruin an empire already verging on its decline.

The disaster which the Angeli brought on their realm was rendered possible only by its complete military and financial disorganization. As a military power the empire had never recovered the effects of the Seljouk invasions, which had robbed it of its great recruiting-ground for its native troops in Asia Minor. After that loss the use of mercenaries had become more and more prevalent. The brilliant campaigns of Manuel Comnenus had been made at the head of a soldiery of whom two-thirds were not born-subjects of the empire. He, it is true, had kept them within the bounds of strict discipline, and contrived at all costs to provide their pay. But the weak and thriftless Angeli were able neither to find money nor to maintain discipline. A state which relies for its defence on foreign mercenaries is ruined, if it allows them to grow disorderly and inefficient. In times of stress they mutiny instead of fighting.

The civil administration was in almost as deplorable a condition, while those two "Earthly Angels" (as a contemporary chronicler called them) were charged with its care. Isaac Angelus put the finishing touch to administrative abuses, which had already been rife enough under the Comneni, by exposing offices and posts to auction. Instead of paying his officials he "sent them forth without purse or scrip, like the apostles of old, to make what profit they could by extortion from the provincials."[28] His brother Alexius promised on his accession to make all appointments on the ground of merit, but proved in reality as bad as Isaac. He was surrounded by a ring of rapacious favourites, who managed all patronage, and dispensed it in return for bribes. When high posts were not sold, they were given as douceurs to men of local influence, whose rebellion was dreaded.

The history of the twenty years covered by the reigns of the two Angeli is cut into two equal halves at the deposition of Isaac by his brother in 1195. It is only necessary to point out how the responsibility for the disasters of the period is to be divided between them.

Isaac's share consists in the loss of Bulgaria and Cyprus. The former country had now been in the hands of the Byzantines for nearly two hundred years, since its conquest by Basil II. But the Bulgarians had not merged in the general body of the subjects of the empire. They preserved their national language and customs, and never forgot their ancient independence. In 1187, three brothers named Peter, John, and Azan stirred up rebellion among them. If firmly treated it might have been crushed with ease by the regular troops of the empire. But Isaac first appointed incompetent generals, who let the rebellion grow to a head, and when at last he placed an able officer, Alexis Branas, in command, his lieutenant took the opportunity of using his army for revolt. Branas marched against Constantinople, and would have taken it, had not Isaac committed the charge of the troops that remained faithful to him to stronger hands than his own. He bribed an able adventurer from the West, Conrad, Marquis of Montferrat, by the offer of his sister's hand and a great sum of money to become his saviour. The gallant Lombard routed the forces of Branas, slew the usurper, and preserved the throne for his brother-in-law. But while the civil war was going on, the Bulgarians were left unchecked, and made such head that there was no longer much apparent chance of subduing them. Isaac took the field against them in person, only to see the great towns of Naissus, Sophia, and Varna taken before his eyes.

While a national revolt deprived the Emperor of Bulgaria, Cyprus was lost to a meaner force. Isaac Comnenus, a distant relative of the Emperor Manuel II., raised rebellion among the Cypriots and defeated the fleet and army which his namesake of Constantinople sent against him. He held out for six years, and appeared likely to establish a permanent kingdom in the island. This revolt was of the worst augury to the empire. It had often lost provinces by the invasion of barbarian hordes, or the rebellion of subject nationalities. But that a native rebel should sever a civilized Greek province from the empire, and reign as "Emperor of Cyprus," was a new phenomenon. By the imperial theory the idea of an independent "Empire of Cyprus" was wholly monstrous and abnormal. The successful rebellion of Isaac Comnenus pointed to the possibility of a general breaking up of the Byzantine dominion into fragments, a danger that had never appeared before. Till now the provinces had always obeyed the capital, and no instance had been known of a rebel maintaining himself by any other way than the capture of Constantinople. Isaac Comnenus might, however, have founded a dynasty in Cyprus, if he had not quarrelled with Richard Coeur-de-Lion, the crusading King of England. When he maltreated some shipwrecked English crews, Richard punished him by landing his army in Cyprus and seizing the whole island. Isaac was thrown into a dungeon, and

---

[28] Nicetas, "Isaac Angelus," book iii. ch. 8 6.

the English king gave his dominions to Guy of Lusignan, who called in Frank adventurers to settle up the land, and made it into a feudal kingdom of the usual Western type.

While Isaac II. was in the midst of his Bulgarian war, and misconducting it with his usual fatuity, he was suddenly dethroned by a palace intrigue. His own brother, Alexius Angelus, had hatched a plot against him, which worked so successfully that Isaac was caught, blinded, and immured in a monastery long before his adherents knew that he was in danger.

Alexius III. never showed any other proof of energy save this skilful *coup d`état* aimed against his brother. He continued the Bulgarian war with the same ill-success that had attended Isaac's dealings with it. He plunged into a disastrous struggle with the Seljouk Sultan of Iconium, and he quarrelled with the Emperor Henry VI., who would certainly have invaded his dominions if death had not intervened to prevent it. But as long as Alexius was permitted to enjoy the pleasures of the table in his villas on the Bosphorus, the ill-success abroad of his arms and his diplomacy vexed him but little.

But in 1203, a new and unexpected danger arose to scare him from his feasting. His blind brother Isaac had a young son named Alexius, who escaped from Constantinople to Italy, and took refuge with Philip of Suabia, the new Emperor of the West. Philip had married a daughter of Isaac Angelus, and determined to do something to help his young brother-in-law. The opportunity was not hard to seek. Just at this moment a large body of French, Flemish, and Italian Crusaders, who had taken arms at the command of the Pope, were lying idle at Venice. They had marched down to the great Italian seaport with the intention of directing a blow against Malek-Adel, Sultan of Egypt. The Venetians had contracted to supply them with vessels for the Crusade, but for reasons of their own had determined that the attack should not fall on the shore for which it had been destined. They were on very good terms with the Egyptian sovereign, who had granted them valuable commercial privileges at Alexandria, which threw the whole trade with the distant realms of India into Venetian hands. Accordingly they had determined to avert the blow from Egypt and turn it against some other enemy of Christendom. The leaders of the Fourth Crusade proved unable to pay the full sum which they had contracted to give the Venetians as ship-hire, and this was made an excuse for keeping them camped on the unhealthy islands in the Lagoons till their patience and their stores were alike exhausted. Henry Dandolo, the aged but wily doge, then proposed to the Crusaders that they should pay their way by doing something in aid of Venice. The Dalmatian town of Zara had lately revolted and done homage to the King of Hungary; if the Crusaders would recover it, the Venetian state would wipe out their debts and transport them whither they wished to go.

The Crusaders had taken arms for a holy war against the Moslems. They were now invited to turn aside against a Christian town and interest themselves in Venetian politics. Conscientious men would have refused to join in such an unholy bargain, and would have insisted in carrying out their original purpose against Egypt. But conscientious men had been growing more and more rare among the Crusaders for the last hundred years. There were as many greedy military adventurers among them as single-hearted pilgrims. The more scrupulous chiefs were over-persuaded by their designing companions, and the expedition against Zara was undertaken.

Zara fell, but another and a more important enterprise was then placed before the Crusaders. While they wintered on the Dalmatian coast the young Alexius Angelus appeared in their camp, escorted by the ambassadors of his brother-in-law, the Emperor Philip of Suabia. The exiled prince besought them to turn aside once more before they sailed to the East, and to rescue his blind father from the dungeon into which he had been cast by his cruel brother Alexius III. If they would drive out the usurper and restore the rightful ruler to his throne, they should have anything that the Byzantine Empire could afford to help them for their Crusade—money in plenty, stores, a war fleet, a force of mercenary troops, and his own presence as a helper in the war with Egypt.

Pope Innocent III. had already been storming at the adventurers for shedding Christian blood at Zara, and tampering with their Crusader's oath. But the prospect of Byzantine gold seduced the needy Western barons, and the desire of keeping the war away from Egypt ruled the minds of the Venetians. They hesitated and began to treat with Alexius, though they knew that thereby they were calling down on themselves the terrors of a Papal excommunication. All now depended on the leaders, and among them the abler minds were set on the acceptance of the proposal of the young Byzantine exile. The three chiefs of the Crusade were the Doge Henry Dandolo, Boniface Marquis of Montferrat, and Baldwin Count of Flanders. In Dandolo the ruthless energy of the Italian Republics stood incarnate; he was the one man in the crusading army who knew exactly what he wanted. Old and blind, but clear-headed and inflexible, he was set on revenging an ancient grudge against the Greeks, and on furthering, by any means, good or evil, the fortunes of his native city. Baldwin and Boniface, the two secondary figures in the camp of the Franks, are perfect representations of the two types of crusader. The Fleming, gallant and generous, pious and debonnair, worthy of a more righteous enterprise and a more honourable death, was a true successor of Godfrey of Bouillon, and the heroes of the First Crusade. The Lombard, a deep and hardy schemer, to whom force and fraud seemed equally good, was simply seeking for wealth and fame in the realms of the East. He cared little for the Holy Sepulchre, and much for his own private advancement. Behind these three leaders we descry the motley crowd of the feudal world; relic-hunting abbots in coats of mail, wrangling barons and penniless knights, the half-piratical seamen of Venice, and the brutal soldiery of the West.

VIEW OF CONSTANTINOPLE. (FROM THE SIDE OF THE HARBOUR.)

Boniface of Montferrat and Doge Dandolo gradually talked over the more scrupulous Baldwin and his friends, and the crusading fleet was launched against

Constantinople, after a treaty had been signed which bound Alexius Angelus and his blind father, Isaac II., to pay the Crusaders 200,000 marks of silver, send ten thousand men to Palestine, and acknowledge the supremacy of the Pope over the Eastern Church. In these conditions lay the germs of much future trouble.

The Crusading armament reached the Dardanelles without having to strike a blow. The slothful and luxurious emperor let things slide, and had not even a fleet ready to send against them in the Aegean. He shut himself up in Constantinople, and trusted to the strength of its walls to deliver him, as Heraclius and Leo III. and many more of his predecessors had been delivered. If the siege had been conducted from the land side only, his hopes might have been justified, for the Danes and English of the Varangian Guard beat back the assault of the Franks on the land-wall. But Alexius III., unlike earlier emperors, was attacked by a fleet to which he could oppose no adequate naval resistance. Though the Crusaders were driven off on shore, the Venetians stormed the sea-wall, by the expedient of building light towers on the decks, and throwing flying bridges from the towers on to the top of the Byzantine ramparts. The blind Doge pushed his galley close under the wall, and urged on his men again and again till they had won a lodgment in some towers on the port side of the sea-wall. The Venetians then fired the city, and a fearful conflagration followed.

Hearing that the enemy was within the ramparts, the cowardly Alexius III. mounted his horse and fled away into the inland of Thrace, leaving his troops, who were not yet half beaten, without a leader or a cause to fight for. The garrison bowed to necessity, and the chief officers of the army drew the aged Isaac II. out of his cloister prison and proclaimed his restoration to the throne. They sent to the Crusading camp to announce that hostilities had ceased, and to beg Prince Alexius to enter the city and join his father in the palace.

The end of the expedition of the Crusaders had now been attained, but it may safely be asserted that the chief feeling in their ranks was a bitter disappointment at being cheated out of the sack of Constantinople, a prospect over which they had been gloating ever since they left Zara. They spent the next three months in endeavouring to wring out of their triumphant protégés, Isaac and Alexius, every bezant that could be scraped together. The old emperor, already blind and gout-ridden, was driven to imbecility by their demands: his son was a raw, inexperienced youth who could neither be firm, nor frank, nor dignified in dealing with any one. He angered the Franks by insincere diplomacy, and the Greeks by his reckless schemes for extracting money from them. The winter of 1203-4 was spent in ceaseless wrangling about the subsidy due to the Crusaders, till Alexius, growing seriously frightened, began exactions on his subjects which drove them to revolt. When he seized and melted down the golden lamps and silver candelabra which formed the pride of St. Sophia, stripped its eikonostasis of its rich metal plating, and requisitioned the jewelled eikons and reliquaries of every church in the city, the populace would stand his proceedings no longer. They would not serve an emperor who had sold himself to the Franks, and only reigned in order to subjcct the Eastern Church to Rome, and to pour the hoarded wealth of the ancient empire into the coffers of the upstart Italian republics.

In January, 1204, the storm burst. The populace and troops shut the gates of the city, and fell on the isolated Latins who were within the walls. They were not long without a leader; a fierce and unscrupulous officer named Alexius Ducas put himself at their head and determined to seize the throne. Isaac II. died of fright in the midst of the tumult; his son Alexius was caught and strangled by the usurper. Thus the Angeli ceased out of the land, and Alexius V. reigned in their stead. He is less frequently named by chroniclers under his family name of Ducas, than under his nickname of "Murtzuphlus," drawn from the bushy overhanging eyebrows which formed the most prominent feature of his countenance.

Alexius Ducas had everything against him. He was a mere usurper, whose authority was hardly recognized beyond the walls of Constantinople. The Angeli had so drained the treasury that nothing remained in it. Twenty years of indiscipline and disaster had spoilt the army; the fleet was nonexistent, for the admirals of Alexius Angelus had laid up the vessels in ordinary, and sold the stores to fill their own pockets. Nevertheless Murtzuphlus made a far better fight than his despicable predecessor and namesake. He collected a little money by confiscating the properties of the unpopular courtiers and ministers of the Angeli, and used it to the best advantage. The army received some of the arrears due to them, and Alexius spent every spare moment in seeing to their drill and endeavouring to improve their discipline. He strengthened the sea-wall, whose weakness had been proved so fatally four months ago, by erecting wooden towers along it, and building platforms for all the military engines that could be found in the arsenal. He ordered, too, the enrolment of a national militia, and compelled the nobles and burghers of Constantinople to take arms and man the walls. To the discredit of the Byzantines this order was received with many murmurs: the citizens complained that they paid taxes to support the regular army, and that they therefore ought to be excused personal service. Little good was got out of these new and raw levies; they swelled the numbers of the garrison, but hardly added anything appreciable to its strength.

Alexius Ducas himself with his cavalry scoured the country round the Crusading camp every day, to cut off the foraging parties of the Franks, and when not in the field, rode round the city superintending the works, inspecting the guard-posts, and haranguing the soldiery. If courage and energy command success, he ought to have held his own. But he could not counteract the work of twenty years of decay and disorganization, and felt that his throne rested on the most fragile of foundations.

The Crusaders took two months to prepare for their second assault on Constantinople, which they felt would be a far more formidable affair than the attack in the preceding autumn. They directed their chief efforts against the sea-wall, which they had found vulnerable in the previous siege, and left the formidable land-wall alone. The ships were told off into groups, each destined to attack a particular section of the wall, and covered with as many military engines as they could carry. Flying bridges were again prepared, and landing parties were directed to leap ashore on the narrow beach between the wall and the water, and get to work with rams and scaling ladders. The attack was made on April 8th, at more than a hundred points along two miles of sea-wall, but it was beaten off with loss. Alexius Ducas had made his arrangements so well, that the fire of his engines swept off all who attempted to gain a footing on the ramparts. The ships were much damaged, and at noon the whole fleet gave back, and retired as best it could to the opposite side of the Golden Horn.

Many of the Crusaders were now for returning; they thought their defeat was a judgment for turning their arms against a Christian city, and wished to sail for the Holy Land. But Dandolo and the Venetians insisted upon repeating the assault. Three days were spent in repairing the fleet, and on April 12th a second attack was delivered. This time the ships were lashed together in pairs to secure stability, and the attack was concentrated on a comparatively small front of wall. At last, after much fighting, the military engines of the fleet and the bolts of its crossbowmen cleared a single tower of its defenders. A bridge was successfully lowered on to it, and a footing secured by a party of Crusaders, who then threw open a postern gate and let the main body in. After a short fight within the walls, the troops of Alexius Ducas retired back into the streets. The Crusaders fired the city to cover their advance, and by night were in possession of the north-west angle of Constantinople, the quarter of the palace of Blachern.

BYZANTINE RELIQUARY.
(*From "L'Art Byzantin." Par C. Bayet. Paris, Quantin,* 1883.)

While the fire was keeping the combatants apart, the Emperor tried to rally his troops and to prepare for a street-fight next day. But the army was cowed; many regiments melted away; and the Varangian Guard, the best corps in the garrison, chose this moment to demand that their arrears of pay should be liquidated; they would not return to the fight without their money! The twenty years of disorganization under the Angeli was now bearing its fruit, and deeply was the empire to rue the next day.

Alexius Ducas, in despair at being unable to make his men fight, left the city by night. He was soon followed by the last Greek officer who kept his head, the general Theodore Lascaris, who endeavoured to make one final attack on the Crusaders even after his master had departed. Next morning the Franks found themselves in full possession of the city, though they had been expecting to face a hard day of street-fighting before this end could be attained.

In cold blood, twelve hours after all fighting had ended, the Crusaders proceeded with great deliberation to sack the place. The leaders could not or would not hold back their men, and every atrocity that attends the storm of a great city was soon in full swing. Though no resistance was made, the soldiery, and especially the Venetians, took life recklessly, and three or four thousand unarmed citizens were slain. But there was no general massacre; it was lust and greed rather than bloodthirstiness that the army displayed. All the Western writers, no less than the Greeks, testify to the horrors of the three days' carnival of rape and plunder that now set in. Every knight or soldier seized on the house that he liked best, and dealt as he chose with its inmates. Churches and nunneries fared no better than private dwellings; the orgies that were enacted in the holiest places caused even the Pope to exclaim that no good could ever come out of the conquest. The drunken soldiery enthroned a harlot in the patriarchal chair in St. Sophia, and made her rehearse ribald songs and indecent dances before the high altar. There were plenty of clergy with the Crusading army, but instead of endeavouring to check the sacrilegious doings of their countrymen, they devoted themselves to plundering the treasuries of the churches of all the holy bones and relics that were stored in them. "The Franks," remarked a Greek writer who saw the sack of Constantinople, "behaved far worse than Saracens; the infidels when a town has surrendered at any rate respect churches and women."

After private plunder had reigned unchecked for three days, the leaders of the Crusaders collected such valuables as could be found for public division. Though so much had been stolen and concealed, they were able to produce no less than £800,000 in hard gold and silver for distribution. The sum was afterwards supplemented by the use of a resource which makes the modern historian add a special curse of his own to the account of the Crusaders. Down to 1204 Constantinople still contained the monuments of ancient Greek art in enormous numbers. In spite of the wear and tear of 900 years, her squares and palaces were still crowded with the art-treasures that Constantine and his sons had stored up. Nicetas, who was an eyewitness of all, has left us the list of the chief statues that suffered. The Heracles of Lysippus, the great Hera of Samos, the brass figures which Augustus set up after Actium, the ancient Roman bronze of the Wolf with Romulus and Remus, Paris with the Golden Apple, Helen of Troy, and dozens more all went into the melting-pot, to be recast into wretched copper money. The

THIS IS WHAT THE ROMAN CATHOLIC FAITH PERTAINS

monuments of Christian art fared no better; the tombs of the emperors were carefully stripped of everything in metal, the altars and screens of the churches scraped to the stone. Everything was left bare and desolate.

Such was "the greatest conquest that was ever seen, greater than any made by Alexander or Charlemagne, or by any that have lived before or after," as a Western chronicler wrote, while the Greeks grew hyperbolical in lamentation, as they saw "the eye of the world, the ornament of nations, the fairest sight on earth, the mother of churches, the spring whence flowed the waters of faith, the mistress of Orthodox doctrine, the seat of the sciences, draining the cup mixed for her by the hand of the Almighty, and consumed by fires as devouring as those which ruined the five Cities of the Plain."

At last the Crusaders sat down to divide up their conquests. They elected Baldwin of Flanders Emperor of the East, and handed over to him the ruined city of Constantinople, half of it devoured by the flames of the conflagrations that attended the two sieges, and all of it plundered from cellar to attic. Four-fifths of the population had fled, and no one had remained save beggars who had nothing to save by flight. With the capital Baldwin was given Thrace and the Asiatic provinces—Bithynia, Mysia, and Lydia, all of which had still to be conquered. His colleague, Boniface of Montferrat, was made "King of Thessalonica," and did homage to Baldwin for a fief consisting of Macedonia, Thessaly, and inland Epirus. The Venetians claimed "a quarter and half-a-quarter" of the empire, and took out their share by receiving Crete, the Ionian Islands, the ports along the west coast of Greece and Albania, nearly the whole of the islands of the Aegean, and the land about the entrance of the Dardanelles. They seized on every good harbour and strong sea-fortress, but left the inland alone; commerce rather than annexation was their end. The rest of the empire was parcelled out among the minor leaders of the Crusade; they had first to conquer their fiefs, and were then to do homage for them to the Emperor Baldwin. Most of them never lived to accomplish the scheme. Meanwhile a Venetian prelate was appointed patriarch of Constantinople, and news was sent to the Pope that the union of the Eastern and Western Churches was accomplished, by the forcible extinction of the Greek patriarchate.

It only remains to speak of Alexius Ducas, the fugitive Greek emperor. He fell into the hands of the Crusaders, was tried for the murder of the young Alexius Angelus, and suffered death by being taken to the top of a lofty pillar and hurled from it. The Greeks saw in this strange end the fulfilment of an obscure prophecy about the last of the Caesars, which had long puzzled the brains of the oracle-mongers.

XXIII. The Latin Empire And The Empire Of Nicaea. (1204-1261.)

Seldom has any state dragged out fifty-seven years in such constant misery and danger as the Latin Empire experienced in the course of its inglorious existence. The whole period was one protracted death-agony, and at no date within it did there appear any reasonable prospect of recovery. Thirty thousand men can take a city, but they cannot subdue a realm 800 miles long and 400 broad. Far more than any government which has since held sway on the same spot did the Latin Empire of Romania deserve the name of "the Sick Man." It is not too much to say that but for the unequalled strength of the walls of Constantinople the new power must have ceased to exist within ten years of its establishment.

But once fortified within the ramparts of Byzantium the Franks enjoyed the inestimable advantage which their Greek predecessors had possessed: they were masters of a fortress which—as military science then stood—was practically impregnable, if only it was defended with ordinary skill, and adequately guarded on the front facing the sea. As long as the Venetians kept up their naval supremacy in Eastern waters, the city was safe on that side, and even the very limited force which the Latin emperor could put into the field sufficed, when joined to the armed burghers of the Italian quarters, to defend the tremendous land wall.

From the first year of its existence the Latin Empire was marked out by unfailing signs as a power not destined to continue. The intention of its founders had been to replace the centralized despotism which they had overthrown by a great feudal state, corresponding in territorial extent to its predecessor. But within a few months it became evident that the conquest of the broad provinces which the Crusaders had distributed among themselves by anticipation, was not to be carried out. The new emperor himself was the first to discover this. He set out with his chivalry to drive from Northern Thrace the Bulgarian hordes, who had flocked down into the plains to profit by the plunder of the dismembered realm. But near Adrianople he met Joannicios, the Bulgarian king, with a vast army at his back. The Franks charged gallantly enough, but they were simply overwhelmed by numbers. The larger part of the army was cut to pieces, and Baldwin himself was taken prisoner. The Bulgarian kept him in chains for some months, and then put him to death, after he had worn the imperial crown only one year [1205].

Henry of Flanders, the brother of Baldwin, became his successor. He was an honest and able man, but he could do nothing towards conquering the provinces of Asia, pushing the Bulgarians back over the Balkans, or conciliating the subject Greek population. All his reign he had to fight on the defensive against his neighbours to the north and south. By the time that he died the empire was practically confined to a narrow slip of land along the Propontis, reaching from Gallipoli to Constantinople. Nor was the chief of the minor Latin states any better off; Boniface of Montferrat had fallen in 1207, slain in battle by the same Bulgarian hordes which had cut off the army of his suzerain Baldwin. With his death it became evident that the kingdom of Thessalonica was no more able to conquer all the old Byzantine provinces in its neighbourhood than was the empire of Constantinople. Boniface's son and heir was a mere infant; during his minority the lands of his kingdom were lopped away, one after another, by the Greek despot of Epirus, the able Theodore Angelus. At last the capital itself was retaken by the Greeks in 1222, and the kingdom of Thessalonica came to an end.

The Latin states in the southern parts of the Balkan Peninsula fared somewhat better. William of Champlitte had contrived to hew out for himself a principality in the western parts of the Peloponnesus, and had organized there a small state with twelve baronies and 136 knights fees. The resistance of the natives in this district was particularly weak, and one battle sufficed to give William all the coast-plain of Elis and Messenia. Yet he did not succeed in subduing the mountaineers of the peninsula of Maina, or the coast towns of Argolis and Laconia, so that the Greeks still had some foothold in the peninsula.

Another small Latin state was set up by Otho de la Roche in Central Greece, where as "Duke of Athens" he ruled Attica and Boeotia. He treated his Greek subjects with more consideration than any of his fellow Crusaders, and was rewarded by obtaining a degree of respect and deference which was not found in any other Latin state. Though the smallest, the duchy of Athens was undoubtedly the most prosperous of the new creations of the conquest of 1204.

Meanwhile it is time to speak of the fortunes of those parts of the Eastern Empire which the Franks did not succeed in seizing when Constantinople fell. The provinces had hitherto been accustomed to accept without a murmur the ruler whom the capital obeyed. But in 1204 it was found that the centralization of the Byzantine Empire, great as it was, had not so thoroughly crushed the individuality of the provinces as to make them submit without resistance to the Latin yoke. Wherever the provincials found a leader, whether a member of one of the ex-imperial houses, or an energetic governor, or a landholder of local influence, they stood up to defend themselves. The Byzantine Empire, like some creature of low organism, showed every sign of life in its limbs, though its head had been shorn off. Wherever a centre of resistance could be found the people refused to submit to the piratical Frank, and to his yet more hated companions the priests of the Roman Church.

Of the nine or ten leaders who put themselves at the head of provincial risings three were destined to carve out kingdoms for themselves. Of these the most important was Theodore Lascaris, the last officer who had attempted to strike a blow against the Franks when Constantinople fell.[29] He might claim some shadow of hereditary right to the imperial crown as he had married the daughter of the imbecile Alexius III., but his true title was his well-approved courage and energy. The wrecks of the old Byzantine army rallied around him, the cities of Bithynia opened their gates, and when the Latins crossed into Asia to divide up the land into baronies and knights fees, they found Theodore waiting to receive them with the sword. His defence of the strong town of Prusa, which successfully repelled Henry of Flanders, put a limit to the extension of the Frank Empire; beyond a few castles on the Bithynian coast they made no conquests. Having thus checked the invaders,

[29] See page 289.

Theodore had himself solemnly crowned at Nicaea, and assumed imperial state [1206].

FINIAL FROM A BYZANTINE MS.
(*From* "*L'Art Byzantin.*" *Par C. Bayet. Paris, Quantin*, 1883.)

Having beaten off the Latins, Theodore had to cope with another who aspired like himself to pose as the rightful heir to the imperial throne. Alexius Comnenus, a grandson of the wicked emperor Andronicus I., had betaken himself to the Eastern frontiers of the empire when Constantinople fell, and obtained possession of Trebizond and the long slip of coast-land at the south-east corner of the Black Sea, from the mouth of the Phasis to Sinope. He aspired to conquer the whole of Byzantine Asia, and sent his brother David Comnenus to attack Bithynia. But Theodore defended his newly won realm with success; Comnenus gained no territory from him, and was constrained to content himself with the narrow bounds of his Pontic realm, where his descendants reigned in obscurity for three hundred years as emperors of Trebizond. A greater danger beset the empire of Nicaea when the warlike sultan of the Seljouks came down from his plateau to ravage its borders. But the valour of Theodore Lascaris triumphed over this enemy also. In the battle of Antioch-on-Maeander he slew Sultan Kaikhosru with his own hand in single combat, and the Turks were beaten back with such slaughter that they left the empire alone for a generation.

Meanwhile a third Greek state had sprung into existence in the far West. Michael Angelus, a cousin of Alexius III. and Isaac II., put in a claim to their heritage, though he was disqualified by his illegitimate birth. He was recognized as ruler by the cities of Epirus, and proclaimed himself "despot" of that land. Raising an army among the warlike tribes of Albania, he maintained his position with success, and discomfited the Franks of Athens and Thessalonica when they took arms against him. He died early, but left a compact heritage to his brother Theodore, who succeeded him on the throne, and within a few years conquered the whole of the Frank kingdom of Thessalonica.

It was soon evident that there would be a trial of strength between the two Greek emperors who claimed to succeed to the rights of the dispossessed Angeli. The Latin Empire was obviously destined to fall before one of them. The only doubt was, whether the Epirot or the Nicene was to be its conqueror. This question was not settled till 1241, when the two powers met in decisive conflict.

By this time Theodore Lascaris had been succeeded in Asia by his son-in-law John Ducas,[30] and Theodore of Thessalonica by his son John Angelus. At Constantinople the succession of Latin emperors had been much more rapid. Henry of Flanders had died in 1216; he was followed by Peter of Courtenay, who was slain by the Epirots in less than a year. To him succeeded Robert his son, and when Robert died in 1228 his brother Baldwin II., reigned in his stead. The young Courtenays were both thoroughly incapable, and saw their empire melt away from them till nothing was left beyond the walls of Constantinople itself.

John III. of Nicaea was an excellent sovereign, a very worthy heir to his gallant father-in-law. Not only was he a good soldier and an able administrator, but by constant supervision and strict frugality he had got the financial condition of his empire into a more hopeful condition—a state of things which had never been seen in Romania since the time of John Comnenus, a hundred years before. In 1230 the troops of Nicaea crossed into Europe, and drove the Franks out of Southern Thrace, while in 1235 John Ducas laid siege to Constantinople itself. But the time of its fall was not yet arrived, and when a Venetian fleet approached to succour it the Emperor was constrained to raise the siege.

---

[30] Sometimes known as John Vatatzes.

FOUNTAIN IN THE COURT OF ST. SOPHIA.

Recognizing that Constantinople was not yet ripe for its fall, John Ducas resolved to measure himself with his rivals the Angeli of Thessalonica. He beat their forces out of the field, and laid siege to their capital in 1341. Then John Angelus engaged to resign the title of emperor, call himself no more than "despot of Epirus," and to acknowledge himself as the vassal of the ruler of Nicaea. This satisfied Ducas for a time, but when Angelus died, four years later, he seized Thessalonica and united it to the imperial crown. The heir of the Angeli escaped to Albania and succeeded in retaining a small fraction only of his ancestral dominions [1246].

John Ducas died in 1254, leaving the throne of Nicaea to his son Theodore II., who bid fair to continue the prosperous career of his father and grandfather. He drove the Bulgarians out of Macedonia, and penned the Albanians into their hills. But he became subject to epileptic fits, and died after a reign of only four years, before he had reached the age of thirty-eight [1258].

This was a dreadful misfortune for the empire, for John Ducas, the son and heir of Theodore, was a child of eight years, and minorities were always disastrous to the state. We have seen in the history of previous centuries how frequently the infancy of a prince led to a violent contest for the place of regent, or even to a usurpation of the throne. The case of John IV. was no exception to the rule; the ministers of his father fought and intrigued to gain possession of the helm of affairs, till at last an able and unprincipled general, named Michael Paleologus, thrusting himself to the front, was named tutor to the Emperor, and given the title of "Despot."

Michael was as ambitious as he was unscrupulous. The place of regent was far from satisfying his ambition, and he determined to seize the throne, though he had steeped himself to the lips in oaths of loyalty to his young master. He played much the same game that Richard III. was destined to repeat in England two centuries later. He cleared away from the capital the relatives and adherents of the little prince, placed creatures of his own in their places, and conciliated the clergy by large gifts and hypocritical piety. Presently the partisans of Michael began to declaim against the dangers of a minority, and the necessity for a strong hand at the helm. After much persuasion and mock reluctance the regent was induced to allow himself to be crowned. From that moment the boy John Ducas was thrust aside and ignored: ere he had reached the age of ten his wicked guardian put out his eyes and plunged him into a dungeon, where he spent thirty years in darkness and misery.

The usurpation of Michael tempted all the enemies of the Greek Empire to take arms. The Epirot despot allied himself with the Frankish lords of Greece, and their united armies, aided by auxiliaries from Italy, invaded Macedonia; moreover the Latin emperor of Constantinople stirred up the Venetians to ravage his neighbours' borders. But in 1260 the troops of Michael won, over the allied armies of the Franks and Epirots, the last great victory that a Byzantine army was ever destined to achieve. The field of Pelagonia decided the lot of the house of Paleologus, for Michael's enemies were so crushed that they could never afterwards make head against him.

Freed from all danger from the West, Michael was now able to turn against Constantinople, and complete the reconstruction of the empire. The city was ripe for its fall, and Baldwin of Courtenay had long been awaiting his doom.

The long reign of the last Latin sovereign of Constantinople is sufficiently characterized by the fact that Baldwin spent nearly half the years of his rule outside the bounds of Romania, as he wandered from court to court in the West, striving to stir up some champion who would deliver him from the inevitable destruction impending over his realm. He gained little by his tours, his greatest success being that, in 1244, he got from St. Louis a considerable sum of ready money in acknowledgment of the liberality with which he had presented the holy king with a choice selection of relics, including the rod of Moses, the jawbone of John the Baptist, and our Lord's crown of thorns.

In 1261 Baldwin was in worse straits than ever. He was stripping off the lead of his own palace roof, to sell it for a few zecchins to the Venetians, and burning the beams of his outhouses in default of money to buy fuel. His son and heir was in pawn to the Venetian banking firm of the Capelli, who had taken him as the only tangible security that could be found for a modest loan which they had advanced to the imperial exchequer. With the government in such a desperate condition there was no longer any power of resistance left in Constantinople. When the Venetian fleet, the sole remaining defence of the empire, was away at sea, the city fell before a sudden and unpremeditated attack, made by Alexius Strategopulus, commander in Thrace under the emperor Michael.

Alexius, with eight hundred regular troops and a few scores of half-armed volunteers, was admitted by treachery within the walls. Before this formidable array the heirs of the Crusaders fled in base dismay, and the Empire of Romania came to an inglorious and a well-deserved end.

Its monarch resumed his habitual mendicant tours in Western Europe, and never ceased to besiege the ears of popes and kings with demands for aid to recover his lost realm. At last Baldwin passed away: his sole memorial is the fact that he made a distressed and itinerant emperor in search of a champion, one of the stock figures in the Romances of his day. No one in Western Europe was ignorant of his tale, and he survives as the prototype of the dispossessed sovereigns of fifty legends of chivalry.

XXIV. Decline And Decay. (1261-1328.)

There was now once more a Byzantine empire, and to an unobservant reader the history of the reigns of the Paleologi looks like the natural continuation and sequel of the history of the reigns of Isaac Angelus and his brother. If the annals of Michael VIII. and his son were written on to the end of that of Alexius Angelus, the intervening gap of the Latin Conquest might almost pass unperceived, and the reader might imagine that he was investigating a single continuous course of events. The Frank dominion at Constantinople, and the heroic episode of the Empire of Nicaea, would pass equally unnoticed.

We need not insist on the perniciousness of such a view. Great as may seem the similarity of the Byzantine Empire of 1204, and that of 1270, it had really suffered an entire transformation in that period. To commence by the most obvious and external sign of change, it will be observed that the lands subject to Michael Paleologus were far more limited in extent than those which had obeyed Alexius Angelus. The loss in Asia was less than might have been expected: Theodore Lascaris and John Ducas had kept back the Turk, and only two districts of no great extent had fallen into Moslem hands—the Pisidian coast with the seaport of Adalia on the south, and the Paphlagonian coast with the seaport of Sinope on the north. Besides these the distant Pontic province had now become the empire of Trebizond.

In Europe the loss was far more serious: four great blocks of territory had been lost for ever. The first was a slip along the southern slope of the Balkans, in Northern Thrace and Macedonia, which had fallen into the hands of the Bulgarians, and become completely Slavonized. The second was the district which is represented by the modern land of Albania. When the Angeli of Thessalonica fell before John Ducas, a younger member of the house retired to the original mountain house of the dynasty, and preserved the independence of the "Despotate of Epirus." Here the Angeli survived for some generations, maintaining themselves against the Emperors of Constantinople by a strict alliance with the Latin princes of Southern Greece.

Next in the list of Old-Byzantine territories which Michael never recovered, we must place Greece proper, now divided between the Princes of Achaia, of the house of Villehardouin, and the Briennes, who had succeeded to the Duchy of Athens. But the Paleologi still retained a considerable slice of the Peloponnesus, and were destined to encroach ere long on their Frankish neighbours. Lastly, we must mention the islands of the Aegean, of which the large majority were held either by the Venetian government, or by Venetian adventurers, who ruled as independent lords, but subordinated their policy to that of their native state.

But the territorial difference between the empire of 1204 and the empire of 1261 was only one of the causes which crippled the realm of the Paleologi. Bad though the internal government of the dominions of Alexius III. had been, there was still then some hope of recovery. The old traditions of East-Roman administrative economy, though neglected, were not lost, and might have been revived by an emperor who had a keen eye to discover ability and a ready hand to reward merit. New blood in the *personnel* of the ministry, and a keen supervision of details by the master's eye, would have produced an improvement in the state of the empire, though any permanent restoration of strength was probably made impossible by the deep-seated decay of society. But by the time of Michael Paleologus even amelioration had become impossible. The three able emperors who reigned at Nicaea, though they had preserved their independence against Turk and Frank, had utterly failed in restoring administrative efficiency in their provinces. John Vatatzes, himself a thrifty monarch, who could even condescend to poultry-farming to fill his modest exchequer, found that all his efforts to protect native industry could not cause the dried-up springs of prosperity to flow again. The whole fiscal and administrative machinery of government had been thrown hopelessly out of gear.

It was the commercial decline of the empire that made a reform of the administration so hopeless. The Paleologi were never able to reassert the old dominion over the seas which had made their predecessors the arbiters of the trade of Christendom. The wealth of the elder Byzantine Empire had arisen from the fact that Constantinople was the central emporium of the trade of the civilized world. All the caravan routes from Syria and Persia converged thither. Thither, too, had come by sea the commodities of Egypt and the Euxine. All the Eastern products which Europe might require had to be sought in the storehouses of Constantinople, and for centuries the nations of the West had been contented to go thither for them. But the Crusades had shaken this monopoly, when they taught the Italians to seek the hitherto unknown parts of Syria and Egypt, and buy their Eastern merchandize from the producer and not from the middleman. Acre and Alexandria had already profited very largely at the expense of Constantinople ere the Byzantine Empire was upset in 1204. But the Latin conquest was the fatal blow. It threw the control of the trade of the Bosphorus into the hands of the Venetians, and the Venetians had no desire to make Constantinople their one central mart: they were just as ready to trade through the Syrian and Egyptian ports. To them the city was no more than an important half-way house for the Black Sea trade, and an emporium for the local produce of the countries round the Sea of Marmora.

From 1204 onward Italy rather than Constantinople became the centre and starting-place for all European trade, and the great Italian republics employed all their vigilance to prevent the Greek fleet from recovering its old strength. Henceforth the Byzantine war-navy was insignificant, and without a war-navy the Paleologi could not drive away the intruders and restore the free navigation of the Levant to their own mercantile marine.

The emperors who succeeded each other on the restored throne of Constantinople were, without exception, men more fitted to lose than to hold together an exhausted and impoverished empire. Their lot was cast, it is true, in hard times; but hardly one of them showed a spark of ability or courage in endeavouring to face the evil day. The three monarchs of the house of Lascaris who ruled at Nicaea had been keen soldiers and competent administrators, but with the return of the emperors to Constantinople the springs of energy began to dry up, and the gloom and decay of the ruined capital seemed to affect the spirit and brain of its rulers.

BYZANTINE CHAPEL AT ANI, THE OLD CAPITAL OF ARMENIA.
(*From "L'Art Byzantin." Par Charles Bayet. Paris, Quantin*, 18`3.)

Michael Paleologus, though it was his fortune to recover the city which his abler predecessors had failed to take, was a mere wily intriguer, not a statesman or general. Having usurped the throne by the basest treachery towards his infant sovereign, he always feared for himself a similar fate. Suspicion and cruelty were his main characteristics, and in his care for his own person he quite forgot the interests of the State. Even contemporary chroniclers saw that he was deliberately setting himself to weaken the empire, because he dreaded the resentment of his subjects. He disbanded nearly all the native Greek troops, and refrained as far as possible from employing Greek generals.

One of his minor acts in this direction may be said to have been the original circumstance which set the Ottoman Turks, the future bane of the empire, on their career of conquest. The borders of the empire in Asia were defended by a native militia, who held their lands under condition of defending the castles and passes of the Bithynian and Phrygian mountains. The institution, which somewhat resembled a simple form of European feudalism, had worked so well that the Byzantine Empire had for a century and a half kept its Asiatic frontier practically intact, in spite of all the pressure of the Seljouk Turks of the Sultanate of Iconium. But the Bithynian militia were known to be attached to the house of Ducas, which Michael had dethroned, and he therefore resolved to disarm them. The measure was carried out, not without bloodshed, but the disbanded levy were not replaced by any adequate number of regular troops. Michael's financial straits did not permit him to keep under arms a very large force, such as was required to garrison his eastern line of forts after the abolition of the previous machinery of defence. Ten years only before Othman, the father of the Ottoman Turks, succeeded to the petty principality which was destined to be the nucleus of the Turkish Empire, the way for him had been thrown open by Michael's suspicious disarmament of the guards of his own frontier.

Michael lived for twenty-one years after the recovery of Constantinople, but he did not win a single important advantage in all the rest of his reign. In Europe he barely held his own against the Bulgarians, the Franks, and the fleets of Genoa and Venice. The troubles which befell him at the hands of the two naval powers were largely of his own creation, for he shifted his alliance from one to the other with such levity and suddenness that both regarded him as unfriendly. Though all through his reign he was at war either with Genoa or Venice, yet such was the distrust felt for him that, when at war with one of the rivals, he could not always secure the help of the other. Venice had been the mainstay of the Frank emperors of Constantinople, and Michael might, therefore, have been expected to remain staunch to the Genoese. On the other hand, the Genoese had designs on the Black Sea trade, which touched the Emperor's pocket very closely, while the Venetians were more connected with the distant commerce of Syria and Egypt, which did not concern him. Balancing one consideration with the other, Michael played false to both the powers, and often saw his coast ravaged and his small fleet compelled to take refuge in the Golden Horn, while the enemy's vessels swept the seas. On land he was less unlucky, and the Duke of Athens and the despot of Epirus were both kept in check, though neither of them were subdued.

But it was in Asia that Michael's rule was most unfortunate. In the second half of his reign the Seljouks, though split into several principalities owing to the break up of the Sultanate of Iconium, united to assail the borders of the empire. They conquered the Carian and Lydian inland, though Tralles and several other towns made a vigorous resistance, and reduced Michael's dominion in South-western Asia Minor to a mere strip along the coast. A similar fate befell Eastern Bithynia, where the Turks forced their way as far as the river Sangarius.

But the ruin of Byzantine Asia was reserved to fall into the times of Michael's son and successor, Andronicus II. This prince had all the faults of his father, levity, perfidy, and cruelty, with others added from which Michael had been free—cowardice and superstition. The main interest which Andronicus took in life was concerned with things ecclesiastical—it would be wrong to say things religious—and he spent his life in making and unmaking patriarchs of Constantinople. No prelate could bear with him long, and in the course of his reign he deposed no less than nine of them.

While Andronicus was quarrelling with his patriarchs the empire was going to ruin. The Seljouk chiefs from the plateau of Asia Minor were pressing down more and more towards the coast, and making their way to the very gates of Ephesus and Smyrna. At last the emperor, growing seriously alarmed when the Turks appeared on the shores of the Propontis itself, and threatened the walls of Nicaea and Prusa, resolved to make an unwonted effort to beat them back.

JOHN CANTACUZENUS SITTING IN STATE.
(*From a Contemporary MS.*)
(*From "L'Art Byzantin." Par C. Bayet. Paris, Quantin*, 1883.)

In 1302 the long war of the "Sicilian Vespers" between the houses of Anjou and Aragon came to an end, and the hordes of mercenaries of all nations which the two pretenders to the crown of Sicily had maintained were turned loose on the world. It occurred to Andronicus that he might hire enough of the veterans of the Sicilian war to enable him to beat back the Turks into their hills. All Europe acknowledged that they were the hardiest and best-disciplined troops in Christendom, though they were also the most cruel and lawless. Accordingly the emperor applied to Roger de Flor, a renegade Templar, the commander of the mercenaries who had served Frederic of Aragon, and offered to take him into his service, with as many of his followers as could be induced to accompany him. Roger accepted with alacrity, and came to Constantinople in 1303 with 6,000 men at his back; other bodies were soon to follow. Andronicus loaded the "Grand Company," as Roger de Flor styled his men, with unlimited promises, and a certain amount of ready money. Roger himself was given the title of "Grand Duke," and married to a lady of the imperial house. After clearing the Turks out of the Bithynian coast-land the "Grand Company" spent the winter of 1303-4 in free quarters along the southern coast of Propontis. Their plundering habits and their arrogance soon brought them into ill odour with the inhabitants, who complained that they were well-nigh as great a curse as the Turks. In the next year Roger moved south with his host, and drove the Turks out of Lydia and Caria; but instead of putting the emperor into possession of the reconquered land, he garrisoned every fortress with his own men, and raised and appropriated the imperial taxes. There can be little doubt that he was plotting to seize on the provinces he had regained, and to reign at Ephesus as an independent prince. At last Roger went so far as to lay formal siege to Philadelphia, because its inhabitants preferred to obey orders from Constantinople, and would not admit him within their gates. Andronicus then lured him to an interview at Adrianople, and in his very presence the great *condottiere*was assassinated by George the Alan, an officer whose son had been slain in a brawl by Roger's soldiers. The Emperor had probably arranged the murder, and certainly refused to arrest its perpetrator [1307].

He was promptly punished. The "Grand Company" was not disorganized by the loss of its leader, and thought of nothing but revenge. Assembling themselves in haste, and abandoning Asia Minor to the Turks, they marched on Constantinople, harrying the land far and wide with fiendish cruelty. The Emperor sent his son Michael against them, but the young prince was disgracefully beaten in two fights at Gallipoli and Apros, and the mercenaries spread themselves all over Thrace and plundered it up to the gates of the capital. It almost looked as if a second Latin Conquest of Constantinople was about to take place, for the leaders of the "Grand Company" got succour from Europe, raised a corps of Turkish auxiliaries, and occupied Thrace for two years. But they could not storm the walls of Constantinople or Adrianople, and at last, after two years of plundering, they had stripped the country so bare that they were driven away by famine. Drifting southward and westward they ravaged Macedon and Thessaly, and at last reached Greece. Here they fell into a quarrel with Walter de Brienne, Duke of Athens, slew him in battle and took his capital. Then at last did the wandering horde settle down; they seized the duchy, divided its fiefs among themselves, and established a new dynasty on the Athenian throne. The empire was at last quit of them, for when once they ceased to wander the "Grand Company" ceased to be dangerous.

This disastrous war with the mercenaries not only ruined Thrace and Macedonia, but was the cause of the final loss of the Byzantine provinces of Asia Minor. While Andronicus was feebly attempting to cope with the "Grand Company," the Seljouk chiefs had conquered Lydia and Phrygia once more, and then advanced yet further north to siege Mysia and Bithynia. By 1325 they had reduced the Emperor's dominions on the east of the straits to a narrow strip, reaching from the Dardanelles to the northern exit of the Bosphorus, and bounded by the Bithynian hills to the south. Five Seljouk leaders had carved out for themselves principalities in the conquered districts, Menteshe in the south, Aidin and Saroukhan in Lydia, Karasi in Mysia, and in the Bithynian borderland Othman, destined to a fame very different from that of his long-forgotten compeers.

While Othman and the rest were turning the once thickly-peopled countries of Western Asia Minor into a desert sparsely inhabited by wandering nomads, Andronicus II. was busied in a war even more uncalled for than that with the mercenaries. He wished to exclude from the succession to the throne his grandson and heir, who bore the same name as himself. But the younger Andronicus took measures to defend his rights, and raised armed bands. Grandfather and grandson were ere long engaged in a long but feebly-conducted war, which was only terminated in 1328, when the old man acknowledged Andronicus the younger as his heir, and made him his colleague on the throne. But his grandson, not contented with this measure of success, made him retire from the conduct of affairs, and assumed control over every function of government. The name of Andronicus II. was still associated with that of Andronicus III. on the coinage and in the public prayers, but he took no further part in the rule of the empire. In 1332 he died, at a good old age, lamented by no single individual in the realm which he had ruled for fifty years. At his death the empire was only two-thirds of the size that it had been at his accession.

XXV. The Turks In Europe.

Andronicus III. was a shade better than the incapable old man whom he supplanted. Though he was given—like all his house—to treachery and deceit, and though his life was loose and luxurious, he was at any rate active and energetic. He may be described as a weak reflection or copy of Manuel Comnenus, being a mighty hunter, a bold spear both in the tournament and on the battle-field, and a great spender of money. If he had not the brains to keep his empire together, he at any rate fought his best, and did not sit apathetically at home like his grandfather while everything was going to rack and ruin.

Nevertheless, Andronicus III. was destined to see the termination of the process which had begun under Andronicus II.—the entire loss of the Asiatic provinces of the empire to the Turks. It was now with the Ottomans almost exclusively that he had to deal; the other Seljouk hordes had no longer any marchland along the shrunken frontier of his dominions.

These new foes of the empire deserve a word of description. Othman, the son of Ertogrul, was a vassal of the Seljouk Sultan of Roum, who had been granted a tract in the Phrygian highlands under the condition of military service against the Greeks. His fief lay in the north-west angle of the great central plateau of Asia Minor. Behind it lay the rolling country of hills and uplands already occupied by the Seljouks. Before it were the Bithynian mountains, with their passes protected by forts, and garrisoned by local militia, till the day when they were so perversely stripped of their defenders by the action of Michael Paleologus. Othman, and his father Ertogrul before him, owned nothing in the hills, nor could they have pushed on if Michael had not made the way easy for them. But after 1270 the native militia was gone, and the followers of Othman, instead of having to face an armed population, fighting to protect its own fields, found to oppose them only inadequate garrisons of regular troops at long intervals.

Othman's life covered two series of great events, the disastrous reign of Andronicus II. at Constantinople, and in Asia Minor the no less disastrous break-up of the power of his own suzerain, the Sultan of Roum. In 1294, Gaiaseddin, the last undisputed sovereign of the Seljouk line, fell in battle against rebels; and in 1307, Alaeddin III., the last prince who claimed to be supreme Sultan, died in exile. This made Othman an independent prince; but he did not take the title of Sultan, contenting himself with the humbler name of Emir.

Othman's field of operation from 1281 to 1326 was the Byzantine borderland of Bithynia and Mysia. He was by no means the strongest of the Seljouk chiefs who made a lodgement within the borders of the empire, and it took him twenty years before he conquered one large town. His wild horsemen harried the open sea-coast plain of Bithynia again and again, till at last the wretched inhabitants emigrated, or acknowledged him as their sovereign. But the towns, within their strong Roman walls, were unassailable by the light cavalry which formed his only armed strength.

The siege of Prusa [Broussa], the capital and key of the region, lasted ten years. The Turks built a chain of forts around it and gradually made the introduction of provisions more and more difficult, till at last a large force was required to march out every time that a convoy was expected. At length the inhabitants could find no advantage in spending their whole lives in a beleaguered town undergoing slow starvation. Prusa surrendered in 1326, and Othman heard of the news on his death-bed. The Turkish frontier now once again touched the Sea of Marmora, which it had not reached since the Crusaders thrust it back inland in 1097.

The reign of Othman's son Orkhan, the second Emir of the Ottomans, almost coincided with that of Andronicus III. All that the one lost the other gained. Orkhan's life-work was the completion of the conquest of Bithynia, which his father had begun. He took Nicomedia in 1327 and Nicaea in 1333, with all the surrounding territory, so that Andronicus retained nothing but Chalcedon and the district immediately facing Constantinople beyond the Bosphorus. Only once did he have to meet the Emperor in pitched battle; this was at the fight of Pelekanon in 1329. Andronicus was wounded early in the day, and his army, deprived of its leader went to pieces and was severely beaten. After his recovery from his wounds the Emperor never faced the Ottomans again.

After conquering Bithynia, Orkhan subdued his nearest neighbours among the other Seljouk Emirs, and then turned to organizing his state. This was the date of the institution of his famous corps of the Janissaries, the first steady infantry that any Eastern power had ever possessed. He imposed on his Christian subjects in Mysia and Bithynia a tribute, not of money, but of male children. The boys were taken over while very young, placed in barracks, educated in the strictest and most fanatical Moslem code, and trained to the profession of arms. Having light horse enough and to spare, Orkhan taught the Janissaries to fight on foot with bow and sabre. They were well drilled, and moved in compact masses, which for many ages no foe proved competent to sunder and disperse. So thorough was the physical and moral discipline to which the Janissaries were subjected, that it was almost unknown for one of them to turn back from his career and relapse into Christianity. To keep them firm in their allegiance there acted not only the military and conventual discipline to which they were subject, but the dazzling prospect of future greatness. The Ottoman sovereigns made it their rule to select their generals and governors, their courtiers and personal attendants from the ranks of the tribute-children. It was calculated that more than two-thirds of the Grand-Viziers of Turkey, in the fourteenth, fifteenth, and sixteenth centuries, had begun their career as Janissaries.

The first generation of the "New Soldiery" [for such is the meaning of the word Janissary] grew up to the military age during the latter half of the reign of Orkhan, and it was he who first utilized them on the European shore of the Bosphorus.

Andronicus III. died in 1241, and left his shrunken dominions to the risks of a minority, for his son and heir, John III., was only nine years of age. If anything had been wanting to aid in the destruction of the empire, it was the arrival of such a contingency. The usual troubles soon set in, and the inevitable civil war was not far off.

MANUEL PALEOLOGUS AND HIS FAMILY.

(*From a Contemporary MS.*)

(*From "L'Art Byzantin." Par C. Bayet. Paris, Quantin*, 1883.)

The evil spirit of the time was John Cantacuzenus, the prime minister of the deceased emperor. He was a clever, shifty, intriguing courtier, with a turn for literature, but had the abilities neither of a general nor of a statesman. However, he had read the tale of the rise of the Paleologi to some purpose, and had resolved to imitate the career of Michael VIII. Now, as in 1258, there was the best of chances for an unscrupulous minister to make himself first the colleague and then the supplanter of his young master. Cantacuzenus did his best to repeat the doings of Michael on Michael's great-great-grandson. He bribed and intrigued, made himself a party in the state, and prepared for a *coup d'état* when the time should be ripe. Unfortunately for himself, Cantacuzenus was not of the stuff of which successful usurpers are made. He had his scruples and superstitions, and showed a fatal habit of procrastination which always led him to act a day too late. The Empress Dowager, Anne of Savoy, succeeded in raising a party against him, and when he threw off the mask and declared himself emperor he found himself unable to seize the capital, though he mustered an army under its walls. Finding that he was playing a losing game, Cantacuzenus took the usual step of calling in the national enemy to aid him. It was for the last time that this was done in Byzantine history, but never before had the result been so fatal. The usurper summoned to his aid first Stephen Dushan, the king of the Servians, and a little later the Turkish princes from across the Aegean—Orkhan the son of Othman, and his rival, Amour, Emir of Aidin.

These allies kept the cause of John Cantacuzenus from destruction, but it was by destroying the empire that John had coveted. King Stephen entered Macedonia and Thrace, and occupied the whole countryside, except Thessalonica and a few other towns. He then pushed further south, conquered Thessaly, and made the despot of Epirus do him homage. The Byzantine government retained little more than the capital, and the districts round Adrianople and Thessalonica. Most of this country was lost for ever to the imperial crown, and it seemed as if a Servian domination in the Balkan Peninsula was about to begin, for Stephen moved south from Servia, made Uscup in Macedonia his capital, and proclaimed himself "Emperor of the Servians and Romans."

It would perhaps have been well for Christendom if Stephen had actually conquered Constantinople and made an end of the empire. In that case there would have been a single great power in the Balkan Peninsula, ready to meet the oncoming assault of the Turks. But Dushan was not strong enough to take the great city, and to the misfortune of Europe he died in 1355 leaving a realm extending from the Danube to the pass of Thermopylae. But his young son Urosh was soon assassinated, and the Servian Empire broke up as rapidly as it had grown together. A dozen princes were soon scrambling for the remnants of Stephen's heritage.

The other allies whom John Cantacuzenus called in were the Turks Amour and Orkhan, and on them he depended far more than on the Servian. He took over into Thrace a large body of Turkish horse, and allowed them to harry the countryside and carry away his subjects by thousands, to be sold in the slave-markets of Smyrna and Broussa. But the depth of John's degradation was reached when he gave his daughter Theodora to Orkhan, to be immured in the Turk's harem. Thrace was rapidly assuming the aspect of a desert under the incursions of the Ottoman mercenaries of Cantacuzenus, when after six years of war the party of the Empress Anne consented to recognize the usurper as the colleague and guardian of the rightful heir. A hollow peace was patched up, and the two Johns could take stock of their dilapidated realm [1347]. The net result of their civil war had been that Macedonia and Thessaly were in Servian hands, and that Thrace was utterly ruined by the Turks. There was nothing left that could be called an empire; all that remained was Constantinople and Adrianople, the town of Thessalonica and the

Byzantine province in the Peloponnesus. Cantacuzenus certainly deserves a notable place by the side of Isaac and Alexius Angelus, as the third of the great destroyers of the Eastern Empire.

But his evil work was not yet done. For seven years he ruled in conjunction with John Paleologus, waging an unsuccessful war against Servia in the hopes of winning back Dushan's conquests. But in 1354 the young emperor, having attained the age of twenty-four, resolved to assert himself, and took arms to dethrone his guardian. Cantacuzenus resisted, and sent over to Asia for the troops of his son-in-law Orkhan, who crossed into Thrace and drove the adherents of the Paleologi out of several fortresses. But a night surprise from the side of the sea put John Paleologus in possession of Constantinople, and by a fortunate chance he got Cantacuzenus himself into his hands. The usurper was, in accordance with the usual practice, tonsured and placed in a monastery; by exceptional good fortune he was spared the loss of his eyes, and was able to spend the remainder of his life in writing a history of his own time.

But it was of little use to sweep away Cantacuzenus while Orkhan's Turks were in Thrace. The Ottomans had come as auxiliaries in the war, but they were resolved to stop as principals. Suleiman, the son of Orkhan, seized Gallipoli for himself, filled it with Turkish families, and made it a permanent settlement. This was the first Ottoman foothold in Europe, but it was not long to remain isolated.

In 1359 Orkhan died, and his successor, Murad I., determined to cross over into Europe, and try the fortune of his arms. John Paleologus was not a worse man than his immediate predecessors on the throne, but thanks to Cantacuzenus he had far less resources than even they had possessed. Two years of fighting sufficed to put Thrace in the hands of Murad from sea to sea. A decisive battle in front of Adrianople in 1361 was the finishing stroke, and the empire became a mere head without a body; its last home-province had been lopped away, and beyond the walls of Constantinople no land acknowledged John V. as sovereign save the district of Thessalonica and the Peloponnesus.

Why Murad I. did not finish the task he had begun, and take Constantinople itself, it is hard to discern. Its walls were still formidable, and the Genoese and Venetians could still protect it on the side of the sea. But a siege pressed firmly to an end must at last have triumphed over the mere inert resistance of stone and mortar, unsupported by an adequate garrison within. However, Murad preferred to press on against worthier adversaries than the weak Paleologus, and spent his life in incessant and successful wars with the Servians, the Bulgarians, and the Seljouk Emirs of Southern Asia Minor. In a reign of thirty years he extended his borders to the Balkans on the north, and annexed large tracts of Seljouk territory from his brother Emirs in Asia Minor.

John Paleologus was his humble vassal and slave. After a vain attempt to get help from the Pope, this emperor without an empire resolved to make what terms he could, and rejoiced when he found that Murad was prepared to grant him peace. The Turk was a hard master, and rejoiced in giving his vassal unpalatablc tasks. Best remembered among the tribulations of John is the siege of Philadelphia. That place had preserved a precarious independence after all the other cities of Byzantine Asia fell into the hands of the Turkish Emirs. Being far away in the Lydian hills, it lost touch with Constantinople, and had become a free town. Murad, wishing to subdue it, compelled John V. and his son Manuel to march in person against the last Christian stronghold in Asia. The Emperor submitted to the degradation, and Philadelphia surrendered when it saw the imperial banner hoisted among the horse-tails of the Turkish pashas above the camp of the besiegers. The humiliation of the empire could go no further than when the heir of Justinian and Basil Bulgaroktonos took the field at the behest of an upstart Turkish Emir, in order to extinguish the last relics of freedom among his own compatriots.

XXVI. The End Of A Long Tale. (1370-1453.)

The tale of the last seventy-five years of the Byzantine Empire is a mere piece of local history, and no longer forms an important thread in the web of the history of Christendom. Murad the Turk might have taken Constantinople in 1370, without altering in any very great measure the course of events in Eastern Europe during the next century. For after 1370 the empire ceased to exercise its old function of "bulwark of Christendom against the Ottomite." That duty now fell to the Servians and Hungarians, who continued to discharge it for the next hundred and fifty years. The Paleologi, by their base subservience to the Turk, protracted the life of the empire long after all justification for its existence had disappeared.

If Constantinople had fallen in 1370, instead of 1453, there are only two ways in which European history would have been somewhat modified. The commercial resources of Genoa and Venice would have been straitened before the appointed time, and ere the Cape route to India enabled Europe to dispense with the use of Constantinople as half-way house to the East. And, we may add, the Renaissance would have been shorn of some of its brilliance in the next century, if the dispersion of the Greeks had taken place before Italy was quite fitted to receive them and turn their learning to account. But in other respects it is hard to see that much harm would have resulted from the fall of Constantinople in the end of the fourteenth rather than the middle of the fifteenth century.

While Murad I. was conquering the Servians and Bulgarians, John Paleologus was dragging out a long and unhonoured old age. His reign was protracted for over half a century, but his later years were much vexed by the undutiful behaviour of his children. His son Andronicus twice rebelled against him, and once succeeded in seizing the throne for a short space. Andronicus allied himself unto Saoudji, a son of Murad I., who plotted a similar treason against his father the Emir. But Murad easily quelled the rebellion, put out the eyes of his own son, and sent Andronicus in chains to John II., bidding him to follow his example. The Emperor did not dare to disobey, and ordered his son to be blinded. But the operation was so ineffectually performed that Andronicus retained a measure of sight, and was even able to venture on a second rebellion against his father.

In consequence of his heir's unnatural conduct, the aged John determined to deprive him of his succession, and when he died in 1391, he left the throne to his second son Manuel, and not to his eldest born. Manuel II. was above the average of the Paleologi, and showed some signs of capacity, but of what use was it to a prince whose sole dominions were Constantinople, Thessalonica, and the Peloponnesus? He had neither military strength nor money to justify rebellion against the Turk, and could only wait on the course of events.

There was, however, one moment in Manuel's life at which the liberation of the empire from the Ottoman suzerainty appeared possible and even probable. In 1402, there burst into Asia Minor a great horde of Tartars, under the celebrated conqueror Timour [Tamerlane]. Sultan Bayezid, the successor of Murad I., went forth to withstand the invader. But at Angora in Galatia, he suffered a crushing defeat, and the Ottoman Empire seemed likely to perish by the sword. Bayezid was captured, his trusty Janissaries were cut to pieces, his light horsemen scattered to the winds. The Tartars swarmed all over Asia Minor, occupied Broussa, the Ottoman capital, and restored to their thrones all the Seljouk Emirs whose dominions Murad I. had annexed. Bayezid died in captivity, and his sons began to fight over the remains of his empire: Prince Suleiman seized Adrianople, Prince Eesa Nicaea, and each declared himself Sultan.

ARABESQUE DESIGN FROM A BYZANTINE MS.

(From "L'Art Byzantin." Par Charles Bayet. Paris, Quantin, 1883.)

This was a rare opportunity for Manuel Paleologus: the thieves had fallen out, and the rightful owner might perchance come again to his own, if he played his cards well. The control of the Straits was of great importance to each of the Turkish pretenders, so much so, that Manuel was able to sell his aid to Suleiman for a heavy price. In order to keep Eesa from crossing the water, the holder of the European half of the Ottoman realm ceded to the Emperor Thessalonica, the lower valley of the Strymon, the coast of Thessaly, and all the seaports of the Black Sea from the mouth of the Bosphorus up to Varna.

For a moment Manuel once more ruled what might in courtesy be called an empire, and so long as the Ottomans were occupied in civil war he contrived to retain his gains. The strife of the sons of Bayezid lasted ten years: Suleiman was slain by his brother Musa, Eesa by his brother Mohammed, and the two supplanters continued the war. By all Oriental analogies their empire ought to have fallen to pieces, for it is very much easier to build up a new state in the East than to keep together an old one which is breaking asunder. But Mohammed, the youngest of the sons of Bayezid, was a man of genius: he triumphed over the last of his brothers, and united all the remnants of the Ottoman realm that remained. Much had been lost to the Seljouk Emirs in Asia Minor, and to the Servians and Manuel Paleologus in Europe, but the rest was back in Mohammed's hands by A.D. 1421. Manuel had very luckily cast in his lot with Mohammed during the later years of the Turkish civil war, and his ally let him enjoy the dominions he had recovered by his original treaty with Suleiman in 1403.

Between 1402 and 1421, Europe had an unparalleled opportunity to rid herself of the Ottomans. Unfortunately it was not taken. Sigismund, king of Hungary, and at the same time Emperor, was the sovereign on whom the duty of leading the attack ought to have fallen. But Sigismund was now engaged in his great struggle with the Hussites in Bohemia. This wretched religious war directed the strength of Hungary northward when it was wanted in the south. Without such a power to back them the Servians, though they recovered their own liberty as a result of the battle of Angora, could do nothing towards driving the Turks from the Balkans. There was never any sympathy between Serb and Magyar, and save under the direct pressure of fear of a Moslem invasion they would not act together. The Hungarian kings had always laid claim to a suzerainty over the crown of Servia, and from time to time tried to convert their neighbours to Roman Catholicism by force of arms. Hence there was no love lost between them, and a crusade to expel the Turks was never concerted.

DETAILS OF ST. SOPHIA.

Mahomet the Unifier died in 1421, and evil days at once set in for Constantinople and for Christendom, when his ambitious son Murad II. came to the throne. Manuel Paleologus was one of the first to feel the change in the times. He tried to make trouble for Murad, by supporting against him two claimants to the Ottoman Sultanate, each named Mustapha, one the uncle, the other the brother of the new ruler. This drew down on the empire the fate which had been delayed since 1370: the Sultan declared war on Manuel, took one after another all the fortresses which had been recovered by the peace of 1403, and finally laid siege to Constantinople. For the last time the walls of the city proved strong enough to repulse an assault. Though Murad levelled against them cannon, then seen for the first time in the East, built movable towers to shelter his troops, and launched his terrible Janissaries to the assault, he could not succeed. The report of a miraculous vision of the Virgin, who vouchsafed to reveal herself as the defender of the city, encouraged the Greeks to resist with a better spirit than might have been expected. At last the pretender Mustapha, whom Manuel had supplied with money to cause a revolt against his brother, began to stir up such trouble in Asia Minor, that the Sultan determined to raise the siege and march against him. He granted Manuel peace, on the condition that he ceded all his dominions save the cities of Constantinople and Thessalonica and the Peloponnesian province. Thus the empire once more sank back into a state of vassalage to the Ottomans [1422].

Manuel II. died three years after, at the age of seventy-seven. He was the last sovereign of Constantinople who won even a transient smile from fortune. The tale of the last thirty years of the empire is one of unredeemed gloom.

To Manuel succeeded his son John VI., whose whole reign was passed in peace, without an attempt to shake off the Turkish yoke; such an attempt indeed would have been hopeless, unless backed by aid from without. As Manuel II. once observed, "the empire now requires a bailiff not a statesman to rule it." Treaties, wars, and alliances were not for him: all that he could do was to try to save a little money, and to keep his walls in good repair, and even these humble tasks were not always feasible.

All the descriptions of Constantinople in the fifteenth century, whether written by Greek natives or by Western travellers, bear witness to a state of exhaustion and debility which make us wonder that the empire did not collapse sooner. The country outside the walls was a desert. Within them more than half the ground was unoccupied, and covered only by ruins which testified to ancient magnificence. The great palace by the Augustaeum, which sheltered so many generations of emperors, had grown so dilapidated that the Paleologi dwelt in a mere corner of it. Part of the porticoes of St. Sophia had fallen down, and the Greeks could not afford to repair even the greatest sanctuary of their faith. The population of the city had shrunk to about a hundred thousand souls, most of them dwelling in great poverty. Such commerce and wealth as still survived in Constantinople had passed almost entirely into the hands of the Italians of Genoa and Venice, whose fortified factories at Galata and Pera now contained the bulk of the wares that passed through the city. The military strength of the empire was composed of about four thousand mercenary troops, of whom many were Franks and hardly any were born subjects of the empire. The splendid court, which had once been the wonder of East and West, had shrunk to such modest dimensions that a Burgundian traveller noted with surprise that no more than eight attendants accompanied the empress when she went in state to worship in St. Sophia.[31]

John VI., in spite of the caution with which he avoided all action, was destined to see the empire lose its most important possession beyond the walls of Constantinople. His brother Andronicus, governor of Thessalonica, traitorously sold that city to the Venetians for 50,000 zecchins. The Sultan, incensed at a transfer of Greek territory having taken place without his permission, pounced down on the place, expelled the Venetians and annexed Thessalonica to the Ottoman Empire [1430].

The chief feature of the reign of the last John Paleologus was his attempt to win aid for the empire by enlisting sympathy in Western Europe. He determined to conform to Roman Catholicism and to throw himself on the generosity of the Pope. Accordingly he betook himself to Italy in 1438, with the Patriarch of Constantinople and many bishops in his train. He appeared at the Councils of Ferrara and Florence, and was solemnly received into the Roman Church in the Florentine Duomo, on July 6, 1439. It had apparently escaped John's notice that Eugenius IV., the pope of his own day, was a very different personage from the great pontiffs of the eleventh and twelfth centuries, who were able to depose sovereigns and send forth Crusades

[31] See Bertrandon de la Broquière quoted in Finlay, vol. iii. p. 493, a very interesting passage.

at their good pleasure. Since the Great Schism the papacy had been hopelessly discredited in Christendom. Eugenius IV. was engaged in waging a defensive war against the Council of Basle, which was attempting to depose him, and had little thought or power to spend on aiding the Eastern Christians. All that John could get from him was a sum of money and a body of three hundred mercenary troops. This was a poor return for his journey and conversion.

Only one thing of importance was accomplished by the apostasy of the Emperor—the outbreak of a venomous ecclesiastical struggle at Constantinople between the conformists who had taken the oath at Florence, and the bulk of the clergy, who disowned the treaty of union. John was practically boycotted by the majority of his subjects; the Orthodox priests ceased to pray for him, and the populace refused to enter St. Sophia again, when it had been profaned by the celebration of the Roman Mass. The opinion of the majority of the Greeks was summed up in the exclamation of the Grand-Duke John Notaras—"Better the turban of the Turk in Constantinople than the Pope's Tiara."

The last years of the reign of John VI. coincided with the great campaigns of Huniades and Ladislas of Poland against the Turks. For a moment it seemed as if the gallant king of Poland and Hungary, backed by his great Warden of the Marches, might restore the Balkan lands to Christendom. They thrust Murad II. back over the Balkans, and appeared in triumph at Sophia. But the fatal battle of Varna [1444] ended the career of King Ladislas in an untimely death, and after that fight the Ottomans were obviously fated to accomplish their destiny without a check. John Paleologus watched the struggle without movement if not without concern. He was too cautious to stir a finger to aid the Hungarians, for he knew that if he once offended the Sultan his days would be numbered.

John VI. passed away in 1448, and Sultan Murad in 1451. The one was succeeded by his brother Constantine, the last Christian sovereign of Byzantium, the other by his young son Mohammed the Conqueror. Constantine was a Romanist like his elder brother, and was therefore treated with great suspicion and coolness by his handful of subjects. He was the best man that the house of Paleologus had ever reared, brave, pious, generous, and forgiving. Like King Hosea of Israel, "he did not evil as the kings that were before him," yet was destined to bear the penalty for all the sins and follies of his long line of predecessors.

Mohammed II., the most commanding personality among the whole race of Ottoman Sultans, set his heart from the first on seizing Constantinople, the natural centre of his empire, and making it his capital. Some excuse had to be found for falling on his vassal: the one that he chose was a rather unwise request which Constantine had made. There dwelt at Constantinople a Turkish prince of the royal house named Orkhan, for whom Mohammed paid a considerable subsidy, on condition that he was kept out of the way of mischief and plotting. Some unhappy inspiration impelled Constantine to ask for an increase in the subsidy, and to hint that Orkhan had claims to the Sultanate. This was excuse enough for Mohammed: without taking the trouble to declare war he sent out troops and engineers, and began to erect forts on Greek soil, only four miles away from Constantinople, at the narrowest point of the Bosphorus, so as to block the approach to the city from the Black Sea. The Emperor did not dare to remonstrate, but when the Turks began to pull down a much-venerated church, in order to utilize its stones in the new fort, a few Greeks took arms and drove the masons away. They were at once cut down by the Turkish guards: Constantine demanded redress, and then Mohammed, having fairly picked his wolf-and-lamb quarrel with his unfortunate vassal, commenced open hostilities [Autumn 1452].

Turkish light troops at once appeared to blockade the city while the Sultan began to collect a great train of cannon at Adrianople, and to build a large fleet of war galleys in the ports of Asia: the siege was to begin in the ensuing spring.

The empire was now in its death agony, and Constantine recognized the fact. He spent the winter in making frantic appeals to the Pope and the Italian naval powers to save him from destruction. Nicholas V. was willing enough to help; now that the Emperor was a convert to Catholicism something must be done to aid him. But all that the Pope could send was a cardinal, a moderate sum of money, and a few hundred soldiers of fortune hastily hired in Italy. Venice and Genoa could have done much more, but they had so often heard the cry of "Wolf" raised that they did not realize the danger to their Eastern trade at its true extent. From Genoa, Giovanni Giustiniani brought no more than two galleys and three hundred men. Venice did even less, only commissioning the bailiff of its factory at Galata to arm such able-bodied Venetians as were with him for the protection of the city. Altogether the Franks, counting both trained mercenaries and armed burghers, who co-operated in the defence of Constantinople, were not more than three thousand strong. Yet either Genoa or Venice could have thrown a hundred galleys and twenty thousand men into the scale if they had chosen.

Constantine's own troops were about four thousand strong, but he hoped to recruit them by a general levy of the male population of the city. He issued a passionate appeal to his subjects to join in saving the holy city, the centre of Eastern Christendom. But the Greeks only remembered that he was an apostate, who had foresworn the faith of his fathers and done homage to the Pope. They stood aside in sullen apathy, and from the whole population of the city only two thousand volunteers were enlisted. Theological bitterness led the blind multitude to cry with Notaras that it preferred the Turk to the Roman.

In April, 1453, the young Sultan, with seventy thousand picked troops at his back, laid formal siege to the city on the land side, while a fleet of several hundred war galleys beset the Bosphorus. The end could not be for a moment doubtful; nine thousand men could not hope to defend the vast circuit of the land and sea-wall against a veteran army urged on by a young and fiery general. Mohammed set his cannon to play on the walls, and it was soon seen that the tough old Roman mortar and stone that had blunted the siege engines of so many foes could not resist the force of gunpowder. The Sultan's artillery was rude, but it was heavy and numerous; ere long the walls began to come down in flakes, and breaches commenced to show themselves in several places.

Constantine XIII. and his second in command, the Genoese Giustiniani, did all that brave and skilful men might, in protracting the siege. They led sorties, organized attacks by water on the Turkish fleet, and endeavoured to drive off the siege artillery of the enemy by a counter fire of cannon. But it was found that the old walls were too narrow to bear the guns, and where any were hoisted up and brought to bear, their recoil shook the fabric in such a dangerous way that the fire was soon obliged to cease.

At sea the Christians won one great success, when four galleys from the Aegean forced their way in through the whole Turkish fleet, and reached the Golden Horn in safety, after sinking many of their assailants. But the Turks had as great a numerical superiority on the water as on land, and the inevitable could only be delayed. Mohammed even succeeded in getting control of the harbour of the city, above its mouth, by dragging light galleys on rollers over the neck of land between the Bosphorus and the Golden Horn, and launching them in the inland waters just above Galata. Thus the inner, as well as the outer, sea-face of the city was beset by enemies.

The end came on May 29, 1453. The Sultan had opened several practicable breaches, of which the chief lay in the north-west angle of the city by the gate of St. Romanus, where two whole towers and the curtain between them had been battered down and choked the ditch. The storm was obviously at hand, and the doomed Emperor was obliged to face his fate. Greek historians dwelt with loving sorrow on the last hours of the unfortunate prince. He left the breach at midnight, partook of the sacrament according to the Latin rite in St. Sophia, and snatched a few hours of troubled sleep in his half-ruined palace. Next morning, with the dawn, he rose to ride back to the post of danger. His ministers and attendants crowded round his horse as he started on what all knew to be his last journey. Looking steadfastly on them he prayed one and all to pardon him for any offence that he might wittingly or unwittingly have committed against any man. The crowd answered with sobs and wails, and with the sounds of woe ringing in his ears Constantine rode slowly off to meet his death.

The assault commenced at dawn; three main attacks and several secondary ones were directed against weak spots in the wall. But the chief stress was on the great breach by the gate of St. Romanus. There the Emperor himself and Giustiniani at his side stood in the midst of the yawning gap with their best men around them, and opposed a barrier of steel to the oncoming assailants. Twelve thousand Janissaries, sabre in hand, formed successive columns of attack; as soon as one was beaten off another delivered its assault. They fell by hundreds before the swords of the mailed men in the breach, for their felt caps and unarmoured bodies were easy marks for the ponderous weapons of the fifteenth century. But the ranks of the defenders grew thin and weary; Giustiniani was wounded in the face by an arrow, and taken on board his galley to die. Constantine at last stood almost alone in the breach, and a forlorn hope of Janissaries headed by one Hassan of Ulubad, whom Turkish chroniclers delight to honour, at last forced their way over the wall. The Emperor and his companions were trodden under foot, and the victorious army rushed into the desolate streets of Constantinople, seeking in vain for foes to fight. The Greeks, half expecting that God would interfere to save the queen of Christian cities by a miracle, had crowded into the churches, and were passing the fatal hour in frantic prayer! The shouts of the victorious enemy soon showed them how the day had gone, and the worshippers were dragged out in crowds, to be claimed as slaves and divided among the conquerors.

Mohammed II. rode through the breach after his men, and descended into the city, scanning from within the streets that so many Eastern conquerors had in vain desired to see. He bade his men search for the Emperor, and the corpse of Constantine was found at last beneath a heap of slain, so gashed and mauled that it was only identified by the golden eagles on his mail shoes. The Turk struck off his head, and sent it round their chief cities as a token of triumph. Riding through the hippodrome towards St. Sophia, Mohammed noted the Delphic tripod with its three snakes,[32] standing where Constantine the Great had placed it eleven hundred years before. Either because the menacing heads of the serpents provoked him, or merely because he wished to try the strength of his arm, the Sultan rose in his stirrups and smote away the jaws of the nearest snake with one blow of his mace. There was something typical in the deed though Mohammed knew it not. He had defaced the monument of the first great victory of the West over the East. He, the successor in spirit not only of Xerxes but of Chosroës and Moslemah and many another Oriental potentate, who had failed where he succeeded, could not better signalize the end of Greek freedom than by dealing a scornful blow at that ancient memorial, erected in the first days of Grecian greatness, to celebrate the turning back of the Persians on the field of Plataea.

At last the Sultan came to St. Sophia, where the crowd of wailing captives was being divided among his soldiery. He rode in at the eastern door, and bade a mollah ascend the pulpit and repeat there the formula of the Moslem faith. So the cry that God was great and Mohammed his prophet rang through the dome where thirty generations of patriarchs had celebrated the Holy Mysteries, and all Europe and Asia knew the end was come of the longest tale of Empire that Christendom has yet seen.

ANGEL OF THE NIGHT.
(*From "L'Art Byzantin." Par Charles Bayet. Paris, Quantin,* 1883.)

[32] See pp. 24, 25.

Norm the Normal by Ben Lemon

What happens when the most useless person in the world gets a reality show, he becomes the most beloved person the world has ever known of course. Now he can't do anything wrong. Bank robberies or attacking TV host must clearly be someone else fault. As the world steps in to help him nothing will ever be the same again. Just watch what happens when celebrity and popular culture starts butting heads with the political, justice and the world order, someone must lose.

The Meaning of Life and Other Useless Crap

This short pamphlet covers many topics that are some of the most important problems things we face in society today from stopping Hurricanes, Flooding and explaining The Meaning of Life.
It will give you a new perspective into many of the problems that we face that are being ignored even though we already have a solution.

The Meaning of Life and Other Useless Crap is Perhaps our generations greatest work as it answers the age old question "What is the meaning of life?" Written simply and straightforward it is easy to understand why Ben Lemon is the most important living philosopher. It hasn't been since A Modest Proposal that a pamphlet can our perceptions so dramatically.

High Rants by Ben Lemon

Coming Soon

The most legal fun you can have in prohibition states.
Well, sucks for you

I RECEIVED THIS GREAT BOOK ON MAY 6, 2019. SENT TO ME BY MY DEAR WIFE KEREN

I FINISHED READING THIS BOOK AT 12:10 AM, ON MAY 10, 2019.

43895702R00108

Made in the USA
Middletown, DE
30 April 2019